A View from The East

Male students of Uhuru Sasa Shule in one of their middle school uniforms. These uniforms consisted of combat boots, jeans, and Malcolm X sweatshirts, while alternate uniforms included a *dashiki* manufactured by the Mavazi Clothing Co-op. Photograph by Osei Terry Chandler. Used with permission.

A View from The East

Black Cultural Nationalism and Education in New York City

SECOND EDITION

Kwasi Konadu

With a Foreword by **Dr. Scot Brown**

Diasporic Africa Press, Inc. | New York
www.dafricapress.com

Copyright © 2018 Kwasi Konadu

Originally published by Syracuse University Press, 2009.

All rights reserved. No part of this publication may be reproduced,
stored in a retrieval system, or transmitted, in any form or by any means,
electronic, mechanical, photocopying, recording, or otherwise, without
the prior permission of Diasporic Africa Press.

LCCN: 2018907758
ISBN 978-1-937306-67-0

THIS BOOK IS DEDICATED TO

Jitu K. Weusi
Yusef Iman
Jim Seitu Dyson
Jumibia Nyahuma
Mama Kuumba Coard
Mzee Moyo

Contents

LIST OF ILLUSTRATIONS | ix

FOREWORD TO THE SECOND EDITION, Dr. Scot Brown | xi

FOREWORD TO THE FIRST EDITION, Dr. James Turner | xiii

ACKNOWLEDGMENTS | xvii

INTRODUCTION | xix

1. Ujima: *Context and Community Control* | 1
2. Nia: *The Birth of The East Organization* | 26
3. Ujamaa: *Enterprises of The East* | 68
4. Kujichagulia: *Uhuru Sasa Shule (Freedom Now School)* | 86
5. Kuumba: *The International African Arts Festival* | 113
6. Imani: *The Challenge of Continuity and The East Legacy* | 124

Epilogue: *The East Family at Present* | 138

APPENDIXES
  A. *The Mashariki and Required Reading Lists* | 143
  B. *Letter from Jitu Weusi to Amiri Baraka, December 12, 1973* | 147
  C. *The East Brotherhood Code Committee* | 151
  D. *The East Collective, Family, and Supporters Responsibilities* | 157
  E. *Uhuru Sasa Shule Protocol, Calendar, Curriculum, Daily Schedules, Praises, Pledges, and Songs* | 161
  F. *Programmatic Content of the International African Arts Festival* | 173

NOTES | 177

BIBLIOGRAPHY | 195

INDEX | 205

Illustrations

Male students of Uhuru Sasa Shule in one of their middle school
  uniforms | *frontispiece*
1. A Black Experience in Sound jazz session at The East, 1971 | 29
2. An East flyer of scheduled jazz and poetry performances | 30
3. Kasisi Jitu Weusi speaking at The East complex, 1970 | 32
4. An ankh-shaped Kwanzaa agenda posted on the door of The East complex,
  1971 | 44
5. Kasisi Yusef Iman wearing a *talisimu* at The East complex, 1970 | 46
6. The Balozi Wazee (council of elders), 1972 | 49
7. Salik Mwando with his Uhuru Sasa middle school students at the Bond Street
  location, 1971 | 71
8. Basir Mchawi and two students of the Central Brooklyn Model Cities summer
  program in Raleigh, North Carolina, 1972 | 74
9. Adding finishing touches onto the "Sweet-East" exterior, 1971 | 78
10. Kununuana (Uhuru Food Co-op) and Mavazi Clothing Co-op | 80
11. A shelf of food items in the Kununuana (Uhuru Food Co-op), 1972 | 81
12. Mavazi Clothing Co-op flyer | 84
13. Kasisi Jitu Weusi, Toola (Edgar Booker), and Maliki (George Robinson) | 106
14. Malika Iman and Adeyemi Bandele in front of The East complex | 110
15. A scene from the first African Street Festival | 117
16. International African Arts Festival promotional collage, 1998 | 120

Tables

1.1. African-Descended Population of Brooklyn, 1698–1960 | 8
2.1. The East's Operations, 1969–1972 | 33
E.1. Uhuru Sasa Curriculum Design | 163
E.2. Uhuru Sasa Shule Curricular Domains | 165

Foreword to the Second Edition

Kwasi Konadu has delivered a fresh and indispensable case study of a central organization of the Black Power movement known as The East. *A View from The East* moves historical discourse to higher levels of clarity and understanding of Black Power and cultural nationalism. The past three decades have seen a wave of research on the Black Power movement of the late 1960s and early 1970s aimed at subjecting this movement to the scrutiny of hindsight. The border between historical inquiry and the movement's own impulse toward self-consciousness is a porous one. Manifestos aimed at detailing the correct path in a movement comprising advocates from a wide political span—for example, Black capitalists, territorial nationalists, ethnic pluralists, cultural nationalists, Black socialists, and much beyond and in between—underscore intra–Black Power debate and contestation. As is the case with any growing historiography timed in relative proximity to (and arguably converging with) the historical phenomena in question, Black Power research is heavily influenced by these ideological debates.

Late 1960s conflicts between self-identified "cultural nationalists" and "revolutionary nationalists" led to a scholarly tendency to reproduce sectarian conceptions of cultural nationalism as fundamentally reactionary. This trend endured through the 1980s—a decade that marked a clear turn toward the historicizing of Black Power whereby most studies regarded the movement as having run its course—while acknowledging the persistence of institutional, political, and cultural legacies. In addition, the Afrocentric movement that gained significant momentum in the 1980s and early 1990s was an important counterpoint to reductive characterizations of cultural nationalism. The growing popular embrace of Kwanzaa and the *Nguzo Saba* (Seven Principles), politicized hip-hop music, study groups, and independent Black schools and bookstores was accompanied by renewed activism and scholarship calling for the transformation of African American consciousness, reminiscent of 1960s cultural nationalist assertions.

Historical research examining cultural nationalism beyond the limits of previous ideological debate has increased dramatically in recent years. *A View from The East* deploys an array of primary sources, oral histories, and ethnographic-styled research methodologies—providing not only a view from The East but one that offers glimpses into the inner workings and culture of the organization. What follows from Konadu's study is a complex portrait of an organization that transcended boundaries between political agitation, education, counterculture, social arrangements, institution-building, creative and artistic production, and pan-African liberation support. The tens of thousands of people who currently attend the annual International African Arts Festival in Brooklyn, New York, are a testimony to the presence of The East—not merely in the form of historical legacy but as a living force in the African worldwide diaspora.

Scot Brown

Foreword to the First Edition

This book about The East is the first serious study of a very important community-based institution, created by dedicated educators who were progressive activists and organizers. The founders of The East came of age during the era of the Black Consciousness/Black Power movements. The period of 1960 to 1975 was a time of extraordinary cultural and political transformation among African peoples, and the United States was one of the focal points. Some scholars have referred to this period as the Second (Black) Renaissance of the twentieth century, or the "Great Awakening." There are always problems of accuracy in making comparisons between different periods of history. It is also problematic to consider one moment in time and the events characteristic of that time as if they were fully unique.

Africans in America have produced a dialectical pattern of history and created a dynamic culture. The 1960s were a critically significant stage in Black social history. The decade opened with the advent of independence of African countries held under colonial domination by the imperialist empires of Britain and France primarily. Portugal was to hold sway over its colonial subjects in Africa well into the 1970s, but the tide was inevitable. The anticolonial struggles were at a high point and had dramatic impact on the freedom movements in the African Diaspora, most particularly in the United States; themes of self-determination and Black Consciousness were stimulated in African American politics. Malcolm X, the Black nationalist political theorist, was most influential among artists, educators, intellectuals, and students, and as a community-based leader he had a mass following at the grassroots level.

By the late 1950s, and the turn of the next decade, the Civil Rights Movement had accelerated to the height of its intensity with the spread of campaigns for civil disobedience and political resistance to the system of segregation and white supremacy in the heart of the old confederacy and the plantation south. The formation of the Congress of Racial Equality (CORE) and the Southern Christian Leadership Council (SCLC) led by Dr. Martin Luther King, Jr., marked the emergence of a national struggle for democratic rights. The Student Non-Violent Coordinating Committee (SNCC) had grown from the Black college student "sit-ins" movement. SNCC (pronounced SNICK), the Black Panther Party, the US Organization, and the Black Arts Movement transformed African American politics to a focus on Black Power/Black Consciousness. Black Power politics articulates an antiracism, anticolonialism ideology that shapes the struggle for power as essential to freedom for African people. By 1970 the Congress of African Peoples was formed as the broad-based united front organization for the Black Power Movement.

It is in this political and sociological context that The East comes into existence. The East was a multiplex community institution, dedicated to the principles of self-determination, nation building, and Black nationalist consciousness. The theoretical analysis of the conditions confronting Africans in America was that we are a subjugated people in all sectors of society, politically suppressed, for the most part powerless, economically exploited, culturally distorted, socially alienated and intimidated, and above all miseducated. An effective liberation movement must have a program that confronts these conditions. The heart of The East was Uhuru Sasa Shule, an independent African-centered school. Its translated name of "Freedom Now" was derived from Kiswahili, the common language in most of East Africa. The school was both a stark contrast to and an alternative to the public schools that were/are so wasteful of the lives of African children. The school mantra was "academic excellence and cultural literacy." If Africans were to resist and seek to release themselves from Eurocentric hegemony, they would have to instigate the first revolution in what the master, Black historian Lerone Bennett, refers to as the revolution in the "winding corridors of the mind." The students were to be imbued with knowledge and values that would encourage critical thinking and positive formation in the dynamic of the Black self-concept. The curriculum and pedagogy were rooted in Kawaida philosophy and concepts of education for self-reliance. Uhuru Sasa, part of a nationwide system of independent African schools, was in the tradition of the African Free School of the mid-nineteenth century. The East provided a day-care center for children of working parents and an evening school for adults.

Black News was a widely circulated news publication, respected for its progressive journalistic analysis, its coverage of news about the community, and its pan-African perspective. It was also the premier organ for politics and education in The East community. The East was a Black nationalist project that defined liberation in terms that emphasized a "stand-up" and "stand-out" position, in bell hooks's metaphor loving blackness as an act of resistance. Blackness is more than a reaction to whiteness as a signifier for white supremacy; it is affirmation of the existence of Black people. But the central issue of moving Black people from a reduction of identity involves an elevated group consciousness whereby Black people think of their existence as necessitating each other. Philosophically, Black nationalists propose that freedom for the slave/the colonial subject/person is to resist being objectified by whiteness; Blackness must become a liberating consciousness at the center of which is the common wisdom that a people seeking to be free should embrace the concept of the necessity of all Black people behaving in accord with the simple notation they must act for themselves. The East recognized that freedom was a struggle at the intellectual and subjective/psychological levels. Preservation and exposure of African culture was/is important to develop fealty to the race. Culture is also the natural pathway to interaction with the people. On weekends, The East was converted to a salon, an evening club, and small concert venue for Black music (jazz) artists. Many of the great musicians performed there, wrote new music there, and read and recited verses/poetry there. This brilliantly successful program brought the culture to the people and the people to the culture. The East had a reputation among the cool and sophisticates; it was a hip site. People traveled from the five boroughs of New York City, and some came from outside of the city to attend the cultural program. In response to wider demand, The East created its own recording label; several of its albums became influential and are now collectors' items.

In this work, dedicated young scholar Kwasi Konadu carefully excavates the legacy of The East. He is one of a growing number of people, referred to as "Black Power scholars," attracted to the study of the African experience in the 1960s. Konadu is among the best of that group. This book will help convey the intellectual and political history of African people at the latter part of the twentieth century. I hope this vital work will stimulate other scholars to study this rich period.

James Turner

Acknowledgments

Mpaee. Odomankoma Oboodee, Asase Yaa, abosompem, nananom nsamanfoo, meda mo ase pii ma mo mmoa ne nhyira bebree. To my parents and siblings, *medaase* (thank you) for support and for challenging me to be committed to family and its development. To Professors James Turner, N'dri Assie-Lumumba, and Mwalimu Nanji, *medaase* for your invaluable time and willingness to work with me as a former graduate student. To The East members interviewed, *medaase:* Jitu K. Weusi, Adeyemi Bandele, Aminisha Black, Job Mashariki, Rosezina Pou, Ngina Mwando (Beverly Blacksher), Mama Kuumba Coard, Latifah (Lauren Callender), Fatima Cynthia Kierstedt, Bernardo Osei Rubie, Gladstone Modele Clarke, Fela Barclift, Martha Bright, Kwesi Mensah Wali, Mzee Moyo, Matthew Holmes, James Williams, Msemaji and Nandi Weusi, Salik Mwando, Basir Mchawi, John Watusi Branch, Kubballa Waliyaya, Baraka Moyo Smith, Alfredo Mitchell, Jumibia Nyahuma (Michael Leonard), Mama Okolo Buyu, Lumumba Bandele, Khadijah Bandele, Yusef Waliyaya, Segun Shabaka, and Nekena and Nadira Evens.

To Leslie Alexander, Scot Brown, and Tom Weissenger, *medaase* for your friendship and support. To the Africana Studies and Research Center faculty and staff, *medaase* for your encouragement. To Ken Glover and the Ujamaa family, *medaase* your friendship. Dr. Mwalimu Shujaa, *medaase* for your insights and for allowing me to utilize the Council of Independent Black Institutions (CIBI) archives. To the late Preston Wilcox, *medaase* for sharing your life's work and access to the Afram archives. To Mama Brenda Isaac and Fatou Seck Isaac, *medaase* for your continued love and guidance. To Michelle Thomas, Solwazi and Adigun Olusola, Mama Carol and Maxine Cenac, *Wofa* Kwasi Odaaku, Kwasi Bempong, and Adjoa

Oriyomi, *medaase* for your friendship and extended family support. If the best is saved for last, then I say *medaase* to Amma (Ronnie), *me do,* for your support of my work and me: *wahoofe de wobeko, wo suban de wo beba.*

Introduction

> Only when we are clear about the kind of society we are trying to build can we design our educational [and institutional] service to serve our goals.
> —JULIUS K. NYERERE, *Ujamaa*

> Nationalism is the love of a people for themselves and their commitment to their group survival. It is the affirmation of the cultural self. It is what motivates the pockets of resistance to European oppression.
> —MARIMBA ANI, *Yurugu*

> The East, a model toward the foundation of a [Black] nation.... Walking into The East is like entering a new Black world. You are engulfed by the aroma of fragrant [i]ncense as you gaze upon entire walls of colorfully painted [m]urals, of Black heroes and symbols. I[n]side there is [u]sually something happening, at The East everyone works. Someone is always at the front selling Black books and periodicals, while in the back there may be a film, a community meeting or jam session with some of the most gifted Black jazz musicians in the world. Upstairs during the weekdays there are classes in session, both in the afternoon and evening and for both adults and children—the young, the old, men and women.
> —*Imani Magazine*, 1971

This book examines the historical and cultural significance of The East organization in terms of furthering our understanding and appreciation of the intersections between cultural nationalism, education, and institution building in twentieth-century African-derived life and culture in general and among people of African descent domiciled in New York City in particular. The book explores the efforts of The East to create and sustain viable community and family-centered institutions in the context of nation(alist) building. *Nation building* is defined here as the conscious and focused application of African and African-descended people's collective resources, energies, and knowledge to the task of liberating and developing the psychic and physical space that they identify as theirs. *Nationalist* is used here to properly situate The East experience in the context and continuum of Black nationalist thought and praxis and its efforts to build upon this often misconstrued yet visionary tradition premised on self-determination.

The activities and challenges of The East experience in cultural, institutional, and nation(alist) building are explored through a sociohistorical case study of the institution and its components. This experience is indicative of the social movements of Africans and their descendants in North America that have expanded their vision and strategy beyond the mode of protest and perpetual dependency to institution building and self-determination. Emerging after the Ocean Hill–Brownsville struggles for community control of schools, but during the Black Power and Black Consciousness era, The East was the direct result of the energies of skilled high school youth and the wisdom of a core group of committed adults. Through the collection of archival documents and interviews of The East family members, the book uses both organizational and experiential data to describe and analyze salient themes, patterns, and activities. The legacies of The East experience are to be found in its methodology of institutional development and the lessons it provided for the intergenerational process of nation(alist) building. Although The East no longer exists as an active organization, its spirit and principles are still vibrant in the character of members who constitute what was and is The East family.

The East began in 1969 as a self-determining cultural and educational organization for African and African-descended people in central Brooklyn, New York. It was armed with the theme "Freedom Now!" and the philosophy of self-reliance under the leadership of Jitu K. Weusi and The East family.[1] Weusi was and is a central figure in the design, expansion, and governance of The East organization in both concrete and ideational terms. Conceptually, The East was a counter hegemonic act toward white cultural and political imperialism through its embodiment of an African spirit of cultural resistance and reconstruction in the North American context. To speak of The East experience we must speak of an appropriate conceptual grounding. The following statement, therefore, represents the conceptual anchor of this text:

> The African-American cultural identity has been and continues to be influenced by the U.S. social context, but it is essential to note that the African-American cultural orientation also represents an experiential context. Thus, while African-Americans exist within the U.S. social context, they also exist within an African historical-cultural continuum that predates that social context and would continue to exist even if the nation-state and its social arrangements were to transform or demise.[2]

Hence, the terms *African* and *African descended* will be used throughout this text as appropriate expressions that elucidate the role of African cultures and Africa-based ideas in The East experience, albeit shaped by diasporic experiences. Terms such as *Black* or *African American* will only be used to maintain the integrity of sources produced by other writers.

Black (Cultural) Nationalism and Racialized Society in Perspective

Some historians of nationalism argue that nations and nationalism are constructed and "modern" phenomena, and it is therefore necessary to distinguish *nationalism* and *nation* because those who claim to study nations are studying specific and contemporary states. For instance, North America is a recent historical invention rather than the product of a natural and long-standing process, and being American has unstable, varied, and conflicting value among its multitude of cultural residents. Nationalism discussions have also focused on the nation-state as the basis of fascism and nationalism or that state-sponsored nationals have produced fascism (e.g., Germany, Italy, and Japan). The bias in these discussions is that proponents do not include U.S. and Western imperialism, colonialism, and enslavement in their discourse. Nationalism tends to essentialize identity, goes the argument, hence, ethnic chauvinism and the notion that nationalism plus race equals racism. However, that tendency, like the bias in nationalism discourse, does not make enough of a distinction between nationalism as a force of resistance to renew humanity and that is not rooted in the idea of the "other" (i.e., people who are minoritized), and nationalism that can be conservative (e.g., U.S. republican patriotism, Neo-Nazi movement, or the Nation of Islam). In Africa, twentieth-century nationalism was part of socially progressive movements to reduce intercultural group conflict and address the European thrust, as was the case for the British, to heighten "tribalism" and promote "traditionalists" in a feudal manner to rule indirectly. In this context, one wonders about the meaning of Asante, Gã, or Fante becoming Ghanaians. Kwame Nkrumah of Ghana and Julius Nyerere of Tanzania attempted to move from "ethnic" to Ghanaian and Tanzanian, respectively, and to African. Nyerere had relatively greater success than Nkrumah; still, no operational concept of "African" exists on the African continent, and the effort to develop that concept has largely been among Africans in the diaspora who live in societies characterized, in large part, by centuries of miscegenation and social exclusion.

The balkanization of the Americas begs the question of why neo-European states in the region were and are so hostile to nationalist movements led by people of African descent but support assimilation into European cultural realities and ways of knowing as the center of the universe. In the African diaspora, peoples of African descent do not have a state structure, so they root notions of nationalism in people and culture. However, some people have moved, have demographically reshaped, and are still moving to urban centers in the United States and the Western world, questioning the very meaning and applicability of notions such as diaspora. Here, the contention that the study of nations and nationalism is really the study of states has validity, particularly when paired with the idea or assumption that only so-called "minorities" domiciled in those states are "ethnic," only "minority groups" deal with "identity politics," and that these groups perpetuate such politics on the larger U.S. society. Identity politics in terms of "whiteness" is presumed as the default and as normative and therefore as an identity without politics, while icons or concepts used to depict North American social history consistently references this same whiteness. Thus, in any discussion of Black nationalism and so-called identity politics, there is a need to unpack "whiteness" and interject that whites or descendants of European colonists too perpetuate structures of identity in that they are the only ones to reduce God and the national ethos in racialized and anthropomorphic terms (e.g., popular images of the Last Supper and Uncle Sam). An insidious consequence of not unpacking whiteness is that the concept of "minority" remains internalized, and those "white lies" planted in the African-descended imagination produce adults and children who see themselves as the demonic inverse of whiteness, while that internalized racism is projected unto other (than white) "minorities" in often violent ways (e.g., gang killings, prison, disease, poverty, feminization of boys and men, masculinization of girls and women).

The East experience suggests that those seeking to address these issues must engender a process for deconstructing their own racialized consciousness with the understanding that the fate of the individual within a cultural grouping is tied to the fate of the group, even though he or she is encouraged strongly to disassociate from that group and engage in competition amongst and within so-called minority groups. By affirming this strategic process of deconstruction, those persons of African descent can reconfigure the group—as individual identity is a function or dysfunction of group identity—so that it empowers both the group and the individual by way of psychological, therapeutic, and voluntary association. Indeed, that process must also confront the fact that there appears to be more social space to move and imagine identities because of the apparent end of U.S. segregation, and that now one can be categorized or self-identify himself or herself as biracial as a result of the greater sense of social movement. If a white woman married a man of African descent in the Black community two or three decades ago, she almost instantaneously lost her citizenship in the white republic and obtained proxy in the "Black republic" through her husband. Today, those relations are of little concern, though uncomfortable, to white elites who shield their daughters but sanction such relations among the nonelite as a mark of their "democratic" society (whatever this, ultimately, means). There is also the pervasive idea of options hinged upon phenotype and within intellectual and artistic circles as well as those who find it necessary to claim some fractional amount of non-African ancestry to vindicate their insistence on mixed heritage or intermediacy. From Ghana to Grenada to Georgia, many still recount with great pride and self-actualization that they had some "white" in them. The phenomena of interracial intimacy and dating on television represent instances of racialized social mobility. The notion of claiming race is now more fluid and flexible; boundaries that proscribed race are not as rigid as they were several decades ago, but this phantom of seeming fluidity and options causes greater confusion wherein, for example, a dark-skinned person of African descent can "imagine" him- or herself to be white, which represents a psychosis, for the empirical and culturally bounded reality within which he or she lives says otherwise.

Race, as a social construct, saturates and regulates contemporary human life in North America and elsewhere, and the very denial or pronouncement of the end of racism is a direct admission of its existence. Race is reified in U.S. society. It forms not only an axis around which human interaction revolves but also the parameters and a coherent explanation for those layered interactions. Choosing who and therefore who not to sit next to on domestic and international flights, trains, buses, and in school cafeterias, movie theaters, restaurants, social and business meetings, and other places of social convergence are often implicit and explicit decisions of race. Even if these decisions are not premeditated, they nonetheless are actions or choices that are "racialized" in contour and content. Thus, racialized decisions performed in the drama of social action suggest that the more substantive issue is that people choose with whom and when to share their social space. And so sitting or sharing a space with someone of another race creates situations of negotiated inconveniences that are tolerated because these temporal moments are (in the minds of the decision maker) not permanent but transitory. That same decision maker, depending upon his or her access to what constitutes valued resources or wealth, may use one of several strategies in this racialized social order: purchase first-class accommodations on most flights or on that exclusive set of train cars, seek out exclusive accommodations, resorts, or beaches where one can be insulated from "them" and their kind (except as servants to be temporarily tolerated). Such strategies not only serve to offer measures of securing social space as personal or group property but also to give the illusion—to both the user and those excluded—that everyone has access, and therefore these strategies are nonexclusive and nonracial.

Those strategies become calcified as "normal," for the power of illusion rests on the fact that concepts that define reality do so by seducing others to accept those definitions as if they were their own. In the equation of social definitions, concepts such as whiteness, minority, and identity politics become not only a part of our living memory but precisely the software that shapes the decision making of the public and individual body or hardware. Interestingly, opponents and proponents of race commit the same act of which they accuse the other: They hybridize Africans and African descendants and biologize race without considering or paying any real attention to the hybridization and ethnicness of whites. For race is real as a marker of social reality and as an expression of culture or a synonym for culture. Race involves that which one feels an affinity in politicized and nonpolitical contexts. For most Black nationalists, race is merely a marker of nationality. Similarly, just as skin color in a society ordered and mediated by race is an identifier of nationality, it partially describes how one appears but not who and what he or she is, culturally speaking. Yet, the notion of race warrants immediate reevaluation; a more accurate descriptor could be "cultural ancestry" because the latter relates to a sort of biogenetic rope that connects Africans and their descendants to an eternal community and consciousness that preceded them yet still informs their collective and personal identity.[3] In fact, the rope analogy would apply to anyone, for everyone has ancestors who imparted specific and shared genetic and cultural material to progenitors who ultimately birthed the person in question. In turn, that person becomes the sum total of all of his or her progenitors' material. The task of affirming an African cultural-historical continuum ("the sum total") is a praxis as well as a cultural and political necessity that some cultural nationalists, such as members of The East, sought to engage through institution building and education. For this reason, Black nationalism is somewhat unique in its proclamation of African identity in the United States and also as a type of nationalism that seeks to redefine group identity and renegotiate the terms of political relationship with the existing social order.

The history of Africans and their descendants in North America is neither a byproduct of nor a footnote to European or white U.S. history and, as such, the former have a distinct nationality that consists of forcibly transplanted colonial subjects who have acquired cohesive identities in the course of centuries of struggle against enslavement, cultural alienation, and the spiritual cannibalism of white racism.[4] From this perspective, the implication is that nationhood is not solely or most importantly defined by the occupation and control of geopolitical space, but rather nationhood is a function of peoplehood. Every people "identifiable and distinguishable by its history, culture, physiology and political/economic status does in fact constitute a nation."[5] Nationalism is the expression of a people's commitment to self-determination in all its scope and dimension. Nationalism among Africans and their descendants in North America can be described as the belief in and vision of independence from being the exploited and expendable segment of a U.S. economic and political order, and as a conscious political and sociopsychological move outside that sphere of influence. The nationalist ideas and praxis among Africans in the United States were and are inextricably linked to the hegemonic context that gave rise to the pursuit of freedom and the idea that they constitute a distinct, cultural nation among other cultural nations within the U.S. borders.

In *Slave Culture: Nationalist Theory and the Foundations of Black America,* Sterling Stuckey describes the convergence of distinct African peoples on plantations in the U.S. South into a composite culture, which flowed from an essentially autonomous value system anchored in indigenous Africa and created a pan-Africanism that provided an identity and an ideology. Stuckey demonstrates that, at the time of emancipation, enslaved Africans still remained essentially African in culture. Vincent Paul Franklin, in *Black Self-Determination: A Cultural History of African-American Resistance,* examined the religious orientation, artistry, music, and statements of Africans in America and found that their core values have always been self-determination, freedom, and resistance to assimilation. The idea here is that slave ships and the plantation system of the United States not only served as natural incubators for revolts but also a nascent pan-African nationalism that grew and assumed different forms, as articulated by numerous proponents, throughout the last two centuries. Historically, the dual themes of assimilation and nationalism have been represented by proponents seemingly at odds in their ideological position relative to liberation for African people in North America. We should note that there were and are African descended "leaders" and ordinary folk who vacillated between these themes and others who positioned themselves (knowingly or unknowingly) between the two. The accommodationist nature of proponents of assimilation has been essentially defeatist and not a viable option for freedom in the United States or elsewhere. Despite the historical shifts from nationalists to accommodationist (and vice versa) as result of the bankruptcy of one movement or the other to advance its cause, Black nationalism has always had a significant constituency in the African and African-descended community in North America, which tends to expand during periods of crisis and contract under overtly oppressive conditions.

Black nationalist movements have also embodied an internal contraction (accommodation) or expansion (pan-African nationalism) in terms of pushing for full rights as citizens, or for a physic and physical space that Africans and descendants would govern, and an unambiguous sense of identity. The so-called club movement of self-help institutions among African-descended women in the early 1800s, as well as the national convention movement, sought to address nationalists concerns in their debates over how Africans and their descendants should culturally identify themselves. It was the appearance of David Walker's *Appeal*, however, that engendered a more unambiguous and pan-African nationalist stance against enslavement, an institution which he saw affecting African people worldwide. Originally published in 1829, the *Appeal* offered a severe criticism of the system of enslavement, a call for revolt by the enslaved, and provided a nationalist alternative to accommodationist perspectives (within the national convention movement) on how Africans should culturally identity themselves. Henry Highland Garnet published his 1847 address and Walker's *Appeal* together. Garnet, like David Walker, viewed nationalism as not simply a means to freedom but an eternal principle to struggle toward. Garnet defended the notion of African humanity and linked the fate of Africans within and outside the United States together, and saw that it was the responsibility of the oppressed to liberate themselves. He later moved toward the idea of emigration to Liberia but remained opposed to the notion of involuntary emigration as a condition of liberation in North America, while cooperating with the New York State Colonization Society. Garnet studied much and was a precursor to W. E. B. DuBois, Paul Roberson, and the scholastic tradition embodied by the late Cheikh Anta Diop of Senegal. In an 1848 speech delivered in Troy, New York, Garnet noted the contributions of Africans to ancient civilization while Anglo-Saxons were living in caves, and called for ideological unity among African descendants in North America.

Between 1830 and 1860, nationalists who articulated the means by which genuine sovereignty might be attained countered the forces of accommodationism. The accommodationist movement contracted and the nationalist movement expanded during this period. The voices of nineteenth-century nationalists, such as Martin R. Delany, Edward Wilmot Blyden, Alexander Crummell, Bishop Henry McNeil Turner, and George Washington Williams reflected pan-African nationalist sentiments as well as ideas that underpinned the accommodationist outlook. Tunde Adeleke, in *UnAfrican Americans*, argues that Crummell, Turner, and Delany combined a strong affection for Africa with an equally strong, if not stronger, commitment to becoming "fully American" because of their ambivalence on the question of identity. Though Alexander Crummell did attempt to Christianize and introduce Western ideas among Africans, Edward Wilmot Blyden pioneered the concept of the African personality, and Henry McNeal Turner taught Black nationalism and pan-Africanism, advocated the view that God was Black, and extended his message of "Black pride" in Africa. Martin R. Delany, a proponent of pan-African nationalism, called attention to the African character of Africans in the North and the U.S. South, and held that the strength of African culture was essential to ending the ambivalence on the question of identity.

Martin Delany and Frederick Douglass, who coedited *The North Star* publication founded in 1847, personify the dual character of African nationality building in North America between accommodationist and nationalist ideologies as well as within the accommodationist and nationalist movements. For instance, Delany called for political independence and the realization of African-descended freedoms in Africa, and Douglass demanded full citizenship in North American; later, Douglass briefly contemplated political independence for African descendants as a "nation," and Delany momentarily tested the path of U.S. citizenship through his participation in the Civil War and the politics of Reconstruction. With the betrayal of Reconstruction and Jim Crowism, the nationalist spirit found expression in movements in the United States to establish all-African-descended towns and Oklahoma as an all-African-descended state. The nineteenth century also saw the emigration of thousands of African descendants from the United States to Haiti. People of African descent entered the twentieth century poised for a new political, cultural, and institutional direction that was not being provided by personalities such as Booker T. Washington, who himself opposed "going back to Africa" but was critical of the Belgium in the Kôngo (Congo) and sponsored programs and opportunities for African descendants in the United States to return to the African continent. It was Washington who inspired Marcus Garvey to come to the United States and who Garvey wanted to meet (but Washington died before Garvey arrived in North America).

The pan-African nationalism of the Garvey movement and the accommodationist nationalism represented by the Communist-oriented African Blood Brotherhood (ABB) directly or indirectly influenced the Harlem Renaissance of the early twentieth century. The ABB was founded by Cyril V. Briggs in 1919 as a result of a split from A. Philip Randolph's *Messenger* publication over definitions of radicalism. (The ABB momentarily leaned toward nationalism rather than the socialism that was advanced by the Communist movement.) Members of the ABB included notables such as Richard B. Moore and Hubert Harrison; Harrison originated the Harlem street corner orator tradition that Malcolm X later embraced, fashioned the slogan "Race First," and provided a platform for Marcus Garvey when he arrived in Harlem. Although Garvey represented the sentiments of pan-African nationalism in the early twentieth century, W. E. B. DuBois, his supposed rival, discovered the Black nationalist tradition in the 1890s through intense study and believed that nationalism was an effective means in the liberation struggles of Africans in America. DuBois viewed African descendants in the United States as a permanent and a distinct group with specific nonnegotiable values, and he viewed the United States as a nation filled with great possibilities of culture and an original destiny based on African ideals. He marked a new development in the nationalist tradition by virtue of his ability to move easily among his people and take part in the sacred settings of their lives, since DuBois was keenly aware that nationalism existed among the grassroots as well. Though he might be considered by some to be a pan-Africanist and an accommodationist, for him, there was reconciliation between Black nationalism and socialism, which he considered to have deep roots in African communalism.

In the 1930s and 1940s, DuBois contemplated the feasibility of Black nationalism in North America on a programmatic basis. He established connections between African culture and Black nationalism and drew upon indigenous values found in West African societies so that African descendants in North America might organize their lives in cooperative communities—a spiritual unity. These efforts derived from a vision of cooperative societies as the primary vehicles for the transformation, through trained leadership, of the majority of the African descendants into leaders. For DuBois, as well as Paul Roberson, African liberation was worldwide in scope. Roberson viewed that African peoples should seek out and build upon their common qualities with the objective of developing a more expansive and composite African culture. Pan-African nationalists such as Carlos Cook and those of the post–Civil Rights era also recognized the relationship between culture, identity, and sovereignty. At a 1959 convention in Harlem, Cook, founder of the Garvey-orientated African Nationalist Pioneer Movement, called for the abrogation of the term *negro*; this term went out of use in the 1960s and 1970s as a result of the efforts of the pan-African nationalist movements of the Black Power era. In hindsight, the ultimate concerns of the Civil Rights and Black Power movements were similar, and the latter was the logical and almost inevitable extension of the former.

More than any other period of Black nationalist activity, the 1960s and 1970s witnessed efforts to form networks of nationalist organizations, the creation of a nationwide system of African-centered schools independent of white control and economically self-sufficient, and a multitude of disengaged organizations of various strands of nationalist thought that vied for ascendancy as the most "correct" ideological path toward liberation. The distinct forms of Black nationalism reflect a matter of emphasis rather than mutual exclusivity. Most nationalists share the goal of liberation and thus, for example, the distinction between revolutionary and cultural nationalism (often personified by the US Organization–Black Panther Party schism) is not really a fundamental one at all. The incoherence of Black nationalist thought exists, in large part, because of a preoccupation with an advocating group's own particular strategy or tactic rather than starting from the goal, and a deficiency in the study of the history and culture of the people for whom they claim to advocate. Komozi Woodard, in *A Nation within a Nation: Amiri Baraka (Leroi Jones) and Black Power Politics*, examined the proliferation of Black nationalism in the urban centers of the late twentieth century, and the dynamics and ascendance of Black cultural nationalism in the broader context of nationality formation. In the final analysis, he regarded nationalism as heterogeneous, linked to day-to-day struggles, and concluded there is no pure nationalist ideology.[6] Nonetheless, it seems the stability of Black nationalism has been its concern with liberation and cultural identity. Dexter B. Gordon, in *Black Identity: Rhetoric, Ideology, and Nineteenth-Century Black Nationalism*, grounded his study in the words and works of nineteenth-century personalities such as Maria Stewart, David Walker, and Henry Garnet, and found that language was used to establish cultural identity in ways that would advance liberation. In the classic text, *Black Nationalism: In Search of an Identity*, E. U. Essien-Odom observed that the Nation of Islam served primarily as a means for poor, urban, African descendants to attain a national identity and a sense of "ethnic" consciousness. However, as Harold Cruse aptly noted in *Crisis of the Negro Intellectual*, Essien-Udom failed to see that culture, economics, and politics had to function in a new and dynamic synthesis, a synthesis that few Black nationalists have been able to effect.

Throughout its history in North America, the overall ideology of Black nationalism lacked coherency and adequate theoretical clarity and, as a result, the Black Power movement was weakened from within by opportunism, ideological conflicts, paranoia, ineffectual leadership, lack of managerial skills, and a weak financial base.[7] Harold Cruse's observation in the 1960s that Black nationalism was fragmented into sects, factions, and cliques that resembled a morass of self-inflicted immobility and frustration still holds true.[8] Amos Wilson, in *Blueprint for Black Power*, also observed that Black nationalists and nationalistic organizations functionally exist but lack a consensually clarified set of goals and a working, well-coordinated system of interdependent nationalist organizations, and the wherewithal to convert ambiguously defined nationalist sentiments into a powerful movement. Wilson advocated the formation of a Black nationalist party to serve as the primary and legitimate leader on behalf of the African-descended community through viable and workable plans, provisions for training and organizing know-how, and as the community's primary political arm, chief negotiator, and principal agency for forming coalitions with others. Some nationalists argue that the United States or its revolutionary potentiality is where efforts should be focused, and others argue that the African continent is the African's and African descendant's only true place to realize freedom and an identity of wholeness. Nationalists of the latter persuasion, such as the Republic of New Afrika, claim five states in the U.S. South on the premise that an African-descended majority owns much of these lands, especially in Mississippi. Yet, quite a few Africans on the African continent and in the Caribbean are overwhelming majorities on their land but still remain conceptual and physical dependents of external thinking, goods, and monetary systems that seemingly govern their lives.

The nationalists that seek to organize the "masses," while their own families and children suffer from acute forms of neglect or abuse, have failed to realize that mass movements have not shown to be sustainable or a viable strategy in freedom movements. Certainly the idea of fighting for compensations through legal means—such as the case for reparations led by the National Coalition of Blacks for Reparations in America—is not new, and the reparations campaign is a tactic rather than a goal that may yield some interesting outcomes. But reparations or not, liberation will remain a different question. Harold Cruse was convinced that the liberation of African descendants in North America ultimately lay in an understanding, appreciation, and assertion of their cultural heritage. Black nationalism is inherently a cultural-ideological statement, and perhaps by drawing upon pan-African nationalist conceptions unambiguously linked to culture, identity, and liberation, nationalists will forge a coherent framework by which to achieve and sustain sovereignty in North America or the larger African world. Indeed, the prime ingredient of nationalism is the will to be a "nation" defined by culture rather than the unstable construct of race for the ends of group consciousness and collective action.

Overview

Chapter 1 provides a historical setting that includes the education and community-based activities of Africans and their descendants in Brooklyn, New York, from largely the nineteenth century to the Ocean Hill–Brownsville struggles of the late 1960s. Specifically, I look closely at African-descended communities such as Weeksville and Carsville and limit myself to the educational concerns of African descendants in Brooklyn. As such, particular attention is paid to community control of school efforts of the nineteenth and twentieth centuries, culminating in a detailed examination of the Ocean Hill–Brownsville Demonstration District struggles from 1966 to 1968. Chapter 2 explores the inception, structure, and subsequent developments of The East organization. This chapter examines the institutional building efforts and challenges of The East in three overlapping developmental phases: emergence (summer 1969–summer 1972), ascension (summer 1972–summer 1978), and decline (summer 1978–summer 1986). In 1976, The East was decentralized, which coincided with the relocation of most of its primary operations to the Sumner Avenue armory (renamed the Uhuru Cultural Center) on Marcus Garvey Boulevard in Brooklyn. The decentralized East had nine departments, each headed by an elected official, and all officials formed the "Family Leadership Council" of The East. These developments, along with key decisions made shortly thereafter, signaled and perhaps hastened the decline of The East organization.

Chapter 3 explores the role and function of the primary enterprises of The East. Though there were (an estimated) twenty to thirty operations that existed under The East umbrella during the life of the organization, many were short-lived while others remained throughout the late 1970s and early 1980s. The enduring enterprises that are explored include the *Black News*, Akiba Mkuu Bookstore, East Publications, East Kitchen and

Caterers, Sweet-East restaurant, Kununuana (Uhuru Food Cooperative), and Mavazi Clothing Cooperative. This exploration underscores the relationship of these enterprises to The East and the larger African and African-descended community. Chapter 4 takes a detailed look at the emergence, the structure, and the educational philosophy and content of Uhuru Sasa Shule, the primary component of The East. It also examines its role in the formative years of the Council of Independent Black Institutions. Uhuru Sasa Shule (Freedom Now School) was developed within the theory and practice of the *Nguzo Saba* ("the seven principles of Blackness") with the objective to liberate the "African psyche" so cannibalized by racism and white hegemony in order to determine and develop a qualitative (African) way of interpreting and relating to the world. Uhuru Sasa Shule began as an evening school and matured into a full-time school in the fall of 1970. The establishment and development of Imani Child Development Center (preschool), Uhuru Sasa Shule's primary, elementary, and secondary levels, and the Evening School of Knowledge (for all ages) are examined level by level.

Chapter 5 explores the formative years of the African Street Festival (now the International African Arts Festival), its growth and its transformations, and the festival's future direction. Few could have imagined that a city "block party" would become what the festival is today. It began as an end-of-the-school-year ceremony designed by the parents of Uhuru Sasa Shule. Today, what was a graduation ceremony at 10 Claver Place is among the most anticipated cultural extravaganzas in Brooklyn, which is attended by approximately sixty to seventy thousand African and African-descended people in a safe, culturally affirming, and communal environment. Chapter 6 addresses the contours of African descendants as a "cultural nation" in the United States, the role and vitality of culture in the context of African-centered education, the power relationships that exist and challenge the development of these realities, and concludes The East experience with its implications and legacy. A brief epilogue on the current status of The East family is presented as well with key documents included in the appendixes. It is hoped that historians and students of the 1960s and 1970s, of freedom and educational movements among African descendants, and of African-descended cultural and social history will find this revised edition useful.

A View from The East

1
Ujima

Context and Community Control

> People of African descent in the United States can only be understood when both the African cultural and Western hemisphere political realities are taken into account together. . . . These factors have affected the culture, the socialization processes, and the very consciousness of African people.
>
> ASA G. HILLIARD, *The Maroon Within Us*

> How shall we turn the ghettos into a vast school? How shall we make every street corner a forum . . . ? How shall we make every houseworker and every laborer a demonstrator, a voter, a canvasser and a student? The dignity their jobs may deny them is waiting for them in political and social action.
>
> MARTIN LUTHER KING, JR., *Where Do We Go from Here: Chaos or Community?*

The year 1967 marked the final publication from Dr. Martin Luther King, Jr., evocatively titled *Where Do We Go from Here: Chaos or Community?* That year also marked the emergence of the community control and independent Black school movements in largely urban centers with sizeable populations of African ancestry. These two movements grew almost simultaneously from the Freedom School efforts of the Civil Rights movement and an earlier tradition of establishing Black educational institutions independent of white control predating the U.S. Civil War, though each affected the scope and direction of the other in different ways. The community control of public schools and the independent Black school movements of the 1960s situated themselves on what

Dr. King called "political and social action" marked by a nebulous distinction between schooling and education, decision-making power and parental involvement, and divergent arguments by African-descended educators and activists who advocated the possibility of transforming urban schools and "making them work" and others who supported the idea of and forged independent Black schools. Former Civil Rights activists transformed by the Black Power movement and Black nationalists of the period constituted the latter group of independent Black school forgers in the 1960s.

The classic and most telling case of the community-control movement was the Ocean Hill–Brownsville Demonstration District in Brooklyn, New York, and several scholars have noted its significance decades after its slow but painful demise in 1968—the year Dr. King was assassinated in Memphis, Tennessee. The central issues of decision-making powers, accountability, and the political and cultural context of schooling are still foremost for many African-descended parents and community activists in New York City, and power struggles of the 1960s suggest that those issues paralleled the control of an educational budget of more than a billion dollars, thousands of nonteaching jobs, the authority of the teachers' union, lucrative construction contracts, curricula content and educational resources, and local and state officials whose interests were at odds with parents and activists. Contemporary struggles over schooling and education predicated on much of the same issues present during the 1960s, and those struggles have specific implications for current debates centered on the ways in which African-descended parents and activists have responded to the struggle over schooling and education by way of vouchers, charter schools, independent schools, private and parochial schools, and home schooling. Indeed, for African-descended parents and other community activists, the issue some forty years ago and "the issue today is a political question involving the accountability and a sharing of power in the decision-making."[1] However, the struggle over schooling and education in New York City in general and Brooklyn in particular must be understood in the historical context of early African-descended communities and the pursuit of a quality education and life.

African American Community and Education in Brooklyn

The descendants of Africans first brought to the Dutch colony of New Netherlands in 1626 came to later occupy some of the earliest communities in Brooklyn, New York. Communities such as Weeksville, Clarksville, Carsville, and Tompkinsville existed in the nineteenth century and perhaps earlier, when Brooklyn emerged as a distinct territory no longer part of Long Island. Brooklyn became incorporated as a city in 1834, and in 1898 it merged with New York City. Throughout the eighteenth and mid-nineteenth centuries, Kings County consisted of six independent towns: Brooklyn, Bushwick, Flatbush, Flatlands, Gravesend, and (New) Utrecht. Between 1870 and 1900, however, Brooklyn came to encompass all of Kings County. The most distinct, independent, African-descended communities that emerged in the vast and semirural region of Brooklyn's ninth ward were known as Weeksville and Carsville, both of which existed in the 1830s.[2] However, owing to white encroachment, the Africans and their descendants in Weeksville no longer formed as distinct a community by the 1870s.[3] The migration of African descendants from Manhattan, owing to the Anti-Draft Riots of 1863, also played a factor in the texture of the Weeksville community in the later nineteenth century. It is unclear to what extent this migration impacted Weeksville community life; since these migrants encountered extant communities, Robert Swan's assertion that "Brooklyn's earliest black community migrated across the river [i.e., Manhattan] and not from Long Island farms" is misleading.[4]

The Weeksville community of the nineteenth century was located in what is now the Bedford-Stuyvesant or Central Brooklyn area. Although there are no conclusions as to the person for whom the community was named, the present consensus is that James Weeks was the founder of the settlement. However, there was another James Weeks and at least eighteen other persons with the surname *Weeks*. Recent evidence suggests that the community or its nucleus dates back to the 1770s, though "the first listing of Weeksville in the Brooklyn City Directory occurred after 1837."[5] The community is known to have provided economic opportunity and charitable institutions by and for African descendants, including a refuge for those who migrated to Weeksville due the Anti-Draft Riots of 1863, in which poor whites blamed the hated Civil War draft on African descendents who resided in Manhattan. Determined to defend their lives and homes against an attack during the riots, the African descendants of Weeksville took up arms and posted guard. Be that as it may, the major educational institution in Weeksville was Colored School No. 2, one of four designated "colored schools." Founded in 1847 at a site between Troy Avenue and Bergen Street, it catered exclusively to the community members of Weeksville and its territory.[6] Around September 1840, community leaders of Carsville, another African-descended community in the rural ninth ward of Brooklyn, formed the African Union Society, which built a small schoolhouse and, subsequently, established African School No. 2. Dominic Nwasike, a professor who worked with the Society for the Preservation of Weeksville founded in 1969, reported, "[The] period between 1840 and 1900 marked the highpoint of the community. These were the decades in which the various social institutions were developed. . . . Most importantly, the period witnessed the demands by blacks for control of the training of their children."[7] Publications such as the *Sunbeam*, the *New York Age*, and the *Brooklyn Sentinel* were established between 1865 and 1885 and formed part of these social institutions.

Founded in 1882, the most prominent and viable financial institution owned and operated by African descendants was the Afro-American Investment and Building Company, which extended its operations into New Jersey and the greater New York area. Yet, many of the social and benevolent organizations were funded by white philanthropy in the latter part of the nineteenth century, as Brooklyn, rather than Manhattan, became the early center of cultural life. In the nineteenth century, white paternalism guided a number of Protestant churches in the establishment of the African Infant School Association, which aimed to plant the "seeds of virtue, the habits of good order and industry, [and] the gain of religious feeling" through a "separate" school for African descendants.[8] From the start of the Dutch colony of New Netherlands to British occupation thereafter, the core curriculum of any schooling that Africans received revolved around the axis of a "civilizing mission." The first of such schools opened in New York City in 1704 for enslaved

Africans; attendance was, however, voluntary. This catechist school was halted because of the African revolt of 1712, where eight whites were killed and others wounded. However, classes resumed shortly after the revolt. From 1760 to 1774, the Anglicans ran a full-time day school for African children in New York City, and reading, sewing, knitting, and the "principles of Christianity" were staples of its curriculum. Some have argued that this was the only known full-time school for Africans in the colonial era.[9]

In 1787, the New York Manumission Society established the African Free School in New York City, which multiplied into several schools, later evolving into the city's Black public school system.[10] Though African-descended community leaders embraced the African Free Schools, "by the 1830s the African-American community had achieved enough cohesion to assert their collective interest in school administration and curricular policies."[11] In 1834, consequently, "African-American demands for community control of public schools, along with logistical problems tied to the rapid expansion of the African Free Schools, led the Manumission Society to drop its role in public schooling . . . and instead focus on extending charity education to the poor."[12] This confrontation was, perhaps, inevitable, not only because the principal and most of the teachers were white, but also because those who wielded power rarely relinquished or shared it without struggle. The African Free Schools were turned over to a white charity society, the New York Public School Society (NYPSS), instead of the community or the African-controlled Society for Education among Colored Children's School (SECCS). The New York City Board of Education would, however, absorb the schools of both the NYPSS and SECCS in 1853.[13]

What historians have called "separate" schools for Africans and their descendants can be problematic because such labeling of institutions owned and operated by Africans as "separatist" structures distorts the reality of early African-based education and community development. There is a distinction between forced association and voluntary association; enslavement, colonialism, and segregation are all forms of a system of forced association. On the contrary, voluntary association is a conscious act or choice on the part of a person or group to build structures, for example, that reflect and affirm who and what they are; forced association is the absence or limitation of such a choice. For instance, the village of Brooklyn opened its district school on May 6, 1816. In 1817, the single building installed a classroom on the top floor for African students; the rest of the building catered to whites, as schools for the latter were separate as an act of policy by white school officials. The room for these African students, totaling forty-five in 1818, was called the "African District School," according to one historian who asserted that this was the beginning of "Brooklyn's separate black public schools" and perhaps "the earliest known black public school in New York State."[14] However, this claim seems dubious, since "from 1819–1825 and after 1827 [to 1845] an African district was not part of Brooklyn's district school system."[15]

In 1827, the African Woolman Benevolent Society (AWBS) built and managed a school exclusively for the "African District School," which had been forced out of the building in which it occupied a room. The AWBS and school officials "hired their own teachers, maintained the building and raised funds for the school by solicitations, subscriptions and exhibitions." From 1817 to 1843, Carleton Mabee argued Africans had "unusual" control over the "Black public school," which ended with the unification of the school districts under an all-white Board of Education in 1843. According to Robert J. Swan, "Generally, most black schools were private schools managed by blacks and were excluded from the white school system until the enactment of the state's segregated school law in 1841. Yet [Mabee] infers that from 1817 to 1843 blacks had control of an 'African Public School.'" Swan further indicates that "from 1815 to 1845 blacks did have control over [their] school but it was not a public school. When it did become a public school blacks ultimately lost control of it. . . . Therefore, blacks did have control over their schools but this was not 'unusual control,' or sharing the administration of their schools with whites."[16] The absorption of these schools by the Board of Education's charter in March 1843 (amended in 1845 to include the "colored schools") resulted in a complete loss of control, and with the civil rights law passed in April 1873, Brooklyn's African descendants sought the right to enter white public schools. On the Black school question, some African descendants wanted to do away with them but were concerned about the teachers in the white public schools; others, though wanting to preserve them, still were not certain about a course of action. On the issue, arguments about whether African-descended teachers should teach students of African descent erupted with similar ambivalence; yet, African descendants in Brooklyn were among those who campaigned for African-descended teachers in their schools.[17] During this period, the African descendants of Weeksville were the first to demand for the supervision (i.e., control) of the schools in their community.[18]

It is important to note that not all African-descended schools were abolished during and after the U.S. Reconstruction era of the late nineteenth century. For example, there was a provision to operate schools for African-descended students in the 1897 charter of the newly enlarged city of New York, a year after the *Plessy v. Ferguson* decision. As more and more African-descended students attended schools with whites, Mabee argues that most did so from 1900 to 1945. This claim, however, is an overstatement, because Mabee himself suggested African descendants who migrated from the south helped to "reintroduce" the very segregation that was being sought for abolishment in the first half of the twentieth century.[19] In fact, "Between 1954 and 1960 the number of segregated [Black] and Puerto Rican Schools in Brooklyn increased from nine to thirty-eight."[20] One of the largest African-descended communities to which these African descendents migrated was the Bedford-Stuyvesant area, which included and still includes most of the Ocean Hill–Brownsville district.

Ocean Hill is the border area between Brownsville and Bedford-Stuyvesant.[21] The then-expansive Bedford-Stuyvesant community originated from the shifting population of the 1920s and, later, the white exodus to the suburbs and the "second great black migration [which] resulted in the urbanization of 4 million more Africans between 1940 and 1970."[22] Between 1950 and 1960, the cultural and racial composition of the Brooklyn population was significantly transformed (see table 1.1). In the 1960s, Brooklyn's African-descended population remained "grossly under-represented despite the rising percentage of the black population and the white exodus from Kings County."[23] As Bedford-Stuyvesant became denser and overcrowded, the phenomena of structural deterioration, high rent in poor apartment complexes, and health problems linked to socioeconomic factors were all symptoms ignored by the established political and social order. Likewise, those who governed the educational system ignored the demands for greater accountability and genuine parent involvement.

African-descended parents, students, community activists, and teachers who advocated the strategy of community control held that the transfer of power from the Board of Education should be vested in the African-descended community to determine the nature of their children's education and the policies governing the educational process.[24] Community control of schools was thus conceived as directly engaging in the policy-making process as an exercise of power. Yet, many activists of the 1960s felt community control should have greater significance beyond the educational system and, indeed, "the notion of control should include a concern for the overall local institutions."[25] In this respect, community control of schools was defined by activists as the power to make and enforce the

Table 1.1 African-descended population of Brooklyn, 1698–1960

Year	Total pop.	African-descended pop.	Percentage
1698	2,017	296	15.0 (KC)
1790	4,549	1,528	34.0 (KC)
1790	1,656	469	28.0
1800	5,720	1,811	32.0 (KC)
1810	2,378	668	15.0
1840	36,233	1,772	5.0
1870	419,921	5,653	1.3 (KC)
1870	396,099	4,931	1.2
1900	1,166,582	18,367	1.6[a]
1910	1,634,351	22,708	1.4
1920	2,018,356	31,912	1.5[b]
1930	2,560,401	68,921	2.7[b]
1940	2,698,285	107,263	4.0
1950	2,738,175	208,478	7.6
1960	2,627,319	371,405	14.1

[a]Population of Brooklyn and Kings County (KC) combined; between 1870 and 1900, Brooklyn encompassed all of Kings County.
[b]Periods of migration of African-descendants from the South, from the Caribbean, and from Manhattan to Brooklyn.

following: (1) the control of expenditure of local, state, and federal funds; (2) control over hiring, firing, training, and the reprogramming of all staff; (3) control over site selection and the naming of schools; (4) control over the design and construction of schools; (5) control over the purchasing of books, supplies, equipment, and food services; (6) control over setting the educational policy, school and community curricula, and educational program activities; and (7) control over merit pay.[26]

The Ocean Hill–Brownsville Struggle for Community Control

The contemporary struggle to control the schools in the Black community began in East Harlem with the opening of Intermediate School (IS) 201 in September 1966.[27] James Doughty asserted, "[this] struggle [had] given identity, purpose, and direction to the Black movement" of the 1960s.[28] However, the effort to assume community control was not an isolated phenomenon. This struggle had its roots in a longstanding Black nationalist tradition, which expressed itself more vigorously in the Black Power and Consciousness movement of the 1960s and 1970s and represented a broad and visionary sociopolitical movement and network. Additionally, the vision of this movement and the liberation struggles of African nations and the heightened sense of pan-Africanism acted as catalysts for further creative and critical responses to prevailing social conditions. The response by parents, students, and community activists to the failings of the school system, futile school reform efforts (i.e., the failure of Open Enrollment, the Princeton Plan pairing, rezoning, better site selection, educational parks, and educational clusters) and the promise of integration was to seek community control.[29] Such was sought under the pretext of the neighborhood school concept. Interestingly, Parents and Taxpayers (PAT), a white organization, supposedly put forth and endorsed "the concept of the neighborhood school [for white children], a concept that advocated that elementary education is about sending your child to local areas to feel a sense of security and cultural identification with the institution."[30] In addition to PAT, there were a number of white organizations that led the citywide coalition against the integration of New York City schools in the 1950s and 1960s. Most notable among these organizations were the

United Federation of Teachers, United Parents Association, Public Education Association (a white elite professional organization), and the Citizen's Committee for Children. All of these organizations had, of course, strong ties with the Board of Education and city and state officials.

The Ocean Hill–Brownsville Demonstration District consisted of eight schools, six elementary schools, and two junior high schools, with an approximately 95 percent African-descended and Latino student population, 540 teachers, and 35 administrators. In the 1960s, the New York City Board of Education was a "massive school system . . . [ran] by an enormous and largely unaccountable and inflexible bureaucracy. The bureaucracy [was] . . . overwhelmingly white and Jewish—over 60% of the teachers, and an even greater percentage of supervisors and headquarter bureaucrats [were] Jewish." In addition, "until 1967, there were only four black principals out of 865 . . . and only 12 black assistant principals in the 1500 positions at the rank."[31] Unlike small suburban districts, the large school districts of New York City were directed by an appointed board; after 1969, members of the board were elected. In 1964, James E. Allen, Jr., State Commissioner of Education, commissioned a report that resulted in shifting the school system "from 6-3-3 (first through sixth grade, seventh through ninth, and tenth through twelfth) to 4-4-4" and directed that "middle schools were to open throughout the district with the purpose of having an integrated school population."[32] The IS 201 complex was the first of these middle schools to take part in this initiative. However, the Board of Education (BOE) went against the parent council of IS 201, an ad hoc council formed to carry out the promise of school integration, and announced that the school was to have a 50 percent African-descended and a 50 percent Latino student population and a (white) Jewish principal.[33] The parent council's request and support for an integrated school was denied, so members opted for the right to control the school. In September 1966, East Harlem parents, students, and community leaders boycotted IS 201 because of unfulfilled promises and accompanying lies with regard to school integration and an educational relationship between a university and IS 201. The BOE sought to find an alternative solution to involve the community. On October 20, 1966, "the Board announced 'a desire to experiment with varying forms of decentralization and community control.'"³⁴ The BOE agreed to allow community participation and, tacitly, it also agreed to the demand for a principal of African descent to be chosen by the East Harlem community.

The United Federation of Teachers (UFT), formed in March 1960 out of a merger between the Teachers' League and a small group of high school teachers, saw these demands as extreme and thus boycotted to counteract the IS 201 group's demands. The BOE and the mayor's office proposed the establishment of a task force, headed by Ford Foundation president McGeorge Bundy, to recommend a solution. Bundy was apparently not persuaded, and the proposal was rejected. However, representatives of the BOE, the Ford Foundation, and the UFT and community groups met informally throughout the winter to develop a realistic plan for community involvement in school policy making. During this period, the BOE officially declared its support for the gradual administrative decentralization of its operations; meanwhile, growing unrest over school conditions increased among community activists and parents. The UFT suggested to the Ford Foundation, the financial backer of the program, that the Ocean Hill group should be included in the pilot program on decentralization. Although the union would suggest Ocean Hill–Brownsville in its support of decentralization, the union was more "interested in the expansion of [their] More Effective Schools program (M.E.S.), by which very substantial extra sums of money (about $600 additional per child) [were] invested in elementary schools."³⁵

After the incident at IS 201 in East Harlem and before the intervention of the Ford Foundation as a broker, "Mayor [John] Lindsay began negotiating with the state legislature for more aid to the city's schools." The mayor requested that the city be regarded not as one but five separate districts (i.e., one for each borough) because state aid to school districts was based on real estate values in the district. Hence, the greater the assessed valuation of the district, the less state aid and vice versa: "If state aid were to be computed by considering each borough separately, however, the city would be entitled to receive an additional $108 million annually." The mayor's request was abandoned once he and the legislature realized that this would create five separate school districts or five powerful bureaucracies instead of one. Thus, a compromise was reached that asked the mayor to submit a plan by December 1 to decentralize the school system. Contingent upon its acceptance, the "city would receive $54 million (not $108 million) in extra state aid."[36] James E. Allen, Jr., in the process of working out the plan with Mayor John Lindsay, converted Lindsay to the idea of school decentralization not only as a fund-raising device but as an educational one as well. Thereafter, the mayor became one of the most animate advocates of decentralization. Accordingly, "the shift in emphasis in the Black community coincided with Mayor Lindsay's attempt . . . to obtain more money . . . by proposing the decentralization of the school system into five, borough-wide districts."[37] Under the guidelines provided by James E. Allen, Mayor Lindsay proceeded to appoint an advisory panel, chaired by McGeorge Bundy, with the mission of formulating a comprehensive study in which the report would become the basis of a decentralization plan. Yet, even before Bundy went to work on this committee, he persuaded the Ford Foundation in June 1967 to finance four decentralization demonstration districts in New York City.[38]

The BOE adopted a mild decentralization plan that included the creation of three demonstration districts: IS 201 in East Harlem, Two Bridges in the Lower East Side of Manhattan, and Ocean Hill–Brownsville in Brooklyn. Three months later, the Ocean Hill Planning Council dropped its original request for the More Effective Schools program after the superintendent of schools, Bernard Donovan, claimed that not all schools in the district could be made MES schools. The teachers on the planning council opposed the change. On August 3, 1967, 1,049 out of 4,000 parents cast their ballots for seven parent representatives to the local governing board as a part of the Ocean Hill–Brownsville experimental school district. These elected representatives then chose five community representatives. As a part of the experiment, two supervisors and four teachers elected by colleagues would complete the membership of the local board.

In September 1967, the Mayor's Advisory Panel on Decentralization completed its report and recommended a drastic overhaul of the public school system. Upon its release, the advisory panel's plan, also referred to as the "Bundy Plan," was widely attacked by school professionals.[39] Subsequently, "the UFT, the Council of Supervisory Associations (CSA), and the Board of Education all successfully lobbied against its passage in the spring legislative session."⁴⁰ Furthermore, the UFT held a strike on all schools for a new contract on the opening day of school. Its contract demands included empowering teachers to expel what the UFT considered "disruptive" pupils from classes to special-service schools in which "teachers would be paid an extra thousand dollars a year to teach these 'special kids'" and expanding the MES program.⁴¹ Suspecting the motivation behind the disruptive-pupil demand, many parents of African descent withheld their support of the strike along with the Ocean Hill–Brownsville governing board. At this time, Albert Vann, president of the African American Teachers Association (ATA), had a heated public exchange with Albert Shanker, president of the UFT, concerning the disruptive child clause and its meaning. ATA was founded as the Negro Teachers Association at the Bedford YMCA on May 10, 1964, and became the African American Teachers Association in the summer of 1966. Though unsuccessful, Shanker sought to convince Vann that the clause would help children of African descent receive "special treatment."

Thus, "with the local district shunning the role of a ready-made M.E.S.-interest group, the union had no further use for the decentralization or local control." The strike ended with a settlement that gave the union a clause empowering it to spend $10 million of BOE money on an educational program. The settlement was significant. For the first time, a union had won a contractual right to make policy and, in so doing, won a shift in power as well as control. Robert Braun, in *Teachers and Power*, indicates that "control by contract requires, [then] at least, no promise of accountability, no real worries about the public's role in the operation of the schools."⁴² Moreover, the lines of vested interest were clearly defined when in "the aftermath of the strike, the U.F.T. forbade union teachers to become members of the governing board."⁴³ The Ocean Hill–Brownsville governing board was comprised of twelve members and chaired by Reverend C. Herbert Oliver. Another instrumental figure in the community-control struggles was the late Preston Wilcox, educator and archivist, who became the principal advisor to the IS 201 and Ocean Hill–Brownsville governing boards, respectively.

During August 1967, the new Ocean Hill–Brownsville governing board appointed Rhody McCoy, a teacher of eighteen years in the public school system, as unit administrator into what was referred to as a "chaotic situation." The situation was further compounded when eighteen assistant principals and five principals, upon being urged by the Council of Supervisory Associations (CSA), requested to be transferred from a district with a "daily absentee rate in the year before decentralization [of] 25 [percent]."[44] Shortly after McCoy became unit administrator, CSA, which consisted of school and assistant principals, district administrators, and upper-level staff personnel, filed a suit against the creation of the category of demonstration school principal, which was made by Superintendent Donovan after receiving approval from State Education Commissioner Allen. The UFT, in its attempt to be the co-plaintiff, was ruled ineligible to act in that capacity. Initially, CSA, joined by the UFT, was successful in the battle. From 1967 to 1969, CSA engaged in an informal alliance with the UFT, which brought together two factions of the pedagogical staff that formerly had been at odds. Not until January 15, 1969, did the Court of Appeals overrule the lower courts and find the central board's creation of the category of demonstration school principal correct on all counts. During the fall of 1967, the founding of the African American Students Association (ASA) embodied the activism and astuteness of high school students embroiled in the community-control struggle under the guidance of Jitu Weusi. Some of those students included John Marson, Sia Behran, and Ronald Breland, among of a list of others who came out of the Ocean Hill–Brownsville experience.

In December 1967, Mayor Lindsay submitted his revised decentralization plan to the state legislature to meet a December 1 deadline given by Allen. By March 1968, the Ocean Hill governing board demanded a clear grant of power instead of the vague mandate under which it was operating in negotiations with the central board; the powers of the experiment districts, however, would not be clarified until sometime in August 1968. According to one writer, "[the] local community boards floundered without direction, demanding clear-cut guidelines for operation, [and that Rhody] McCoy threatened to close the schools unless he had some idea of how they were supposed to be run. John Bremer, unit administrator at Two Bridges, quit in disgust, unable to obtain even some idea of what these experiments were supposed to be testing."[45] Bremer's resignation did not persuade Charles Wilson, unit administrator at IS 201, or Rhody McCoy. Both continued in their position, determined to make the "experiment" work. In the spring of 1968, the incidents and provocation between the UFT and the governing board reached their pinnacle. On May 10, 1968, the Ocean Hill governing board requested the involuntary transfer of thirteen teachers, five assistant principals, and one principal to central headquarters for reassignment. The UFT protested, claiming that the transfers were in fact firings and were done in violation of due process. The UFT then proceeded to strike, and approximately five hundred teachers walked out, with Albert Shanker vowing that they would not return until the experimentation was over. It was members of the African-American Teachers Association who went into the Ocean Hill–Brownsville district and kept the schools open while UFT teachers were on strike.

The actions taken by the Ocean Hill governing board and the UFT punctuate the most critical juncture in the case. For the governing board, this would explicitly mark the end of its beginning. "The U.F.T. had made the experiments a failure; the experiments themselves were inconclusive because they were destroyed before they bore fruit." However, was the governing board's transfer of the teachers and principals an "act to determine, through one test or another, exactly what powers it had"?[46] One report argues that the timing of the decision to transfer the teachers and the principals—just before the Albany legislature was to vote on the various decentralization plans—and the very provocativeness of the challenge implied that the dismissals were a deliberate test of the governing board's authority.[47] Yet, a transfer was not a dismissal or a firing. By failing to clearly define the authority and the function of the governing board and by refusing to cooperate with it, the central board was framing a confrontation. In a nebulous predicament, the local governing board was bound to overstep its vague authority and thus come into inevitable conflict with the central board.[48] The attempt by the Ocean Hill governing board to transfer the teachers and principals out of the district was "a common practice in the New York City school system, yet the central board denied Rhody McCoy, as demonstration district supervisor, the powers normally given to district supervisors."[49] In fact, none of the teachers and principals lost a day's pay, and the letter informing them of their transfer not only offered them an opportunity to appeal—the central board did not provide transfers on appeals—but also instructed them to report to the central board for reassignment.

The Bundy Plan was discarded, and the legislature substituted the plan advocated by the New York State Board of Regents, the technical overseer of all public education in the state. The legislature passed the Marchi Law, which postponed action for one year and authorized the BOE to formulate an interim plan. In turn, some authority was given to local school and demonstration districts, in addition to the membership of the nine-member mayor-appointed central board, which was expanded to thirteen. Central Board president Alfred Giardino resigned and thus left opponents of the Bundy Plan with a one-vote advantage over the Lindsay appointees. Yet, Mayor Lindsay, a strong advocate for decentralization, and his forces did not lobby against the Marchi Law because "Marchi was the chairman of the Senate Committee on New York City and an important keeper of the keys for Lindsay's perennial begging for more state aid for the city."[50] After two resignations in August 1968, the Lindsay pro-decentralization forces now commanded control of the new central board. Subsequently, the Ocean Hill governing board received permission to recruit new teachers to replace striking teachers to staff the schools in the fall. Even though most of the teachers hired during the governing board's tenure were white, they also hired the first Puerto Rican and Chinese principals in New York City history.[51]

By September 4, 1968, the new central board announced an interim decentralization plan that gave some local control to thirty local school boards and the three demonstration school districts with the exception of electing school board members in regular school districts. Between September 9 and November 17, the UFT held three strikes, resulting in some of the most adverse effects on public schools in New York City history. The UFT strikes were aimed at "what had been considered very promising experiments in community control of the public schools."[52] After the second strike on September 13, which negated the voice of a African-descended caucus in the UFT that opposed the strike, James E. Allen proposed a compromise: He suspended the local governing board and temporarily transferred several teachers out of the district. By this time, "most ATA members [had] already disassociated themselves from the UFT."[53] Considering Allen's compromise, the UFT only accepted the latter portion of his decision. Despite this, Commissioner Allen ordered the BOE to suspend the local board. Afterward, the local board was suspended a second time for failing to assign the disputed teachers to classroom duties, though all nineteen of them transferred to other districts in February 1969.

Throughout all the negotiations, each and every agreement between the central board and the UFT was reached without the participation of the local board. On October 8, 1968, Rhody McCoy and seven of his eight principals were relieved of their duties and reassigned to the central headquarters. However, McCoy refused to be reassigned and remained in the Ocean Hill–Brownsville district. After the seven principals were reinstated and Junior High School (JHS) 271 reopened from its two-day closure, the UFT struck for the third time and demanded that:

1. JHS 271 be kept closed, and only principals who will abide by previous agreements with the central board should return;

2. The Ocean Hill–Brownsville project was to be termed a failure;

3. The governing board, unit administrator, teachers, and supervisors in the schools who were guilty of threats of violence and intimidation should be permanently removed;

4. The eight schools in the district should be returned to the central school system.

In a pointless attempt to resolve the situation, Mayor Lindsay appointed a fact-finding panel headed by Theodore Kheel. However, the panel quit after only four days. The third strike ended with the central board and the UFT, without the participation of the local board, agreeing on a plan that would place the district under state trusteeship. Arising from such agreements, the UFT received a guarantee that, pending the negotiation of a mutually satisfactory clause, the arbitration machinery of the contract would cover involuntary transfers. Several weeks after the foregoing settlement, Rhody McCoy was reinstated as unit administrator, yet the Ocean Hill–Brownsville governing board remained suspended until March, while others faced charges of harassment. The "School Decentralization

Bill" adopted by the New York State Legislature on April 30, 1969, stated that the then-present community boards were to remain in force until February 16, 1970. The new decentralization bill maintained that (1) the employment and placement of educational personnel will be carried out by the central Board of Education; (2) the local boards would have a limited role in the curriculum development; (3) the demonstration districts would be absorbed into the new structure of thirty-two local school districts to be governed by elected school boards; (4) a new interim central Board of Education, consisting of one member appointed by each of the five borough presidents, would serve for a period of one year; and (5) a new seven-member board would be established—one member from each borough and two to be appointed by the mayor for a four-year term. As the position of chancellor came to replace the superintendent as head of schools, the 1969 legislation remained in place for twenty-seven years until it was reversed by action of the state legislature on December 18, 1996.

Jitu Weusi, a teacher at JHS 271 during the Ocean Hill–Brownsville struggle, concluded, "The Ocean Hill–Brownsville confrontation of 1968 had the most profound impact in New York City of any incident within the past 50 years."[54] The struggles not only served as a unifying force within and between African-descended and Latino communities but, as Mwalimu Shujaa and Hannibal Afrik indicate, the "struggles over control of schools in settings such as the Ocean Hill–Brownsville Experimental School District in New York City brought the power of whites to control African schooling into clear focus."[55] This clarity, furthermore, revealed not only the vested interests of the UFT, the Board of Education, and state and city educational and governing bodies, but it also revealed that some teachers of African descent would not risk their position for a purpose greater than themselves, despite the responsibility that they have to their students and the community they serve. According to one educator, such teachers "helped transfer the victory [of seemingly improved education] into defeat."[56]

The Ocean Hill–Brownsville case offers an instance where the ideological assumption that liberal whites, educators, and politicians would be the alternatives to the policies of the established sociopolitical order proved to be painfully false. Indeed, the case came down to the issue of power. Again, the control of more than a billion dollar educational budget, thousands of nonteaching jobs, the dominance of the teachers' union, lucrative construction contracts, curricula and content and educational resources, and the continued hegemony of the white political structure were all being challenged. With the common denominator of power in the equation, the defense mechanisms of the state and city educational and political structure signaled a call to arms and declared war. As one writer remarked, "[if] it means, as it did in New York City in 1968, keeping teachers out so long that the school children suffer measurable damage ... then that is war."[57] The nature of the struggles were so pronounced in scope that one high school student, synthesizing the feelings of so many other high school students, stated, "This is only a power play and we students are being used as pawns. I feel so helpless."[58] Indeed, only "fools and those in control of the schools are willing to say the free public system is in reality both free and public."[59] The struggle that began at IS 201 in Harlem and crystallized in Ocean Hill–Brownsville acts as a mnemonic for popular movements in that an "ironic aspect of black popular movements is the way in which white (western) elements act as catalysts in the emotional reaction which [produces] nationalist feelings."[60] The historical struggles for community control of schools in Brooklyn reveals that the issue of central importance "is not merely socialization, but the nature of the socialization process for African [descended] children."[61]

Education and Schooling in Perspective

All human experiences occur in the context of culture, and education or socialization is no different. Cultural and educational institutions are centers of socialization that intentionally engage the challenges of identity formation and build a commitment to one's culture and community. The importance of this aspect of education and culture, as Fu-Kiau and Lukondo-Wamba have argued, is that "[w]hat the childhood of a generation is will be what that generation becomes in its adulthood. A ruined childhood is a ruined society. . . . [Thus,] what is true for the life of a child is also true for the life of a nation."[62] Among African and African-descended people in North America, the power to determine the nature of quality education in the context of one's culture is an imperative no less than being self-determinative to a certain quality of life.[63] By quality education, we are referring to a process whereby the intellectual, spiritual, and physical development of a person and group occurs in the context of competence in one's community and culture and, as a corollary, the preservation and continuity of that culture and sense of community. Contemporarily, the form that this thrust for quality education has taken not only illuminates our understanding of schooling within the present social and political arrangement, but also illuminates the power of relationships involved in the processes of schooling and education. Education, within the context of one's culture, is the transmission of cultural knowledge from one generation to the next; a people must be able to transmit culture, in all its implicit and explicit forms, so as to exist as dynamic agents of their own development. It is the umbilical cord that provides further life and potentiality and, therefore, determines a cultural group's ultimate destiny.

Certainly, a design for education cannot be separated from the aspirations and goals of a people. As such, African and African-descended people in North America and their basis and construction of identity, and the means by which to approach and clarify "national" interests, cannot be divorced from the outcomes of the educational process. Furthermore, one cannot ignore the complexities of nationalism and the process of building a cultural nation—underlying themes in any discussion of quality and independent educational efforts among African and African-descended people in North America. Insofar as nation building is seen as a process toward nationhood and its preservation, likewise, education must be recognized as

> a process that should reflect our own interests as a cultural nation and be grounded in our cultural history. It should be a process of identity development within the context of pan-African kinship and heritage. Education is our means of providing for the intergenerational transmission of values, beliefs, traditions, customs, rituals, and sensibilities along with the knowledge of why these things must be sustained. Through education we learn how to determine our interests from those of others, and recognize when our interests are consistent and inconsistent with those of others. Education prepares us to accept the staff of cultural leadership

from the generation that preceded ours, build upon our inheritance, and make ready the generation that will follow.[64]

Historically, African and African-descended people in North America have pursued two forms of educational efforts: one has been independent of white control and the other has sought participation in those institutions organized and dominated by whites. Most scholars of the independent African-centered education movement of the 1960s trace its roots to Prince Hall's efforts in the late eighteenth century. In Boston, Massachusetts, an independent school was established by Prince Hall in the home of Primus Hall in 1789 and continued there until 1803, when it moved to the quarters of the African Society House because of increased student enrollment.[65] The work of James Anderson further substantiates the fact that "freed" Africans of the nineteenth century, in general, initiated and supported education for themselves and their children, and also resisted external control of their educational institutions.[66] In fact, these Africans preferred sending their children to independent schools controlled by their own rather than supporting the less expensive, northern, white-dominated "free" schools. However, as Anderson notes, "Black education developed within [the] context of political and economic oppression. . . . [Thus,] the basic form, philosophy, and subject matter of black education reflected the [Africans'] intent to restructure and control their lives. Yet their struggle to defend and advance themselves was undertaken as oppressed people."[67]

In addition to schools established independent of white support, Evelyn Higginbotham argues, "Sabbath schools [which operated in the evening and on the weekend] constituted another example of independent efforts to promote literacy during and after the Reconstruction era" (1865–77).[68] These Sabbath schools taught adults as well as children, providing a core curriculum in reading, writing, and arithmetic. In contrast, the contemporary African-centered school movement marked a shift in the cultural orientation of the curricular content; indeed, this clarity of focus represented the reinstituting of an African-centered perspective throughout the operation of a school and the substance of its educational programs. With the assumption that schooling was neither without interest nor acultural, this attention to the cultural context of schooling was, in fact, largely missing from the school desegregation movement of the 1950s and 1960s.[69] Likewise, the impact of the *Brown v. Board of Education of Topeka, Kansas* (1954) Supreme Court decision, which legally ended apartheid or racial segregation in the domain of education, remains questionable for many reasons. The Brown decision, among others, did not challenge the power relationships within the existing educational system or social order. The reasoning is that change or transformation of the social order "is acceptable to those who wield power within them only if it can be managed in a way that does not disrupt the systems' workings and extant power relationships." Therefore, institutional building in the form of independent African-centered institutions was and is "organized resistance against the European-centered cultural hegemony and intellectual control that [represented] school desegregation. . . . [Moreover,] institution building became a means of establishing 'liberated zones' or 'free spaces' where the process of education would be insulated from the cultural assault of Western hegemony."[70]

Yet, the above perspective on institution building and education has not been shared by a majority of African-descended people in North America. Perhaps this is because of an insufficient "understanding of the role that [the strategic distinction between education and schooling] . . . can play in the success of African-American resistance to political and cultural domination and in guiding the development of our cultural nation."[71] Meaning, the act of going to school does not necessarily mean that one will be educated for competence in one's culture and community by merely partaking in the process. In a recent study on parental choice in independent schools and African-centered awareness, Mwalimu Shujaa concluded, "By assigning dual priority to academic preparation and cultural awareness, the informants in this study demonstrated their capacity to differentiate between schooling and education. . . . It should be noted, however, that this analysis is limited to parents' expressions at a particular moment in their lives."[72] Thus, the concern is not whether education is taking place but the nature of the education and the ultimate products of the learning process.

In addition, we must also consider the impetus for how African and African-descended people in North America approach the question of quality education in or out of the context of their own culture. This approach, I would argue, is largely determined by how African and African-descended people view their relationship—and themselves in relation—to the social order. On this point, Mwalimu Shujaa contends, "African-Americans view their relationship to the social order in different ways. [A] . . . key factor influencing such views is the tension between individualistic and group orientations."[73] In a recent publication on nineteenth-century Black nationalism, the author observed, "although both were tormented and victimized by slavery and racism, integrationists and [so-called] separatists responded differently" in relationship to the social order.[74] The tension between group and individualistic orientations is a product of the cultural and historical experience of African-descended people in a racialized social order under white political and cultural hegemony and how they have approached the question of nationality. The national question refers to how a group defines its aspiration for national identity and its struggle for national sovereignty or self-determination. The question of group consciousness and cultural identity finds its relevance, most significantly, in how that group approaches the socialization process and with whom it is entrusted, and why the group does not support or feel the need for "independent" institutions.

Education is not for education's sake, but "education, in contrast to schooling, is the process of transmitting from one generation to the next knowledge of the values, aesthetics, spiritual beliefs, and all things that give a particular cultural orientation its uniqueness. Every cultural group must provide for this transmission process or it will cease to exist."[75] In addition, education is for the development of intellectual competence in the context of community and culture, and its appropriate application. Therefore, African-centered education can be defined as the "means by which African culture—including the knowledge, attitudes, values and skills needed to maintain and perpetuate it throughout the nation building process—is developed and advanced through practice. Its aim, therefore, is to build commitment and competency within the present and future generations to support the struggle for liberation and nationhood." In contrast, schooling within the U.S. social order is viewed as a "process intended to perpetuate and maintain the society's existing power relations and the institutional structures that support these arrangements. [However,] . . . when multiple cultural orientations exist within a nation-state, it is the leadership among the adherents to the politically dominant cultural orientation that exercise the most influence on the concepts, values, and skills that schools transmit."[76] Education and schooling are not mutually exclusive; nonetheless, each serves distinctive functions within the social order as it relates to the ability to preserve and perpetuate one's culture under hostile conditions. Accordingly, cultural-educational institutions become that more vital in the socialization processes of African-descended people in North America. One might argue that the building of such institutions is a matter of life and cultural death.

The East, a cultural-educational institution that emerged after the struggles in the Ocean Hill–Brownsville Demonstration District and during the larger Black Power and Consciousness movement of the 1960s and 1970s, offers us a vital case in the study of education and cultural nationalism in a historical period marked by a strategic shift from seeking school and social integration and to community control or the creation of institutions under the premise of self-determination and self-reliance. Jitu Weusi, then a teacher known as Leslie Campbell in the Ocean Hill–Brownsville district and later founder of The East organization, captured the transformations some felt necessary to solidify the foregoing shift as it relates to educators of African descent: "If we as black educators are going to further the goals of black power and prepare our youth for the role in moving toward black nationhood, we must undergo a complete change in thinking pertaining to our positions in the society. As educators we should begin to examine the existing educational structure and start revising it to meet the needs of our youths and our communities."[77] This statement emanated from a social and political climate that was more reflective of the post-Brown period than the legal end to educational apartheid in North America and the coming of integration as a social phenomenon. Nonetheless, as Kofi Lomotey comments, "We didn't become free at the end of this [Civil Rights] period. And the evidence of [this] is that we've regressed in terms of the few gains that we got during that period.

The other evidence is that there is no institutional remembrance of that era, other than independent schools. We [did not] maintain control of the electoral politics, we [failed to] maintain control of any institutions in our community, other than independent African-centered schools."[78]

2 Nia

The Birth of The East Organization

> To recreate an Afrikan mind is to create an Afrikan lifestyle that is consistent and compatible with the life and death struggle we're engaged in daily. . . . [It is to create] a consistency among Afrikan people that will allow us to think, act, create, and build in the best interests of the Afrikan world.[1]
>
> HAKI MADHUBUTI, *From Plan to Planet*

During the struggles for community control of schools in Ocean Hill–Brownsville, an organized group of high school students came together to form the African American Student Association (ASA) under the guidance of Jitu Weusi. Weusi, a member of the African-American Teachers Association (ATA), recalls that the fall of 1967 constituted "an internal development phase . . . [wherein] the student association was born [and] . . . would become very instrumental in the organizing that would begin around February [1968]."[2] The movement for quality education as well as the challenge regarding the cultural context of schooling was a fierce one. The increased levels of cultural and political consciousness expressed in the organizing and institutional building efforts were equally intense. As one writer noted, "The 1960s witnessed an unprecedented fusion between the nationalism of the grassroots and the nationalism of the emerging college-educated elite."[3] The fusion, in our case, occurred between a group of astute students and committed adults who would soon struggle to develop an appropriate institutional and cultural context for education for nationhood. One writer of the historical period commented, "The key to the building of a nation is the fervor and rebellious character of the youth and the proper training and direction of the youth by courageous Black adults."[4] The lives of these youths and adults would confirm this statement.

The political and organizational developments that ensued were augmented by a symbiotic relationship between Weusi and the youth of ASA, whereby the bond enabled them to foresee the results of the Ocean Hill–Brownsville confrontation and begin to forge the groundwork for what would become The East. As a result of the media in Brooklyn, the United Federation of Teachers, and the Board of Education slandering his reputation as a teacher, Weusi officially left the New York City Board of Education in November 1969 and would not return until September 1985.[5] In April 1969, ASA held a citywide strike against the New York City high schools, lasting approximately two months. During the strike, the youth presented fifteen demands to the Board of Education. Some of the demands called for one inclusive high school diploma (instead of the three), firearms training in schools, and that teachers should only instruct classes in which they were licensed or trained to teach.[6] In the summer of 1969, Weusi took the opportunity to attend the Black Power conference held in Bermuda. According to him, this trip not only broadened his international perspective through his interactions with "people of a longer stature in the movement" but also posed a critical question: "which path would his life take from here on?"[7] One idea was to relocate to East Africa and perhaps start a business with friends who did similar work. For unknown reasons, this idea never materialized. Then there was the group of ASA students who decided that their current headquarters was insufficient due to their increased political activity. In addition, many students were being expelled and suspended for their political activism, thus creating a large contingent of students unoccupied with meaningful work and an appropriate place to go. ASA members who worked during the summer of 1969 saved portions of their earnings toward a building and bail fund, which included monies from Jitu.[8] That fund helped initially to finance an old abandoned three-story building, which would become the facility of The East in July 1969. The building, a former art gallery called Studio O, was acquired through a two-year lease with an option to buy.

Throughout the summer, Weusi, the students of ASA, and a number of people "involved in the struggle in the area, also put in personal money so that almost $10,000 was raised. Skilled men in the community donated their services to do the electrical work, the painting, the plumbing and the carpentry, and in October 1969 the group moved in to use the building for meetings."[9] Additionally, furniture, sound equipment, and kitchen appliances were purchased. Yet, with the newly acquired space, plans for its usage and development were still vague. As Weusi recalls, "We knew that we wanted an institution, but we weren't clear about what type and form and how this institution was going to jump off and what it was going to be about."[10] However, by November 1969, a number of persons began working at The East, organizing schedules and staff, in an effort to design a structure that would uniquely respond to Weusi's foregoing questions.

The Emergent Years (Summer 1969–Summer 1972)

With the establishment of the cultural annex of The East, initially called the Black Experience in Sound, there were weekly musical performances by local and well-known artists such as Freddie Hubbard, Betty Carter, McCoy Tyner, Pharaoh Sanders, Max Roach, Sun Ra, Lee Morgan, Dewey Redman, Roy Ayers, and Rahsaan Roland Kirk. The East officially began as a cultural center on December 31, 1969, and featured singer Leon Thomas, who usually performed with Pharaoh Saunders, opening what would be the weekend cultural program. (Interestingly enough, Pharaoh Saunders had a hit song called "The Creator Had a Master Plan.") This opening weekend show drew a crowd of approximately three hundred people. East member Kwesi Mensah Wali booked most of the jazz artists. On Friday and Saturday nights, there were usually two shows—one at 9 P.M. and one at 11 P.M.—and a third to accommodate enormous crowds. The music was coupled with presentations of poetry, artwork, dance, dramatic plays, drumming, and lectures from persons such as the late Kwame Ture, Sundiata Acoli, and H. Rap Brown. Ron Worrill and the late Jim Seitu Dyson, two of the most brilliant artists, helped to visually transmit The East message to the larger community. During the Black Experience in Sound, the musicians, who were also extremely politically conscious, were called "messengers" due to what was called their "teachings" between musical sets. To some, these musicians were the "musical proof that the politics of Black Nationalism and Nationhood [were] being practiced in all walks of life."[11] Moreover, the Black Experience in Sound attracted people from various levels of the community not only to the music and performances but also to the cultural and political education that took place at The East.

The founding of The East was the result of a collective effort on the part of many key persons, all of whom assumed various roles and responsibilities to make tangible the vision of the collective effort. For the most part, the leadership came through Jitu Weusi until the late 1970s. However, to posit that Weusi was *the* leadership of The East is inaccurate. In the organization's formative years, Weusi was "entrusted with carrying out the major decisions reached by the core of The East family. There [were] no written rules defining his authority. The entire operation of

1. A Black Experience in Sound jazz session at The East with vocalist Andy Bey, Reggie Workman (?) (*center*), and saxophonist Gary Bartz, 1971. Photograph by Osei Terry Chandler. Used with permission.

2. An East flyer of scheduled jazz and poetry performances.

The East [was] based on the trust implicit in the relationships existing between the people." The leadership consisted of the men, women, and children who built and sustained the organization, oftentimes referred to as "The East family." The institution provided for the basic needs of individuals in the core of The East family, who devoted all of their working hours to the organization's operation.[12] The East family, initially, consisted of the youth of ASA and a core group of adults that initiated the actual building. Prior to its process of becoming an institution, there was "a theoretical revolution [that] founded The East and from there a small group went on to research and develop a structure."[13] Designers of the institution knew that they "wanted a cultural-educational center for people of African descent, [but they] didn't know what [they] were going to call it."[14] One evening, after juggling a multitude of names, the group came up with "The East," which was a direct response to "the West" (i.e., European thought and culture and the Western Hemisphere as it relates to the United States). The reasoning on the part of The East family for the concept of "The East" derived from two fundamental sources: (1) The East family's cultural and political disposition; (2) for the sake of simplicity, a name that was short and "culturally rhythmic," which the average person could remember.

The international African political and cultural events of the 1960s also provided inspiration for the naming ceremony of The East. Symbolically, African political figures such as Kwame Nkrumah, Julius Nyerere, and Jomo Kenyatta became prominent icons in the organization's political culture. Its architects took examples from the Republic of Guyana, in the form of their cooperative government and institutions, and newly (politically) independent Ghana as working models. From Ghana, The East drew from its pan-African legacy in that the republic represented the fountainhead of intellectual and worldwide pan-Africanism. Historically, this was partially the ideological foundation of The East. In addition, Julius Nyerere's writings on *Ujamaa*—often referred to as African socialism or cooperative economics—and the Kiswahili language became strong elements of its configuration. In this context, the primary institution of The East emerged as an educational institution called Uhuru Sasa Shule (Freedom Now School). *Uhuru sasa* (freedom now), which was also a phrase of the historical period, signaled the move toward self-determination and a genuine expression of Africanity.

During 1970, Uhuru Sasa Shule emerged as the primary nation-building component of The East. Its establishment coincided with a

3. Kasisi Jitu Weusi speaking at The East complex, 1970. Photograph by Osei Terry Chandler. Used with permission.

number of economic, cultural, and political operations that expanded the scope of The East and its level of activity. Between October 1969 and February 1972, The East built and developed these operations with some becoming institutions themselves under its umbrella. See table 2.1 for a general outline of The East's operations during this period, including the year and month of creation.

Though it is an arduous task to capture this energy and this level of activity in print, Martha Bright, a teacher at Uhuru Sasa, explains it best: "this [phenomena] was an explosion, because everything was done in the span of about two years."[15] Initially, each of the operations was generated to meet the growing needs of East family members. However, each soon became a vital service for the larger or extended African community. In fact, a number of the primary operations of The East, particularly the ones that generated revenue, became economic enterprises outside of the institution. In addition to these institutional developments, The East sponsored several key events between 1970 and 1972, some of which remain an integral part of Brooklyn's African life. A number of these annual activities were and are Black Solidarity Day (developed by

Table 2.1. The East's operations, 1969–1972

Year	Month	Operation
1967	September	African American Student Association
1969	October	*Black News*
	November	Clerical Office of The East
1970	February	Renting out of The East facility[a]
	February	Akiba Mkuu (The East bookstore)[a]
	February	Weekend Cultural Programs[a]
	February	Uhuru Sasa Shule
	March	First Uhuru Sasa Parent Council (meeting)
	April	East Kitchen
	May	*Black News* Typesetting Services[a]
	September	East Records (The East recording studio)[a]
	September	East Printing Service[a]
	September	Evening School of Knowledge
	November	Black Solidarity Political Party
	November	Kununuana (The Uhuru food cooperative)
1971	January	*Black News* Distributions[a]
	April	East Catering Service[a]
	June	Tamu Sweet-East (restaurant and dessert shop)[a]
	June	Universal Temple of Thoughts (Prophet Isaac Stokes's Soul Temple or Church)
	July	African Youth Village
	September	East Publications[a]
	September	Saturday Movies at The East[a]
	October	Haribu Dawa Na Hai ("Destroy drugs and live")[a] (High School and College Drug Council)
	October	*East Family Newsletter*
	November	Committee to Elect Responsible Candidates
	December	Mavazi Clothing Cooperative[a]
1972	February	Black National Education Series[a]

Source: Adeyemi Al-Muqaddim, *The East Mental Ministry Report* (Brooklyn, N.Y.: The East, 1972), 10.
[a]Income-generating operations for The East.

Dr. Carlos Russell in 1969), Malcolm X memorials on February 21, and Marcus Garvey Day on August 17. Other activities, such as African wedding and funeral ceremonies, summer programs, Sunday Umoja Karamu (unity feast), East Brotherhood and Sisterhood meetings and events, and seasonal trips to the Republic of Guyana were more germane to The East. Of particular importance, the initial trip to Guyana, and those thereafter, "had a tremendous, monumental and historical impact on The East."[16]

The first trip in 1970 occurred as the result of a meeting in Georgetown, Guyana, which was announced as a conference or seminar of pan-Africanists and Black revolutionary nationalists. This conference was the design of Anne King and Eusi Kwayana (formerly Sidney King). Eusi Kwayana was a prominent political figure in Guyana as well as the president of the African Society for Cultural Relations with Independent Africa (ASCRIA), which hosted the conference. Though the conference was reported as a "poorly attended affair," some of the persons in attendance included the late Queen Mother Moore, James Turner, Acklyn Lynch, Sonny Carson, and Jitu Weusi and Adeyemi Bandele as delegates of The East. The Guyanese government, represented by Prime Minister Lynden Forbes Sampson Burnham, also supported the conference. Prime Minister Burnham assumed the leadership of Guyana in 1964, a year after the "rebellion" of 1963. In 1966, Guyana gained political independence from the British. By 1970, it had declared itself the Cooperative Republic of Guyana and, thereafter, sought to establish and develop its domestic policy of feeding, clothing, and housing the nation through cooperative formations. ASCRIA developed several self-sustaining programs, including efforts along the Guyana countryside in rural and village farming, garment making, cattle rearing, and mining cooperatives. The national slogan of "make the little man the real man" was indicative of the Burnham administration's efforts and, perhaps, the mission and subsequent development of Cooperative Republic of Guyana. However, it must be noted that by the mid-1970s, Burnham's efforts and interests collapsed into the political defense and perpetuation of his national authority. Previously, Burnham had proclaimed himself a nationalist who supported the efforts of ASCRIA, which was an African cultural and political organization that dealt primarily with the African grassroots population. With Burnham's abandonment of his nationalist posture, Eusi Kwayana, who supported Burnham when he gave genuine support to the development of Guyana's African-based population, was now in opposition to the prime minister.

During the ASCRIA-sponsored conference, a key meeting was held with Prime Minister Burnham to discuss the possibility of providing a secure location for African political prisoners. In a private meeting, Burnham, who had monetarily and politically supported Southern African liberation movements, confirmed his commitment to this possibility; thereafter, it became a reality. The significance of this development made it possible for numerous political prisoners, including Herman Ferguson and several South Africans, to relocate to Guyana. Moreover, "ASCRIA [had] called on the Caribbean countries and Suriname to lift their bans on Black [nationalists] and [nationalists] publications" such as *ASCRIA Speaks* and *The Message*, which was published by the African Cultural Association of Trinidad.[17] Yet, for example, Trinidad's prime minister Eric Williams would not answer this call; in fact, he ensured that few nationalists were able to visit, much less reside in Trinidad. Nonetheless, The East delegates were able to make a brief stopover in Trinidad and, as a result, developed a relationship with Geddes Granger and Dave Darbeau of the National Joint Action Committee. This relationship was based on the kinship of African struggle and would be sustained for many years. For Weusi, the conference deepened his understanding of protracted struggle and, for the first time, gave him an authentic connection to a pan-African movement. In fact, as a result of this transformative experience, Weusi decided to commit his life's work to African people.

"After subsequent visits," Adeyemi Bandele wrote, "we arranged with the Guyana government to lease 300 acres of land in [Yarakita, located in] the Northwest District [i.e., South Riumveldt Park, Georgetown, Guyana]. This is an area [that] the government is attempting to populate. So here we are with 300 acres of land to clear, plant, harvest crops, build houses, and above all, experience nation building beyond the theory." Clearly, with this "large but underpopulated nation [needing] people committed to a progressive development," The East saw this as a "situation where whatever [a culturally focused person] did could be useful in helping [the] nation-building process."[18] Why Guyana? The East not only saw it as a place "to test [their] theories about self-reliance and sacrifice for the struggle," but also to transform the land into a viable base where they could "demonstrate all the things [they] said [they] wanted to be about in the development of 'a nation.'"[19] Thus, plans were set to establish a cooperative farm of over 300 acres with livestock and other facilities called the Uhuru Sasa Land Project. A person or group seeking to develop land in Guyana had to apply for it and then describe how the land would be utilized, by whom, for what purpose(s), and why, in addition to having the terrain surveyed. In 1974, The East filed for land and received confirmation. According to one source, the fees to survey the land were paid in the following year.[20] As a part of the plans for the land project, the recruited persons engaged in its development were required to abide by laws, regulations, and procedures; maintain financial and physical requirements; decide upon clothing and type needed; and schedule land-project working hours. Every three months each person was to submit an in-depth evaluation report to be reviewed by a designated person at The East.

In addition to serving the purpose of developing the necessary nation-building skills through personal and institutional work, the land project was also a rehabilitative or renewing enterprise for those (in the United States) who were experiencing some form of "mental and physical breakdown."[21] Moreover, the cost of living in Guyana was considerably less in contrast to a decent quality of life for most in America. By 1977, East members were still "for the most part overjoyed at the potential for growth in Guyana."[22] Toward the end of the 1970s, however, the project collapsed from insufficient funding and a lack of concerted effort, in the context of the African struggle to maintain governmental control in Guyana. Indeed, all of these ingredients contributed to what some have called the natural death of an "era project," and "the era was gone."[23] The East's relationship and interactions with Guyana were not only indicative of the thrust of Africans there to maintain national sovereignty but also consistent with the principles of nation building and communal-based institutional development. Although the Uhuru Sasa Land Project was no more, *Kununuana* or the Uhuru Food Cooperative, which was modeled after comparable efforts in the Cooperative Republic of Guyana, remained until 1992.

The idea of communal and cooperative formations did not end with the establishment of the Uhuru Food or Mavazi Clothing cooperatives. In an effort to expand operations and build a network of cooperative and community-sustained and African-based institutions, The East sought to establish these institutions beyond Brooklyn and New York City. In the early 1970s, two tangible institutional extensions of The East existed in New York City and one was located in Memphis, Tennessee. The Far-East was located at 192-15 Linden Boulevard, St. Albans (Queens), New York. An ASA member directed the institution.[24] As The East began to expand as an umbrella organization, ASA soon faded into the texture of the institution as members assumed more active roles in the direction and governance of The East. After 1973, The East discontinued its active engagement, recruitment, and interaction with local high schools, and so ASA naturally melded into The East and ceased to exist as an organization. Yet, as ASA faded out of existence, the African-American Teachers Association (ATA) was facing a civil suit from the United Federation of Teachers (UFT), charging defamation of the teachers' union. The UFT won the case and was awarded a financial settlement, which allowed it to take all of ATA's assets and dissolve the organization in its execution. Clearly, the dissolution of ATA through political defamation originated from the cultural and political conflicts that surfaced between the Ocean Hill–Brownsville governing board and the UFT. However, the UFT's action was and is indicative of the schooling, professional, and political arrangement and the power relations that are involved in the governing and continuity of these social structures. Unfortunately, many "looked at Ocean Hill–Brownsville as being a situation that was going to develop into a very beautiful thing. [They] did not realize all of the aspects of the struggle" they were engaged in.[25]

The Far-East, in the midst of these occurrences, emerged from the needs of ASA members who lived in Queens and who viewed The East as a model of what could and should be done in their own locality. As such, The Far-East sought to initiate "a Uhuru Sasa pre-school and [envisioned] going into programs full force."[26] The Far-East, however, did not have the same support base, among other things, as did The East and merely fell off the scene in 1974. Nonetheless, it did become the local forerunner of the Afrikan Poetry Theatre, established in 1977 and also modeled after The East.[27] In the early 1970s, Yusef Iman developed The Mid-East as an extension of The East in the Brownsville section of Brooklyn. The structure was a storefront located several blocks from where he lived. Iman had also formed the Weusi Kuumba Dance Troupe, which consisted of members of his family as well as other talented members of the community.

Under Iman's direction and persistence, The Mid-East engaged in similar activities as The East, but never to the same extent as the "parent" institution. The establishment of a "Rhythm and Blues Center" at The Mid-East was proposed; however, this project, according to available sources, did not come to fruition. Similarly, despite the fact that the details of the institution are obscure, "The Mid-East continued until the council [of The East] could no longer carry the weight of its responsibility."[28] The last of the known extensions of The East was the Uhuru-East Bookstore and Cultural Center in the city of Memphis, Tennessee. Robbo Jumatatu initiated the bookstore and cultural center in the early 1970s. One of the few available sources reported that "the Uhuru-East [was] slowly working on hooking-up a program designed to service the residents of Memphis. [They were] hoping that the bloods [i.e., the average brother and sister] of Memphis [would] come out and support the Uhuru-East and help to bring strong Black nation-building to that area of the country."[29] Although the particularities of this project, including its structure and duration, were uncertain, The East's attempts to build or to become a part of a self-determining institutional network did not cease with these efforts. During the early 1970s, The East became a part of a national network of nationalist organizations through its relationship with the Congress of African People (CAP) under the leadership of Amiri Baraka.

The East and the Congress of African People

The relationship between The East and CAP began in September 1970. The official severance of this relationship occurred on April 3, 1974, while CAP was under the leadership of Baraka.[30] It was primarily through Yusef Iman, as a member of Baraka's Spirit House Movers and Players, that The East and Jitu Weusi became involved with the CAP collective. In the aftermath of both the National Black Power Conference and the Newark, New Jersey, uprising of 1967, Baraka and a few of his associates formed the United Brothers. Under the guidance of Maulana Karenga, the United Brothers became the Committee for United Newark or

NewArk (CFUN), a politically motivated organization headed by Baraka, Balozi Zayd Muhammad, and Mfundishi Maasi.³¹ Before CFUN became CAP's national headquarters, Karenga had a profound impact on Amiri Baraka's development and the structure of his organization between 1966 and 1970. More precisely, as one author wrote, "Baraka had become fanatical, almost religious, in his faith in Karenga's leadership and doctrine."³² Consequently, among other things, Baraka configured CFUN in ways similar, if not identical, to Karenga's US Organization.³³ Since a number of core and contrasting elements of the US Organization and CFUN funneled down to The East and became some of its defining characteristics, we must consider their origin, form, and character.

Karenga founded the US Organization in 1965 in Los Angeles, California. In contrast to the Black Panther Party for Self Defense, the organization was (and is) often characterized as cultural nationalist. Karenga, as architect of US, developed the organization's ideological-philosophical statement called *Kawaida*, literally meaning "usual thing or customary" in Kiswahili but interpreted by US to mean "tradition and reason." According to Karenga, "Kawaida is essentially an ongoing synthesis of the best of Black nationalist, Pan-Africanist and socialist thought and practice."³⁴ At its core, Kawaida is "a theory of cultural and social change." The structure and order of allegiance of the US Organization was the leader (Karenga), the doctrine (Kawaida), and the organization (US). According to one member, it was never conceptualized as a mass organization; it "was always conceptualized as an organization that would have people trained to go out and programmatically influence things that were going on in the community."³⁵ Prospective members or advocates came into the organization through its advocacy class. In these classes, advocates were taught the doctrine, its areas, and the organizational structure, and they were expected to make monetary contributions as well as join one or two committees. Supportive, associate, and active advocacy were the three ascending levels of being an advocate. The level a member chose would determine one's degree of participation and, in turn, what would be expected of him or her.

In the minds of US members or advocates, the leader spoke the word (i.e., the doctrine), and the word was the basis of the structure, substance, or symbolism of the organization. Consequently, after speaking, the advocate employed the following protocol: "If I have said anything of beauty, or anything of value, all praise is due to Maulana Ron Karenga and only the mistakes have been mine." For the advocate, "the idea of giving reference to . . . Karenga as the source of all the organization's ideas and images [was] an important aspect in the development of US Organization." Therefore, the title Karenga designated "the highest of the high priests of the Kawaida faith." The organizational structure and leadership of US consisted of *Maulana* (master teacher), *Imamu* (priest), *Walimu* (teachers), *Wanafunzi* (students), *Ishilangu* (security force), *Simba* (youth/paramilitary wing), and a circle of administrators. Karenga first awarded the title of *Imamu*, assigned the meaning of high priest or spiritual leader, to the head of the spiritual arm of US and later to heads of each *hekalu*.[36] Kiswahili for temple, a *hekalu* was an affiliate of the national temple (i.e., the physical location) of the US Organization, which was "The Hekalu." CFUN, for example, was such a *hekalu*, and Amiri Baraka was given the title of *Imamu*, hence references to him as Imamu Amiri Baraka.

Kawaida's philosophy of "tradition and reason" was based on what Karenga perceived of African traditions and the use of reason as a way of adjusting these traditions to contemporary dynamics. Narratives or myths that were the underpinnings of the ideological contours of the organization support this philosophy. For example, there is a character named *Nkulunkulu* in Kawaida mythology, which, according to Karenga, is a Zulu concept meaning "the first born, the first ancestors of our people." In Kawaida mythology, "*Nkulunkulu* is referred to as the first ancestor [and] . . . as the founder of the African community. He is considered [the] first ancestor who organized the first African community around the Seven Principles. From this community all other communities sprang. This African myth explains why the Seven Principles are the basis of all African life."[37] Clearly, this narrative serves as an explanatory principle as well as an indoctrinating tool for the aggregation of US members. The seven principles of the organization were called the *Nguzo Saba*. The organization's "philosophy *Kawaida* poses the *Nguzo Saba*—or seven principles—as a moral minimum value system necessary for the development of African-American national culture."[38] Many persons within the

African-based community refer to the *Nguzo Saba* as either the seven principles of Blackness or the seven principles of Kwanzaa. The seven principles are *Umoja* (unity), *Kujichagulia* (self-determination), *Ujima* (collective work and responsibility), *Ujamaa* (cooperative economics), *Nia* (purpose), *Kuumba* (creativity), and *Imani* (faith).

As with the *Nguzo Saba*, the essential teachings of Kawaida were presented in seven levels or functions, such as the seven principles, or in types of three, such as Blackness is based on "color, culture, and consciousness" and culture supplies "identity, purpose, and direction" to all peoples.[39] Essentially, the doctrine was taught in terms of catechisms, therefore making it simpler to remember and impart these categories. Consistent with these structural nuances, the colors of the US Organization were "Black, Red, and Green" (derived from Marcus Garvey) and its motto was "Anywhere we are, US is." A carved, wooden symbol known as a *talisimu* was created in collaboration with Chestyn Everett, Karenga's brother, and worn by advocates and affiliates of the US Organization. According to US members:

> The symbol is the head of an Africanoid man inside a triangle. The triangle is symbolic of the pyramids, which in turn is symbolic of our traditional greatness. The three triangles represent the ends of Black power [self-determination, self-respect, and self-defense], the star is for our first principle Umoja—unity, the seven lines represent the Seven Principles and the head represents the modern Africanoid man.[40]

The holidays and ceremonies of the US Organization included *Arusi* (wedding ceremonies), *Akika* (naturalization ceremony for children), *Maziko* (funeral ceremonies), and *Kuzaliwa* (Birth of Malcolm X, May 19). Moreover, the organization observed Uhuru Day (celebration of the 1965 revolts in Watts—August 11), *Kuanzisha* (commemoration of the founding of US by Karenga, September 7), and *Kwanzaa* (the first fruits celebration from December 26 to January 1).

In the first version of his autobiography, Amiri Baraka recalls, "very quickly I had assimilated the Kawaida doctrine and began pushing it wherever I went. . . . I myself became one of the chief proselytizers of Kawaida."[41] Yet, as Baraka and CFUN came into national prominence with the 1970 founding of the Congress of African People in Atlanta, Georgia, the alliance between Karenga's US Organization and Baraka's CFUN started to dissipate. As a result of internal dissension amongst the two groups, and perhaps aggravated by Baraka going ahead with the founding meeting of the congress and thus disobeying Karenga's direct orders to call it off, the relationship between US and CFUN came to an end. One writer, on CFUN's part, offers an account of the breakage:

> On the weekend of the Congress, Karenga sent several of his men from Los Angeles to Atlanta to intimidate Baraka's leadership. Ominously, Karenga's men carried briefcases ostensibly filled with firearms—briefcases with concealed weapons had become a nefarious trademark of the US Organization. . . . Fortunately, even after several confrontations, there was no bloodshed in Atlanta. Although there was no shooting, behind the scenes Baraka called CFUN together in Atlanta to announce the formal split between his group and the US Organization.[42]

Recalling the split, Baraka admits, "we could not work with him [Karenga], but we were still committed to Kawaida and its multiple lists and the Nguzo Saba and Kwanzaa."[43] On May 26, 1971, Maulana Karenga was found guilty of aggravated assault for allegedly torturing former US members, and he was imprisoned until 1975. Between 1969 and the 1970s, a substantial number of members left the US Organization as a result of the US-Panther conflict, FBI activities, and the reported shift from "development to defense" posture of the organization.[44] Shortly after Karenga's incarceration, Baraka began to elevate the meaning of *imamu* to that of *maulana*, in addition to forging his own interpretation of the Kawaida philosophy. Though Baraka mentions in passing that Karenga had accused him of revisionism, US members were more explicit in terms of the ownership and what they perceived to be the proper interpretation of Kawaida and the *Nguzo Saba*. In an edited text on Kawaida, they wrote, "for US the seven principles are absolute. By absolute we mean nothing can be taken away from them. . . . The seven principles . . . are already defined." As such, Kwanzaa, for example, "evolved as tradition adapted and developed out of Kawaida principles."[45] The US Organization spelled the celebration of Kwanzaa with two *a*'s to distinguish it from the term *kwanza*, which means "first," and to accommodate the seven principles as well as the "seven children in the [US] organization" in its very beginning.[46]

Yet, even with Kwanzaa, there were discrepancies or modifications relative to nationalist organizations that adopted and practiced the Kawaida philosophy or Kwanzaa. For CFUN and The East, Kwanzaa was spelled with one *a* for reasons unknown. The only speculative purpose this could serve was to situate the Kiswahili term in its proper context, in which Kwanza would simply mean "first" and be a reference to the "first fruits" celebration. Nonetheless, we find further adjustments, specifically in the phrase "all praises due to Maulana," which was modified by Baraka to read, "all praises due to Imamu."[47] All available records indicate that The East neither revised nor continued the use of these salutations. According to Jitu Weusi's recollection, "[The East] never had this messianic leadership thing like Baraka and [Karenga] had and that was part of what hurt them. [For example,] people used to tell us you don't have them bowing low enough and all that kind of jive. We were more like an African-centered democratic organization."[48] Yet, the question of "extended-family" (polygynous) relationships among the members of both The East and US did ignite criticism by CFUN/CAP, eventually leading to further fragmentation within the ranks of CAP.

As the successor of the National Black Power conferences, CAP decided to federate the organization that attended the foregoing conferences, creating chapters such as The East in Brooklyn and other urban enclaves. In CAP's mass political campaign in anticipation of the National Black Political Convention in Gary, Indiana (1972), there were several decisive meetings in this initiative, "particularly the Black Political Convention held at 'The East' in Brooklyn, New York, on the July 4th weekend of 1971." It was at this meeting that Amiri Baraka presented his position paper, "Strategy and Tactics of a Pan-African Nationalist Party," en route to the development of the National Black Agenda advanced at the Gary convention. As a result of the second international CAP meeting in San Diego, California, in September 1972, "the national leadership was reorganized along the

4. An ankh-shaped Kwanzaa agenda posted on the door of The East complex, 1971. Photograph by Osei Terry Chandler. Used with permission.

lines of an executive committee (EXCO) and ministries. The EXCO consisted of three at-large positions, some regional coordinators, and eight work council leaders."[49] Jitu Weusi led the Education (*Elimu*) Work Council, one of CAP's major areas of concern, and The East was a member of the northeastern region.

Few sources speak to the contacts or relationship between Weusi, director of The East (Brooklyn chapter of CAP), and Baraka, chairman of CAP. Baraka himself only recalled that he and Weusi "had begun to communicate on a limited basis, particularly through [Sonny] Carson in the Continuations Committee meetings" of the Black Power Conference.[50] Although the details of this relationship are unclear, a December 12, 1973, letter addressed to Amiri Baraka as CAP's chairman outlined several of the more salient internal differences between the two groups and, in turn, became the "divorce letter" (see appendix B). On the same date, there was also a meeting held with Baraka in Uhuru Sasa's secondary classroom on 1231 Bedford Avenue.[51] The details of the meeting are unknown, but more than likely the meeting became a ground for the withdrawal of The East from CAP. During a midwestern CAP meeting in Chicago, Baraka made a speech calling for the inclusion of the teachings of Karl Marx and Mao Zedong to be added to what he called "revolutionary" Kawaida. At the end of the meeting, as Baraka recalls, "both Jitu Weusi of The East and Haki Madhubuti of IPE [Institute of Positive Education] resigned."[52] By March 1974, Baraka wrote, "I was now openly including elements of Marxism in this 'Revolutionary Kawaida.'"[53] In the spring of 1974, the Congress of African People was dismantled with Baraka's faction embracing what they considered "revolutionary Marxism/Kawaida," renouncing Black nationalism and nationalists as essentially "reactionary." Of those "reactionary" nationalists, Haki Madhubuti and Jitu Weusi were criticized in Baraka's *Unity and Struggle* newspaper as result of them both resigning from CAP after Baraka's ideological shift. In February 1975, the New York State Black Assembly board of directors "voted to remove Imamu Amiri Baraka as Secretary General of the National Black Assembly" on account of his and CAP's "attempt to force their ideology of scientific socialism upon the National Black Assembly."[54]

Although Baraka and Weusi stand out as the primary protagonists, the relationship between The East and CAP did not begin with them but through Yusef Iman. Beginning in September 1970 and following Baraka's prompts, Iman became very active within The East and enticed Weusi and The East into the CAP collective. According to Weusi, Iman "had a tremendous impact upon The East and its development."[55] In fact, he became such a central figure that many of the cultural protocols and practices of The East and Uhuru Sasa—such as marches, oaths, songs, and other elements—were products of his creativity. From 1970 until he passed in the early 1980s, Iman contributed greatly to the development of The East.

Although The East adopted the celebration of Kwanzaa, the *Nguzo Saba*, and undetermined portions of the Kawaida philosophy through the CAP relationship, to suggest that The East was merely a replica of Baraka's CFUN or Karenga's US Organization would be inaccurate. According to East members, the institution's foundation and value system was the *Nguzo Saba*. Yet, The East was built around the development of Uhuru Sasa and was the product of the initiatives of its members, prior to and after the relationship with CAP. The adopted cultural elements, such as

5. Kasisi Yusef Iman wearing a *talisimu* at The East complex, 1970. Photograph by Osei Terry Chandler. Used with permission.

Kwanzaa and the *Nguzo Saba,* were spread throughout many parts of the African world by East members and were combined with existing components to fortify their composite.

The Ascension of The East (Summer 1972–Summer 1977)

The formative years of The East provided the institutional basis for the organization, but the management and nature of its activities remained questionable in light of their rapid emergence. In reflecting upon this concern for the organizational management of the various concurrent operations, a number of East members explained that as a part of the institution's weakness, there was not an identifiable or effective process for acclimating prospective members in ways that would enable them to work with others.[56] Although the validity of these concerns continued to plague The East throughout its existence, there were a number of structural attempts made to address them. With The East's strong emphasis on *kazi* (work) and continual study, there existed at least two lists of regimented readings as an orientation to the philosophy and workings of the institution. In fact, through the auspices of the Uhuru Sasa Evening School, there was an East course entitled *"Mashariki* Introduction," which provided an orientation to The East. Additionally, all new arrivals were provided with a reading list, and their first requirement was to catch up on their reading(s). I came across two distinct reading lists: the *"Mashariki* Reading List," which was divided into six levels, and a required reading list organized into topical categories, with an East member heading each respective category.[57] (The *Mashariki* Reading List and the required reading list can both be found in appendix A of this book.)

Even though new arrivals became a part of The East, to many the institution was borne out of the work and sacrifice of the present and incoming youth community. Assignments both intellectually and physically challenging were selected for them; yet, according to one source, the youth were only given responsibilities that they were able to handle. Nonetheless, under the guidance of and in cooperation with the organization's adults, the youth responded well beyond their chronological age and proceeded to develop in the context of The East family. With the development of The East as an institution as well as a family, the organizational structure and governance began to naturally take on form through its familial relationships. The structures of the primary operating and decision-making bodies consisted of the *Balozi Wazee* (council of elders) and later the *Waziri Baraza* (leadership council), East Brotherhood and Sisterhood, *Super Simbas* (super lions; young men), and *Malaikas* (good spirits; young women)—the youth groups aged twelve to sixteen.[58]

The East began with a large contingent of men, and thus its leadership was male-dominated in its formative years. As more women joined the family, the institution developed structures in an attempt to organize the families and their responsibilities to The East. Before the establishment of the *Balozi Wazee*, there was a system of seven counselors, to which seven men were individually and collectively assigned. Perhaps this system was necessary on account of the large male population. The counselor's responsibilities were to get the most out of the men; to build and develop them through the establishment of meaningful relationships; and to deal with those who needed to be dealt with on a personal level. In the second year of The East's operation, it was decided at a *Balozi Wazee* meeting that The East Brotherhood was not to be used as the decision-making body by the council members.[59]

According to an internal document, the *Balozi Wazee* began in July 1971 "to make The East leadership more circular and democratic." The document went on to state that The East had "gone through a period of development characterizing any body attempting to grow. The way the *Balozi Wazee* can truly lead is by their example. While the overwhelming majority have [sic] taken this initiative, some have not taken this initiative and have shown *bad* example. They don't understand the concept of continuity."[60] Approximately two weeks after this statement, according to the minutes of a council meeting, the establishment of criteria in the three principal areas of mental, physical, and spiritual was believed to be needed as the basis for "purging" the *Balozi Wazee*.[61] From an East Brotherhood document that took up the task of establishing codes of behavior in the context of the above three areas as well as a social area, there appears to be evidence of a concerted attempt at balanced leadership. This attempt, of course, is noteworthy given the uniqueness of The East's formation primarily through its male members.

Toward this balanced leadership, the Brotherhood Code committee held that no one should be exempted "from *kazi* [work] because of position or past accomplishments. . . . [Therefore,] Brothers placed in leadership positions [were] responsible to see that all expected work [was] finished. Leadership [was] also responsible to see that all Brothers and Sisters placed under their command know what functions they [were] to fulfill." In initiating these policies after some analysis, the committee saw themselves as walking "a new path guided by Kawaida," a path on which they would "never misuse the Spiritual Doctrine of Kawaida to meet some personal need." Though the document stressed these members being "advocates of the Doctrine of Kawaida [striving] to grow and develop by its guidance," the authors were more convinced that it was necessary to "provide a basic code of behavior to assist the Doctrine and make it more concrete."[62] The codes established by the committee are significant in that they underscore

6. The Balozi Wazee (council of elders), most if not all of which derived from The East Brotherhood, at the late Queen Mother Audley E. Moore's Mt. Addis Ababa encampment in Parksville, New York, September 13, 1972. Photograph by Osei Terry Chandler. Used with permission.

the orientation and the specific historical development of The East. The codes appear in appendix C.

In fact, these developments were not confined to the institution but also sought to address the tangible and intangible realities of each member's existence. Materially, the established codes spoke to the need for active "participation in self-defense," the observance of "dietary rules," and the imperative of wearing "African clothing as much as possible."[63] Immaterially, the committed wrote, "We must develop our spiritual selves because it is the spirit that gives us the power and Imani [faith] to act correctly. . . . Our spirituality must be developed just as well as our mental and physical selves."[64] In fact, the committee felt that "spirituality and politics [were] not necessarily contradictory. [Their] new politics [was] a spiritual thing, dealing with the highest values."[65] Irrespective of the male leadership of the institution in its formative years, these perspectives and policies served as institutional signposts and the possible or intended direction of The East. More precisely, these statements emanate from (and are consistent with) The East seeking to (1) consolidate its nationalist position; (2) project itself as a legitimate political force within the African-based community; (3) be clear and purposeful in its appearance (including clothing and hairstyle); (4) remain on top of reading materials; and (5) transform from what-they-want to what-will-get-the-job-done.[66]

In the latter part of 1972, the governmental structure shifted from the *Balozi Wazee* to the *Waziri Baraza* (leadership council), which dealt with the topical activities of The East. All *Waziri* (ministers) and *Naibu* (counselors) were expected to attend *Bazara Kazi* (council work) classes.[67] The next level of the structure consisted of The East Brotherhood and Sisterhood, which were premised on the ideology of Kawaida and the necessity of men's and women's training and development. Both The East Brotherhood and Sisterhood had separate meetings on Wednesdays and Mondays, respectively, but they communed as a family on Sundays with an *Umoja Karamu* (unity feast). The East Sisterhood was:

> The component of women within The East Organization that [helped] to fulfill the organization's function as a cultural and educational institution for people of Afrikan descent. As Afrikan women, they [played] a

vital role in the organization's day to day operations, which include the Uhuru Sasa school, a bookstore, a clothing store, a cooperative food buying service, and the newspaper *Black News*.[68]

According to council-meeting minutes from as early as 1971, The East Sisterhood structure consisted of "initiation" meetings, a council body of five to seven women, and allocations of work assignments in the areas of secretarial, housekeeping, kitchen, child care, food and nutrition, and *Kuumba* (creativity).[69] Programmatically, it had designed a conference on "Organizing the Black Family" and held retreats that engaged the priorities of their home, children, and institution.[70] In addition, the sisterhood was able to procure the necessary funds to send one of its members, Alberta, as a representative of The East Sisterhood to the 1972 All Africa Women's Conference held in Dar-es-Salaam, Tanzania. Both the Brotherhood and Sisterhood were convinced that "the primary role of womanhood [was] motherhood."[71] Toward the late 1970s, The East Brotherhood and Sisterhood faded into the overall management of the institution, perhaps signaling another attempt to be more balanced in terms of family and work relationships.

Members of The East Brotherhood had a twenty-four-hour schedule that involved assignments related to work and supervision. Early reports indicated that to some men, the assignments were beyond their expectation and, consequently, they could not manage the responsibilities.[72] In addition to establishing the principles and institution of *Baba Umoja* (fatherly unity), which functioned to provide "visible male concern" and "parental assistance and respect for family, race and nation," the men also performed security duties for The East and its related facilities.[73] The security uniforms consisted of red dashikis, black pants, combat boots, and a green East arm patch.[74] Additionally, in the context of the early male orientation of The East, dress codes were established, and members were expected to observe these codes in accordance to protocol. Parenthetically, personal hygiene and grooming were strongly emphasized for the men. It was felt that the men were "responsible for their appearance at all times," since they were "reflections of the *Mashariki* Family [i.e., The East family] and should mirror appropriate values." The general clothing for males consisted of optional *kufis* and hats, which were discarded for the appearance of unity; Black nationalist suits; black dress and khaki work pants; dress and work boots or shoes; Kwame Nkrumah sweatshirts; green and dark red dashikis; and silver *talisimus*.[75] The *talisimus* were "worn at [The East], when representing family among other African people, and at any other time [members wished] as long as the symbol [was] not endangered."[76]

Based on the principle of *Ujamaa* (cooperative economics), The East members shared their financial resources and attempted to distribute them according to the needs of the various families. At its height, The East employed approximately a hundred full-time workers. As Weusi noted, "[e]veryone who came to [The East] seeking work, found a job. They may have been underpaid or minimally paid, but they found meaningful work, warm friendships, safety, security, cultural identity, training in job tasks, and self-assurance."[77] The family atmosphere, structure, and work provided a level of organizational management and, although unclear to some members, did allow for each person to know his or her dynamic role since no one had an actual position at The East. Though certainly not the case for all members, there was an outline of the multileveled responsibilities of The East collective, the family, and the supporters, which explained the requirements and benefits granted to each level of membership.

The outline of the institution's responsibility to its members and the member's responsibility to the institution clearly identified and made a distinction between the levels of involvement (see appendix D). Among the levels, The East collective was the highest, expecting participation in all areas of requested work. It was responsible for electing the leadership and ratifying its policies when necessary. At the next level, the family consisted of all paid staff members. Members of this body were considered to have not yet developed the level of participation necessary to be in the collective. In addition, full-time and part-time members were entitled to certain benefits as well as being expected to adhere to organizational standards and policies. Lastly, The East supporters consisted of women and men outside of The East collective and family who were interested in supporting the goals and ideals of the institution through services or finances. Although these distinctions may have helped to clarify a member's level of involvement, everyone who worked at The East was considered a part of the composite family structure.

Family Life and Relationships at The East

The East optionally practiced what it referred to as "extended-family" living arrangements wherein a male could be married to more than one woman, considering that he and they could marshal their resources to effectively manage the "large family" and its accompanying responsibilities. Given that men and women operate in distinctive social spheres, as it relates to the culturally determined behaviors and duties that constitute womanhood and manhood, The East appeared to have been more inclined to the notion of women being taken care of as opposed to providing the proper space for personal and familial development. Both the notion of being taken care of and the spheres or domains in which women and men function are usually based on the culture and philosophy around which a people's lives are organized. At The East, polygamous relationships were structured around "the concept of the extended family" to the extent that it was a "must [to] put this belief into practice."[78] Numerically, the polygamous relationships were the smallest contingent, yet these relationships caused the most concern. Clearly, confusion and abuse will emerge when men are free to engage in multiple relationships under the guise of polygamous marriage without the obligation(s) that polygamous law prescribes. The evident confusion and abuse appeared to be a function of gender inequality, but was in fact a result of cultural confusion. This confusion existed in the complementarities between women and men (or lack thereof), the gender specificity of culturally constructed roles and responsibilities, and the protocols for resolving familial conflicts.

To many involved in these extended-family arrangements, the 1960s was a time of experimentation with relationships in general, but more specifically with relationships within the context of (what most considered to be) the practice of African cultural traditions. In fact, this extended-family arrangement was one of the major unresolved concerns that ended the relationship between The East and CAP-CFUN.[79] Generally speaking, there were numerous polygamous relationships in addition to little, if any, real hesitation in participating in institutions where these familial arrangements existed. Parenthetically, as far as The East was concerned, this was certainly true for the young adults who became integral to the institution. According to Jitu Weusi, The East, as a way to approach relationships, "began to codify things such as laws of marriage, courtship, divorce, and responsibility toward an offspring. The East held a strong position on relationships such as fathers to their sons [and] even in divorces; they had to make provisions to take care of such responsibilities."[80] In 1973, The East Sisterhood conducted a "Male-Female Relationships" lecture series that featured such persons as Nathan Hare and Sonia Sanchez in an effort, more than likely, to proactively address that topic within The East.

For The East, the knowledge base of their extended-family arrangement derived primarily from books and presentations concerning African social organization and traditions. Yet, books and presentations are never adequate substitutes for the cultural setting in which specific African practices exist and are experienced. Those sources of information, nonetheless, did allow for the instituting of naming ceremonies, rites of passage, and wedding ceremonies (i.e., the joining of multiple families). The East came to see the family as a very important part of the institution and engaged its development through discussions, workshops, events, speakers, and structures (protocol) as preventive and procedural frameworks. One such structure was a process of courtship that included no intercourse; one source, though uncorroborated by others, suggests that this procedure was instituted in 1972 and continued thereafter.[81] It is clear that The East greatly emphasized familyhood, since the family was the nucleus of the cultural nation. However, the manner in which these relationships were approached and the challenges that emerged had the effect of fragmenting some families, while the intention or objective was to create and bring them together. As a consequence of the historical period and the political and cultural stance taken by the youth and adults that became The East family, many were, in varying degrees, severed from biological members of their families. In a few cases, some were completely estranged; in other cases, such as that of Tamisha, her biological family—former Garveyites and members of the Communist Party—and she never lost touch for one moment.[82]

Given the initial male orientation of The East leadership in the formative years, Khadijah Bandele, a member of The East Sisterhood, stated that the organization "started out quite chauvinistic, but for the most part, it changed." Bandele further went on to state, however, that a number of the men did not understand the totality of the extended family arrangement and, as a consequence, practiced it simply to have more women.[83] Women such as Aminisha Black had initially "really bought this thing about we can build a nation" and later realized that it was an attempt "to adopt a culture and kind of put it on like clothing and not really take into consideration the internal contradictions." Though disappointed in the end, Black admitted that the extended family structure is viable and "workable if people are committed to doing the work on themselves that is required." In addition, she noted that the men occupying leadership roles did make attempts to incorporate a number of women on the leadership council.[84] Basir Mchawi also points out that there were clear attempts to "try to move sisters into decision-making roles," but in "some cases, [they] moved sisters who were not ready. . . . to assume decision-making roles and [move] into the leadership of the organization." Additionally, Mchawi noted that, in most cases, the men carried themselves principally in these matters of leadership and relationship. In other cases, men who did otherwise were forced to leave the institution.[85]

Other male members, such as Modele Clarke, who was on the leadership council, stated, "on the surface, the relationships seemed to be male-dominated [and that]. . . . this appearance of male domination was evident at social and public events. In private, however, most mates and spouses adopted control and decision-making in those areas where they had the most expertise."[86] Women of The East did occupy leadership roles in the council and through major divisions of the institution, though; for many of them, one of the most important components was The East Sisterhood, which provided the women a safe space to bleed and to address matters related to themselves, their families, their relationships, and their relations with men at The East. It also provided opportunity for them to contribute their skills and their creativity within the East and the broader community. These women formed healthy and affirming bonds through comforting each other and caring for each other's children, cooking vegetarian dishes, sharing natural remedies and laundry duties, provided clothing and a place to stay when needed, and understood that they and the men were "not merely biological parents but sociological parents—responsible for all the children [of The East family]."[87]

Many of the women are still very much connected across the North American landscape through their experience as part of The East Sisterhood, which attracted many of the women who came to The East after its inception and provided a "port in the storm" during turbulent moments within the organization. According to the testimony of a sizeable number of East Sisterhood women, most "have healed the wounded relationships [where necessary] and are able to appreciate the friendships that were formed and that continue to this day."[88] Most of the women were not entirely subservient or silenced at The East, but, as Fela Barclift mentions, there were abusive relationships wherein the women's creativity was suppressed and issues surrounding duties relegated by gender were not fully addressed.[89] Gender specificity was never sufficiently contextualized in a way that the aggregated duties were clear and consistent with the institution's mission. Yet, despite what conclusions may be drawn from this experience in "extended families," the children of these living arrangements were the beneficiaries in the minds of several present East members.[90]

Family and Community Relationships

The wholeness of a community is generally reflected in the lives and values of its families. Likewise, the strength and weakness of a family-based community institution, such as The East, would be most evident in the life of its major activities. The community school of Uhuru Sasa Shule was the centerpiece of The East and, as such, its stability and development (or lack thereof) reflected the direction of the organization. According to Lumumba Bandele, a student of Uhuru Sasa, the institution provided not only a sense of being a responsible and disciplined member of a community but also the collective "identity as a people and nation within the U.S. borders."[91] The extended family structure of Uhuru Sasa attempted to build family and community from inside out, and thus the focal point began with the intimate and the familial relationships that emerged at

The East. Since many of the teachers were either parents or East affiliates themselves, it was possible to build and maintain a consistent cultural and political framework—one that provided a design for living—shared by family members between home and institution life. The extended family that was the particular outcome of polygamous relationships was, in part, responsible for sustaining this type of environment. Yet, this large family arrangement was practiced on an optional basis; monogamous relationships were more the norm. Although polygamy is neither necessary nor required to develop a sense of belonging to a large family, it did provide the children of The East and Uhuru Sasa with a storehouse of *babas* (fathers) and *mamas* (mothers) and a pragmatic understanding of African cultural and communal life. Notwithstanding, only two interviewees attributed the factor of the large family arrangements and the challenges surrounding them to the decline of The East. A number of respondents did, however, express valid concerns about the nature and consequences of these relationships.

One of the few striking responses was a criticism regarding the lack of balance and openness in male-female relationships, unresolved contradictions, and the absence of provisions for healing to occur within such relationships.[92] By healing, the meaning here is the appropriate means to confront and resolve the emotional, psychological, and spiritual damage and conflict that result from unhealthy relationships. Attention must, therefore, be brought to the shortcomings and emotionally detrimental consequences that take place when relationships are approached with certain intentions and are not given the time and space to develop in a healthy manner. The East attempted to provide vehicles of resolution through its Brotherhood and Sisterhood divisions of the governing family, guided by the wisdom "that women must work with women in order to build a feminine identity and that men must work with men in order to build a masculine identity. This way, when a man and a woman come together, they are better able to relate to each other."[93] Nevertheless, a number of the relationships did not allow for the necessary developmental time and space for them to functionally mature. Likewise, the lack of effective protocols on how to approach and resolve challenges and rituals for reestablishing healthy relationships seems to have also been a factor.

For example, in the context of polygamy, a few men of The East brought women into their home(s) to be second wives without first consulting their first wife; similarly, some women even sabotaged relationships in order to obtain a certain husband. Moreover, the foregoing criticism regarding male-female relationships inferentially asks if relationships are based on certain principles, what are they, and what is the substance behind them? What are the benefits and shortcomings of certain relationships? How will potential challenges be dealt with and within the context of what structure?

To determine to what extent these questions were entertained or responded to is difficult. Most of the respondents held positive recollections of the large family structure and atmosphere at The East, along with some honest concerns that these relationships could have been better organized and handled. Yet, these recollections should not obscure the fact that there was dissension and in-fighting as a result of the unresolved challenges within those familial structures. One female member simply left The East rather than endure feelings of uneasiness with the large-family living arrangements.[94] Many large-family members claim to have established an intergenerational pool that has not only kept the traditions of The East alive but has remained within the African-based community and continues some of the organization's cultural and political work through various organizations.

One measure of success, in the context of nation(alist) building, is the intergenerational transmission of culture and institutional leadership and a commitment to institutional development by those who accept the responsibilities of cultural leadership. To echo the words of Modele Clarke, The East family did not provide the necessary "provisions for continuity" of the institution.[95] Even though there were attempts to forge a structure of organizational leadership that would, in fact, provide a basis for institutional continuity, there was a lack of building horizontal and complementary leadership and commitment among the youth of the families. Meaning, and in unison with approximately half of the interviewees, the appointment of Dr. E. Curtis Alexander as headmaster of Uhuru Sasa was a harmful decision in relationship to institutional continuity and perhaps to common sense. This is not to say that Dr. Alexander lacked effective leadership skills, but if institutional and family development is the primary objective, then development should have been determined from within The East family structure in order to ensure continuity. Further, one cannot build a commitment to institutional development and leadership from outside of the target institution, particularly if it does not have a process of developing the necessary skills and sensibilities within an external candidate over a sufficient period of time. Clearly, The East demonstrated that institutional building is serious work, but it also suggests that provisions for continuity demanded purposeful action and intergenerational processes to perpetuate efforts to expand, defend, and project institutions beyond the threshold of survival.

Purposeful intergenerational processes would have made clear the mission and purpose of the institution, its defining characteristics, and how its mission and vision would be realized. In other words, the philosophical and cultural underpinnings of the institution and how they manifested themselves in its structure must be made clear, consistently refined, and "ritualized" in the living memory of the members. For institutional self-study and development, as The East experience suggests, the philosophical foundations must determine the institution's goals and objectives, which would assess the actualization of its mission. Thus, as a constantly changing institution, The East perhaps did not fully address its mission in very unambiguous and concrete terms and, as a result, its goals and objectives.

The Decentralization of The East

From all the institutional activities and advances made in the infrastructure, The East was in a mode of constant development. As Aminisha Black observed, The East was "something in the making.... It was something to be shaped and molded.... It was something that was organic and it was evolving."[96] In 1976, The East sought to make further internal changes through the decentralization of the institution, which coincided with the relocation of most of its primary operations to the Sumner Avenue armory (renamed the Uhuru Cultural Center). The decentralized East was comprised of nine departments and *Waziri* (ministers), or elected officials who provided leadership for each particular department.

Those officials collectively formed the "Family Leadership Council."[97] The departments were organized around the areas of education (Uhuru Sasa/Cultural Center), buildings and grounds, culture, family affairs, Uhuru Food Cooperative, Imani Child Development Center, political affairs, economics (East Caterers and Akiba Mkuu bookstore), and communications (*Black News*). Yet with decentralization, the questions that usually arise when an institution expands or becomes a more complex entity were certainly apparent. Black, author of a rare evaluation report of 1977, offered the following criticism:

> We are unquestionably a recognized Black organization and we are respected by many. I observe that our issue raising has decreased and in its place there has been more preoccupation with the organization itself visible in terms of expanding businesses. Expansion itself is not bad provided that it is occurring in line with designated political goals. With this self-interest theme, we have attracted more people who are here out of their own self-interest rather than seeking a place to serve a political commitment to Black people. . . . Within these conditions, decentralization could only serve to heighten the contradictions.[98]

Generically speaking, decentralization at The East was an attempt to share the leadership and decision-making authority within the institution. However, some perceived problems that stemmed from a one-man leadership, such as envy, lack of cooperation, and competitiveness, were unresolved prior to decentralization, which itself offered no firm resolution.[99] Others felt that the attempt at decentralization was an attempt to restructure the leadership of The East and, therefore, adequately marshal its primary institutional responsibilities and resources. As Basir Mchawi explains, "One of the things we attempted to do at The East organization [was to] decentralize as many operations as we possibly could so that each operation would be more or less independent, self-determining [and] self-standing."[100] According to the recollection of some members, there seem to have been a number of structural concerns that, perhaps, made decentralization appear to be a healthy response to these challenges.[101] One member suggested that The East existed in a historical context charged with urgency, which consequently gave way to the deficiency in the institution's long-term planning.¹⁰² Whether decentralization was strategically planned and executed or was the subsequent outcome of this urgency is uncertain. Black's evaluation report is revealing in that it highlights many internal challenges, which either emerged as a result of decentralization or existed prior to it. The report states, "Much time was spent in hassling [as it related to] what one department owed to another. This was reduced to definite individualism since there [were] no organizational principles to decide the issues. . . . All in all there were many skirmishes to solidify this newly shared power and the workers in the organization were kept at a non-participating level of decision-making and involvement."¹⁰³

As a result of the shared power brought about by decentralization, political in-fighting and unresolved personal battles seemed to have disconnected and fragmented members further from one another and from the institution's purpose.¹⁰⁴ Decentralization did, however, bring about a number of positive developments, which included the establishment of the Department of Record Keeping, Accounting and Personnel Bookkeeping (DRKAPB). This department provided insights into the consequences of decentralization, but these insights are limited due to the lack of internal documents. It was reported in the formative years of the institution that The East only had an informal system of record keeping. One East member reported that the institution was, in fact, plagued with poor business planning and management.¹⁰⁵ At decentralization, the DRKAPB was created to deal effectively with this lack of business sophistication. The department was largely an outcome of the increased activity of the institution with state and city agencies, which required maintenance of related records and the filing of regular reports; a secretarial staff, confronted with a heavier workload related to the school's day-to-day activities; and the institution's intention to become a nonprofit organization, which dictated that more detailed records be kept.¹⁰⁶

The DRKAPB filed and handled the various monthly reports; kept records of deeds, loans, contracts, and business agreements; maintained the checkbooks; and collected fines where necessary. Yet, the reported lack of clear institutional goals also applied to this department despite its seeming achievements. According to one report, "Bookkeeping was generally hampered by lack of knowing the ultimate aims of the organization. At most [the staff] kept superficial records."[107] The significance of the bookkeeping department is considerable in light of the fact that many self-determining institutions have met an abrupt demise due to a lack of sophistication in business and organizational management, particularly in the areas of fiscal responsibility and personal interactions. The challenges of this department may have certainly been indicative of the challenges of other departments, given the analysis of the evaluation report and the fact that many members began to leave the institution in 1977 for various reasons.

During this period of leave, one East member concluded that these departures were the result of "the question of nationalism versus spiritualism," since a number of members began to pursue their study and practice of the Yorùbá and Akan traditions of spirituality to find "a spiritual base."[108] Other members, however, felt that it was the "lack of political education [that] forced people to involve themselves in religious pursuits and other forms of occultism.... [and suggested] that continuous political education in general be brought back into [The East,] particularly political education that [would] eliminate metaphysical thought and allow [them] to be more analytical and scientific in thought and practice."[109] These ideological, organizational, and culturally confusing idiosyncrasies exacerbated unresolved conflicts and gave way to external intrusion and the eventual collapse of the organization. Most of all, the lack of business management or competency, "clear organizational aims," and "sophistication in consistently defining what The East was about" paved the way for the institution's decline.[110]

The Decline of The East (Summer 1977–Summer 1986)

The East maintained substantive and mutually beneficial relationships with national and international African communities, despite an ironic but ambiguous relationship with small segments of its immediate community, which indicated the lack of support that would come when The East needed it most. Community and institutional development defined The East in the formative years, but in the late 1970s the institution took on a life of its own and became primarily concerned with its survival. As a consequence, it did not fully recognize the realities and impact of its local and national existence. The outcome was an inability to adapt adequately to transformations that occurred within that existence—precisely, the sociopolitical transformations in Brooklyn, New York, New York State, and the United States. The East also became more detached and insulated from its community, that is, beyond those who constituted The East family. Generally speaking, when institutions become introverted, their vision for development can only span as far as survival will allow. This somewhat paralyzing form of development can be further aggravated when there are stable institutions and transient members who use the institution as an appendage of a phase that they are going through. This is one of the reasons why relationships within institutions should be approached with the utmost sincerity through appropriate processes that allow for optimal personal and community development. Institutions are people-driven and engender an atmosphere where personal interactions are intimate and intensive or have the potential to be. Thus, as a result of inadequate or nonexistent processes for sufficient member orientation, members have left institutions due to unresolved challenges in personal relationships, which was certainly the case for a number of East members.

Some left the institution because a personal or conjugal relationship did not materialize as expected. Regarding allegiances to personalities and power struggles, one-third of the members interviewed attributed the changes in attitude and lack of support and will to sustain the institution to the decline of The East. A slightly higher percentage of interviewed East members credited the spiraling decline of The East to the shift in school leadership from Jitu Weusi to Dr. E. Curtis Alexander and Dr. Alexander's manner of leadership and organization. A smaller number of respondents indicated changes in the political and social climate, while others cited the lack of fiscal responsibility and business management as factors leading to the organization's demise. Lastly, only two East members viewed its demise as a "natural death." These unique responses were the most metaphoric of all. One of these respondents concluded, with an analogy related to the sun's path, that The East was supposed to rise for a period of time, provide models, and set (decline).[111] The other respondent noted that all organisms have a time, and The East and Uhuru Sasa Shule could not live forever, since as part of life, every organism dies. Moreover, the respondent was of the opinion that The East and Uhuru Sasa lived as long as they should have before dying. However, just as a mother who has offspring, The East and Uhuru Sasa left a legacy behind.[112]

The history of The East strongly suggests that it was a multifaceted, nonsectarian institution. As such, it had a certain openness to African people from most if not all segments of the immediate and larger community. From its inception, its position was that "we accept [African] people of all religious and political backgrounds and levels if they are willing to make a contribution."[113] This willingness to create a "liberated area" for African people to commune and develop, especially an African cultural orientation, resulted in the rapid indoctrination of members. Yet, on some levels, due to the "nebulousness" of the institution, as Job Mashariki called the lack of processes for immersing some of those very same persons into the culture of The East, many complications were created. Some included the infiltration by agent provocateurs, the inclusion of several belief systems without organizing or unifying principles, and a cacophony of personal experiences and issues, all of which produced diverging views on management and direction. As a consequence of a lack of clarity around these challenges and a lack of a consistent means through which resolution could be sought, many East members left or became involved in the Yorùbá and Akan traditions, Islam, and later the Kemetic or Ancient Egyptian philosophy of the Ausar-Auset Society.[114] The East did not necessarily have ideological classes—which would have been distinct from political educational classes offered through the auspices of the Evening School of Knowledge in the 1970s—nor was it rigid on ideology.[115] The East was steeped in the philosophy and practice of the *Nguzo Saba* and held a firm Black nationalist and pan-Africanist orientation. However, it did not have a spiritual or philosophical system rooted in African concepts of spiritual-temporal reality, which might have given it a basis for (a) approaching relationships and methods to resolve challenges that arise; (b) developing institutional protocols; and (c) the intergenerational transmission of knowledge and skills of leadership, including competency in African cultural and community development.[116]

In an attempt to grapple with the question of determining what The East was about, a purpose and standards committee was established at a December 1978 organizational meeting. The "Purpose and Standards Committee" defined its function as a body assembled to (1) develop a statement of purpose for The East and all its institutions; (2) develop organizational principles, goals and objectives, criteria, and performance standards to be practiced throughout the institutions; and (3) design a system of monitoring performance and enforcing policy.[117] At the conclusion of the meeting, assignments to develop a written statement of purpose for The East and to gather written materials on the umbrella institution were given out to each committee member. Whether a written statement of purpose came out of the committee's next scheduled meeting is unknown. Some of the interviewed East members mentioned an organizational document called the *Mashariki* (Kiswahili for *East*); others had no recollection of it. If such a document were in the interviewed members' possession, they were either unwilling or unable to produce it.

In August 1978, Jitu Weusi officially resigned from his duties as director of The East and headmaster of Uhuru Sasa. Approximately two years before this date, Weusi had also relinquished his role as chairperson of the Council of Independent Black Institutions (CIBI), the umbrella organization of independent African-centered educational institutions established in 1972. After Weusi's resignation, Dr. E. Curtis Alexander assumed the role of headmaster of Uhuru Sasa, and Adeyemi Bandele took on the responsibility of directing The East. When in 1976 the Sumner Avenue armory became known as the Uhuru Cultural Center, all the operations of The East were moved to the armory, with the exception of *Black News* and The East Catering. Within two years, *Black News* would move to the cultural center, while The East Catering remained at 10 Claver Place, the original facility of The East.[118] In 1976, the Claver Place structure caught or was set on fire, which resulted in the roof of the building needing repair, among other things.[119] Meanwhile, the Uhuru Cultural Center not only expanded the school and made full use of the larger facility but also rented out the space to other community groups for concerts and cultural performances. Ultimately, some of the incidents that took place during the rental of the facility led to the collapse of The East's image and longevity.

One of these incidents, known as the "New York Eight," involved a group of men who were members of the "triple angle" (pyramid) gun club. Unbeknownst to the leadership of The East, Howard Barnes allowed the club access to an unused shooting range downstairs in the armory.[120] The group, which was under government surveillance, left shell casings in the vicinity and consequently jeopardized The East's occupation of the armory. The surveillance reports and shells were used as evidence in the group's subsequent trial. Viola Plummer of the December 12th Movement, a reparations group based in Brooklyn, and the New York Eight was tried on conspiracy to commit bank robbery in the early 1980s. However, both the gun club and the reparations group were acquitted of most charges, with the exception of gun possession. For The East, unfortunately, the irresponsibility of the aforementioned groups led to increased state and city scrutiny, particularly by Mayor Edward Koch and his administration, and the eventual seizure of the armory.

Between 1979 and 1983, East leadership shifted from Adeyemi Bandele to Robbo Jumatatu to Segun Shabaka; Dr. Alexander had relinquished his headmaster duties in or about 1979. Thereafter, the directing of Uhuru Sasa shifted from Jumibia Nyahuma to Lubaba Ahmed to Rashida Kierstedt, who was the headmistress in 1983. What is important to note is that East members "always felt that the school was the heart of the institution" and thus "it was the most important entity" as far as they were concerned.[121] In fact, most, if not all, of the operations of The East revolved around the maintenance and development of the school. Consequently, when it began to unravel from internal conflicts and external assaults from city and state agencies, The East began to reflect the instability in leadership and organizational management. The feeling that "every time somebody [new] took over, [they] had to learn how to do things their way" was certainly present among East members from 1977 to the early 1980s.[122] In addition, a number of "people did not come [to The East] with their heart and mind to build, to grow, develop, [and] help build an institution."[123]

In the final analysis, the unresolved challenges discussed throughout this chapter contributed to the demise of The East as an institution in 1986.[124] The only viable operation that remained, and that still exists, is the International African Arts Festival. As a consequence of being forced out of the armory in 1986, Segun Shabaka explained that the operation of the festival "worked out of [his] living room for about two years and used the back of [his] house" for storing its equipment.[125] Thereafter, festival coordinators established an office and also made an attempt to acquire The East structure at 10 Claver Place. However, the attempt did not quite work out, and the original building was eventually sold at an auction. Based on an understanding of the organization's birth and development, we may ask if its respective components followed the same trajectory.

3 Ujamaa

Enterprises of The East

> We must inoculate our people with nation building concepts of Land, Tools and Labor (work). We must also be ready and able to defend what we are building. We must develop and strengthen our communities around the economic principle of [Ujamaa].
>
> AN UHURU SASA SHULE BULLETIN

Communication within the African World Community: *Black News*, Akiba Mkuu Bookstore, and "A View from The East"

Although *Black News* did not begin as the official communication organ of The East, it would assume this distinction in October 1969. In August 1969, a political conference took place in Brooklyn, where thirty-five community activists came together to discuss the idea of a publication. This group, among them Jitu Weusi and Jim Williams, met with the aim of putting in motion the seven principles of the *Nguzo Saba*. The main purpose of the meeting was to establish a communication link within the African-based community, and it resulted in the emergence of *Black News*.[1] The publication was born under the principle of *Umoja* (unity) with the intention that it would be "a dynamic voice in the liberation struggles of [African] people."[2] The overall idea derived from a late-1960s publication called *Rebellion News*, which came out of Boston, Massachusetts.[3]

Armed with the slogan of "Agitate, Educate, Organize," *Black News*, under its first editor Jim Williams, began with four men and women on the third floor of The East facility. Some of the staff members under Williams included Ante Brown, Martha Bright, Addie Rimmer, Monifa King,

Fujii Breland, Penda Aiken and her husband, Rasheed. Williams taught these men and women the fundamentals of copy layout, artwork, reporting, and all of the other necessary skills associated with putting out a quality publication. The first issue of *Black News*, which contained eight pages, was sold for ten cents a copy, with approximately five thousand copies issued in October 1969. Distribution manager Jitu Weusi soon initiated a vigorous subscription campaign, and subscriptions began to arrive from literally all over the world. The local method of distribution consisted of young men and women stopping by The East, taking fifty to one hundred copies of *Black News*, and selling them at subway stations, playgrounds, schools, and other appropriate locales. Robbo Jumatatu succeeded Weusi as the distribution manager.

Black News's increase in subscriptions, from five thousand to fifteen thousand, demanded more space than what The East facility could accommodate, so its operations moved to the African-American Teachers Association (ATA) office at 1064 Fulton Avenue. Shortly after, the structure that became known as the *Black News* building was rented at 1281 Bedford Avenue with the option to buy. Interestingly, in a process akin to training an apprentice, Jim Williams had each staff member complete an issue from start to finish. With the idea of expansion and the hopes of having a complete printing press, *Black News* became incorporated, and a board of directors was established.[4] The organizational meeting for the incorporation was held at 1064 Fulton Street on December 20, 1972, with a board consisting of Jim Williams, Donald Blackman, Leroy Bowser, Les Campbell (Jitu Weusi), George Dudley, Maurice Fredericks (Msemajei Weusi), Andre Womble (Salik Mwando), and Frank Richards. Among the board members, the officers of the *Black News* organizational structure were Msemaji Weusi (president), Leroy Bowser (vice-president), Frank Richards, (treasurer) and Salik Mwando (secretary).

The need for a new location, better machinery, and the reality that paid staff members were required compelled *Black News* to seek a loan from the Bedford Stuyvesant Restoration Center, which never materialized. In addition, the wasted time and energy it took to have people trained and then have them leave the operation became problematic. Nonetheless, the core staff continued the work and later sought to acquire a three-story building at 1281 Bedford Avenue. With the acquisition of a building, projections were made to establish a printing plant on the first floor, an art department and composing area on the second floor, and a research library and a meeting room on the third floor. During this time, *Black News* was lodged on the third floor of The East building at 10 Claver Place. What is uncertain is whether *Black News* bought the building at 1281 Bedford Avenue.

Certainly, the publication did not always come out on schedule, but the overall effort of those committed to the necessary work was always evident. The core policy at *Black News* was underscored by the principle of *Ujima*. The staff, however, did not agree on every article that went into the paper or the position taken by the publication on certain matters. The official position of the paper stated, "The only 'ism' that *Black News* would embrace would be that of Black Nationalism."[5] Yet, this position was the primary source of why Jim Williams left or was ousted. Apparently he worked exclusively with *Black News*; in doing so he was not actively engaged in the "culture" of The East or its institutional extensions. In very simplistic terms, The East was a nationalist organization. *Black News* was the official communication organ of The East, not Jim Williams. Nonetheless, Williams articulated his criticism of certain nationalists' tendencies through the publicaton. In a July 1972 article entitled "Whose Puddle Do I Be Standing In," he stated, "the position of *Black News* on this African Nationalist–Negro politician new political direction had been spelled out in [two] previous issues. Lest anyone think we've changed our position or have lessened our opposition to it, we haven't. If anything we're going to be intensifying our opposition to this brand of political maneuvering which we see as being based on sheer expediency, opportunism and rank evidence of the bankruptcy of African nationalism as is now being practiced by most such motivated organizations."[6]

Salik Mwando, who assumed the role of editor after Jim Williams, confirms, "There were internal conflicts between Jim Williams and his philosophy and that of The East."[7] Additionally, Williams himself admits that his position, as it relates to The East, was "from the outside because [he and the *Black News* staff] were always so busy" with the publication.[8] The conflict between the ideological positions of Williams, *Black News*'s founding editor, and The East is indicative more so of the ideational and physical security concerns of The East rather than a resolvable political disagreement. By the mere fact of the organization's existence and its activities, The East had to maintain and defend its operations from those who would compromise or seek to extinguish its life. During Williams's tenure, a man named George Dudley, but who was more commonly known as Brother Z, worked at the publication. After a few suspicions about his residence and inconsistent work schedule, *Black News* and The East discovered that he was a police officer and, therefore, an agent. This discovery came at an undisclosed "soul food" eatery, while Dudley was congregating with ten to eleven young police recruits. The outcome remains unclear.

After Williams's departure, Salik Mwando took on the role of editor, though Basir Mchawi and Segun Shabaka along with other staff members aided him. Mwando indicated that each volume of *Black News* corresponded to a respective editor.[9] Typically, a volume was one year's worth of issues, but for the editors of *Black News*, one volume encompassed several years.

7. Salik Mwando with his Uhuru Sasa middle school students at the Bond Street location, 1971. Photograph by Osei Terry Chandler. Used with permission.

Thus, according to Mwando's account, volume one was edited by Jim Williams, volume two by Mwando, volume three by Mchawi, and volumes four and five by Shabaka. Excluding the fact that volumes four and five overlapped, Mwando's recollection was certainly accurate. Considering the factors of year(s), volume(s), and editor(s), the life of *Black News* would be chronicled as follows: volume one (Jim Williams, 1969–72); volume two (Salik Mwando, 1972–74); volume three (Basir Mchawi, 1974–78); volume four (Segun Shabaka, 1978–83) and volume five (Segun Shabaka, 1983–84). Shabaka's tenure was broken into two periods as a result of being the *Black News* editor for two distinct volumes.

Up until the decentralization of The East in 1976, the revenue from the sales of *Black News* was allocated into two categories: (1) money that was set aside for publishing the next issue; and (2) revenue (the balance) that went to aid the operations of Uhuru Sasa and The East. With decentralization, *Black News* had to become self-sufficient in terms of salaries and production.[10] While an international publication that included circulation in five countries with an estimated maximum circulation of fifty thousand, *Black News* was mostly sold on the streets of New York City.[11] The monthly publication, which began as a biweekly, also created institutionally and economically supportive relationships through its sales in that most members of The East family, including students of Uhuru Sasa, sold *Black News*. The prominent features of the publication were the columns "Around Our Way" and "*Black News* Briefs," which provided coverage and analysis of local, national, and international events in relation to the African world community, and *Fundisha*, the official news organ of the Congress of African People (CAP). *Fundisha*'s feature in *Black News* ended with The East's departure from CAP in 1974. Additionally, *Black News*'s "POWs Forum," a column for African-descended prisoners detained in American prisons, and its "Brooklyn Family Schools" newsletter provided mediums for information sharing and informed community members of essential political and educational concerns, respectively. In sum, the real meaning of *Black News* in terms of liberating and developing the African-based psyche must be seen in its dissemination of pan-Africanist and nationalist thought and practice in a way or language that could be understood by the average person.

Throughout the life of *Black News*, the foregoing features of the publication, coupled with local and consistent advertisers, were responsible for its endurance and its readership. Parenthetically, it is important to note that advertisers too were conscientiously held to a cultural and value-based standard. By way of illustration, one *Black News* ad read: "We're choosey about ads. If you don't satisfy Black dignity, they don't satisfy *Black News*. Therefore, we forward all peddlers of bleach creams, goofy dust, and wigs to the *Amsterdam [News]*."[12] In 1976, *Black News*'s editor reported, "We have become The East Department of Information, Propaganda and Culture (IPC).... The Department has only been in existence since September [1976].... Aside from *Black News*, we are responsible for most of the program that The East has become famous for."[13] With these new changes, editor Basir Mchawi proposed that a more visually pleasing format, with increased international news coverage and periodical reports from African-based communities across the United States, would now define the publication. Since *Black News* utilized color and black/white layouts and gave coverage to these proposed areas beginning in as early as 1972, Basir's proposal was not new but an enhancement of prior activities and developments.

The *Black News* remained at The East facility until 1978, two years after most of the institutional components moved to the Sumner Avenue armory. In that year, Segun Shabaka assumed the role of editor. As editor and assistant director of the institution, Shabaka admits, "I came in with limited skills."[14] Nonetheless, in light of the decentralized organizational structure, Shabaka was able to transform *Black News* into a self-sufficient operation, which was one of the objectives of decentralization. According to Shabaka, this self-sufficiency meant typesetting duties, printing the paper, and managing business-related services, in addition to incurring the bill for new IBM typesetting equipment that Mchawi had bought, which replaced the contracted typesetter used by *Black News* until this time.[15] Clearly there was a struggle to maintain the publication and all the other areas, which required similar commitment, time, and energy. In the context of its historical and archival value, *Black News* published invaluable information on matters internal as well as external to The East and, as such,

8. Basir Mchawi and two students of the Central Brooklyn Model Cities summer program run by The East at Shaw University in Raleigh, North Carolina, where three hundred junior high school students from Brooklyn spent eight weeks, 1972. Photograph by Osei Terry Chandler. Used with permission.

has left a substantial knowledge-based legacy. *Black News* discontinued its operations in or about 1984.[16]

As the logical extension of *Black News* activities, the Akiba Mkuu bookstore was established in February 1970. Its origins can be found in the closing of another local bookstore. A woman named Wendy Richardson and her late husband, Fred Richardson, had a bookstore called Richardson's Bookstore, located on Atlantic Avenue. At one point, Fred decided to go out of business but died before doing so. After he passed, Wendy sold the items from the bookstore to The East and, thereafter, the Akiba Mkuu bookstore came into existence.[17] The bookstore was located in a storefront at 1310 Atlantic Avenue, when The East operated out of that space. It was also reported that Akiba Mkuu Bookshop ("the knowledge bookshop") was located at 6 Claver Place. In its early stages, a person by the name of Hakim Bomani managed it. Akiba Mkuu carried books, records, papers, and other related materials published by The East Publications, which had a *Black Nation Education* and a *Our Nation's History* series that were very popular activities of the press. Other publications included *A Message from a Black Teacher* (1973) by Jitu Weusi, *First Book of Kwanza* (1975), and *Afrikans for Communications*, a language arts text edited and published by The East. Essentially, the bookstore was the arm of The East for the dissemination of political and cultural information.

As to its maintenance and development, we are told that "in a lot of cases, the people that took on the business responsibility, they didn't necessarily have . . . the background, the drive [or] whatever it [took]."[18] Additionally, the store was not sufficiently exposed, except if a person was able to frequent The East. For unknown reasons, it was not accessible to the larger community. Clearly, a business entity has to be accessible to potential consumers and can only fail when insulation becomes the operative principle of business conduct. In 1982, the insulation was further elevated when the store moved to the Uhuru Cultural Center at 357 Sumner Avenue (renamed Marcus Garvey Boulevard). With its decline inevitable, the bookstore closed shortly afterward. Yet, The East's drive to communicate its ideas and to engage the community with matters of importance from a nationalist position did not stop with its efforts in print media.

The East felt that it was critical for "the Revolutionary Nationalist/Pan-Africanist position to get airtime on radio and television."[19] Beginning in 1975 or 1976, it held a weekly radio program called "A View from The East." This program aired on Sunday mornings from approximately 9 A.M. to noon on WLIB (1190 AM). The global African broadcast was first hosted and produced by Basir Mchawi. At times, the program would be taped and then aired; on other occasions, the host-producer would go on the air live. Though "A View from The East" was not a business entity per se, it did provide a necessary medium for the communication of ideas and pertinent information. In contrast, business operations such as The East Kitchen and Caterers were profitable ventures that helped to sustain the institution and its member-employees.

The East Kitchen and Caterers, Tamu Sweet-East Restaurant, and the Uhuru Sasa Food Cooperative

The East Kitchen began in April 1970, coinciding with the weekend cultural programs and jazz performances at The East. Its first year, Jitu Weusi recalls, "was rough due to lack of organization."[20] However, this was soon transformed for the better and actually placed The East Kitchen in a position to help sustain the institution with the employment of a cook named Lottie Hicks Brown. To understand the full meaning of this event, the brief story behind it needs to be revealed.

One day, Weusi was walking toward The East from his home and noticed the mother of a child who attended a number of summer programs he had supervised. The mother said, "Hi, Les Campbell [Jitu Weusi], you don't remember me, do you?" Weusi replied, "Yes, I do. You're Eleanor's mother. What's your name [again]?" She said her name was Lottie (or Loddie) Hicks Brown and asked, "What's the matter? Looks like you got something on your mind." Weusi said, "Yeah, these people are wearing me out. This ... kitchen is [also] wearing me out." "Kitchen," says Lottie. "[Well,] I am a cook." That afternoon both agreed that she would be the cook of The East Kitchen. Lottie insisted that she [get] paid $125 a week, but during this period, no one at The East received that much. In fact, the teachers of Uhuru Sasa Shule only received $200 a month.[21]

Yet, the problems of the kitchen were so immense that Lottie got what she demanded. According to Weusi, he had never made a wiser decision in his life. In so few words, Lottie took over the kitchen, which flourished thereafter. In 1972, The East Kitchen took its services to the National Black Political Convention in Gary, Indiana, the first African Liberation Day held in Washington, D.C., and the second international Congress of African People meeting in San Diego, California. It was economically successful at all three gatherings. Lottie was assisted by Khadijah Bandele and Esenga, along with kitchen helpers such as Abimbola Wali and Malika, who created The East Recipe Book. Lottie is also the person who created such dishes as Kawaida Rice—a popular East dish composed of sautéed brown rice, green and red peppers, onions, chopped broccoli, and fresh mushrooms. The East Kitchen also pioneered in making a memorable green salad, carrot cake, and the famed "East fruit punch."[22] The revenue generated by The East Kitchen supported the institution for many years. According to Weusi, the kitchen was the reason why the International African Arts Festival existed in its formative years, since the organizers had no other way of making a profit. The East Kitchen was the parent of The East Caterers, which was based out of the kitchen and dealt primarily with external services.

The East Catering began in April 1971, a year after the founding of The East Kitchen. Mzee Moyo, who managed the catering operation in the early 1980s, reported, "The East Catering . . . was one of the main focuses of the institution."[23] It operated as an institutional entity as well as a business activity through its services of summer lunches and dinners at feasts, dances, weddings, and programs for individual persons, families, and institutions. The East Caterers not only catered to a variety of affairs but also for some years fed a large contingent of the Brooklyn nationalist community. By way of illustration, The East Catering breakfast-lunch program fed not only the students at Uhuru Sasa Shule but also the students from Weusi Shule (now Johnson Preparatory), Al-Karim, Modern Academy, Robert Conner Memorial, and Shule ya Mapinduzi. In fact, it fed most of the independent educational institutions throughout the Brooklyn community beyond the regular school year. The vital role it played cannot be overlooked or be minimized. In essence, The East Catering was the mobile unit of The East Kitchen.

Along with the kitchen and catering operations of The East, there was also the Tamu Sweet-East, which functioned as a food and dessert shop. The Tamu, meaning "sweet," began in June 1971, offering such items as ice cream, candy, cobblers, sweet potato and bean pies, and small sandwiches. Moreover, for a modest price, often referred to as "Black prices" (affordable prices), the Tamu Sweet-East offered a catering service for group and individual affairs. In the early years, the Tamu was located at 8 Claver Place and operated during the week from 10 A.M. to midnight and on Friday, Saturday, and Sunday from 10 A.M. until there were no more customers. Records indicating changes in hours of operation, structural modifications,

9. Shukuru Copeland adding finishing touches onto the "Sweet-East" exterior, 1971. Photograph by Osei Terry Chandler. Used with permission.

or other related matters are unavailable. Therefore, the Sweet-East's development, or lack thereof, is just as uncertain as its demise.

Uhuru Food *(Kununuana)* and Mavazi Clothing Cooperatives

The food-buying program of The East called *Kununuana*, which means "buying together or with each other," was formed through the operative principle of *Ujamaa* or cooperative economics. *Kununuana* was organized in November 1970.[24] According to Kwesi Mensah Wali, who ran the co-op during the daytime at 10 Claver Place,

> the food coop came about as a result of the trip to Guyana and we observed their cooperative operation and thought that we could create something of that sort here with the family that we had built in. Basically, what we did was agree on a minimal fund, say twenty dollars, and we would pool these twenty dollars together, [go] to the [Bronx Terminal

Market at Hunts Point], buy the supplies and products, [and] bring them in [and] divvy them up evenly.[25]

In light of the recognition of the high prices and poor quality of foods in African-based communities, The East formed the food co-op with the purpose of buying "fresher food [and better quality food] at a lower cost to the Black people in the community."[26] In addition, "The major purpose of the program [was] to show Black people what they can do when they unite for the collective benefit of all. It [was] a model [that could have been] easily used by Black people in all Black communities."[27] When the program began, a person would place his or her order(s) at The East by Monday night and pick up and pay for it on Thursday or Friday. All the food items were wholesale and sold in pounds unless otherwise indicated. Yet, as Kwesi Mensah Wali suggests, the process from order to pick up became cumbersome due to the fact that The East jazz performances on the weekend required the space used to store the purchases. Wali explains, "We would go to the market on Thursday mornings and divvy up the products on the ground floor at [10] Claver place Thursday during the day. Everyone was supposed to pick up, say midday, on Friday. It [would] go to the point where we knew the weekend sets [started] Friday nights at 9 P.M. and folks wouldn't pick up. . . . It got a little bit overbearing after a while and [was] occupying space. Then we found a space around the corner and we built a store there called the *Kununuana* food co-op. . . . [When the co-op moved around the corner,] certain aspects of it still remained co-op. In other words, people would pool their money in for particular products, but in general, the store was just open to the public [wherein natural foods were introduced to the community]".[28]

What began amongst The East family expanded when parents also started to include their monies with the existing amount, which consequently resulted in the food co-op moving into a storefront located at 1115 Fulton Street between Franklin and Classon avenues. According to an advertisement, goods such as herbs and spices, dry fruits, fresh fruits and vegetables, organic and whole wheat products were made available under the theme of "food for life, shopping in tradition." Due to unresolved structural weaknesses in the former building, the food co-op was

10. Kununuana (Uhuru Food Co-op) and Mavazi Clothing Co-op on Fulton Street, Brooklyn, New York. Photograph by Osei Terry Chandler. Used with permission.

11. A shelf of food items in the Kununuana (Uhuru Food Co-op), 1972. Photograph by Osei Terry Chandler. Used with permission.

relocated to 1107 Fulton Street, at the corner of Fulton Street and Claver Place, in 1975 and was now called The East Co-op Food Store.[29] In the same year, one report indicated that "fifty families currently participate in the food co-op and since its expansion to larger headquarters on Fulton Street—more families are expected to be accommodated."[30]

According to written sources, the store was open to the community from Monday through Saturday, during the operating hours of 9 A.M. to 8 P.M. At an unknown date, The East Co-op Food Store became known as the Uhuru Food Cooperative. The earliest appearance of this change is in October 1978. With the support of The East, the Black Community Congress, and the Black United Front, writes Jitu Weusi, the Uhuru Food Cooperative "embarked upon an ambitious program to develop cooperative retail stores and a wholesale food packaging and distribution center in Central Brooklyn." It focused on food as the commodity of choice, since it was an item consumed by all. The central idea was that "if only 1 percent (one thousand families) of the family units shopped at the Coop Store and spend an average of $20 per week, we would have a successful business," given the fact that there were over one hundred thousand estimated family units in Central Brooklyn.[31] The calculations would look something like this: 1,000 × $20.00 × 52 (weeks) = $1,040,000 (per year). The cooperative was open to nonmembers; however, members received a 10 percent discount, and workers received a 20 percent discount. Significantly, the program called for these stores to become health-information and nutrition centers as well, encouraging community members to start cooperative stores in the areas of clothing, furniture, and home improvement (e.g., plumbing, carpeting, and electrical). Since The East had already begun a family clothing and food cooperative, the institution offered its experience and insight as a part of the proposed program.

According to Weusi's recollection, the Uhuru Food Cooperative or *Kununuana* closed in 1992; the latest written indicator of its existence can be found in an advertisement placed in the January 1979 edition of *Black News*.[32] In 1979, the Uhuru Food Cooperative had improved upon its goods and services to now include soy products, beauty aids, fresh organic produce, and a host of preventive and curative literature. On the point of the co-op's closure, Mzee Moyo offers the following analysis, in light of the health food revolution that emerged in the late 1980s and continues today: "I just think that in some cases we weren't as prepared as we should have been for what was to take place. There was another revolution, like the health food revolution that's going on. Had we just stayed with it, we would have been in the forefront [now], because we were there then. But, at that time, everybody wasn't ready for it. It was a small niche; we just had to be consistent with it and we just didn't hang with it long enough."[33]

During the mid-1970s, though in small numbers, food cooperatives were being formed when consumers were faced with the alternatives of watching prices rise and quality food become a luxury item or forming food cooperatives. The Uhuru Food Cooperative was one of the few in New York City to operate a store. Many were formed in opposition to supermarket policies and their history of poor-quality and processed foods. The Uhuru Food Cooperative, in part, was no different, especially toward the local A&P supermarket. Yet, and akin to the demise of the

Mavazi Clothing Cooperative, Mzee Moyo points out, one had to "be consistent [because] with anything it takes [a great deal of] consistency. If you don't [hang] with it, it's going to go."[34] This, including a number of other factors, such as lack of foresight, contributed to the collapse of the Mavazi Clothing Cooperative and later the Uhuru Food Cooperative.

In December 1971, the Mavazi Clothing Cooperative was established at 1117 Fulton Street. Job Mashariki supervised the operation during its early development. The African boutique and international gift shop sold incense and body oils, pants and shirts, dungarees, dashikis, underwear, Kwanzaa kits (*Kinara*, mats, candles, *Umoja* cups, and horn of plenty), drum, flutes, imported statues, African records and carvings, paintings, Kwanzaa cards and elephant bone jewelry. Mavazi, which means "clothes," also dealt with the designing, producing, and selling of African and African-inspired clothing. Some of these attires included Nkrumah and Nyerere suits, which were complete outfits worn and popularized by the late Kwame Nkrumah of Ghana and Julius Nyerere of Tanzania.[35] The family clothing cooperative not only sold the above items, but also it offered ready-made and made-to-order services.[36]

Despite the range of products, the longevity of the clothing cooperative was hampered by the fact that Mavazi "never really caught on like the other businesses" of The East. A plausible reason is that Mavazi was only a "business that was popular among The East organization."[37] Bear in mind that during the 1970s and 1980s, to wear African clothing and even to proclaim "being African" was a phenomenon distant from the minds of most community members, even though they supported the efforts of The East. Perhaps if Mavazi had persevered, the clothing cooperative could have been in a position similar to Moshood. The Moshood clothing store seems new to many; however, the designer and owner of Moshood has simply been consistent with his work for the past twenty-odd years.

Another factor in the decline of Mavazi and other enterprises, which is also applicable to The East, was that members worked at very low wages. Mzee Moyo stated that people worked for as little as two hundred dollars a month, which is roughly fifty dollars a week. Although many came to The East without families of their own, subsequently families did begin to proliferate and required care through parental and fiscal responsibilities.

12. Mavazi Clothing Co-op flyer.

Additionally, there was a prominent tendency among local nationalists that such persons by their ideological position had to be generally poor and subsist off bare minimums. In other words, the statement "being in the struggle" had to be symbolically and literally true for these nationalists. The prototypical nationalist was thus expected to wear "combat boots, fatigues, and turtleneck shirts," and he or she was defined as "sacrificing for the community."[38]

This tendency only complicated matters to the extent that the lack of economic sophistication and marshaling of resources gave way to members seeking means to sustain their livelihood outside of the institution. Likewise, in the words of Mzee Moyo, "If you . . . start out [at a certain point], twenty years later you still can't be bringing in fifty dollars a week. You have got to take care of your family, and that was one of the shortcomings [of The East]. We didn't make the change fast enough . . . [in order to take] care of the people's needs. . . . [As an African in America] you have to find out how to live in society, but yet outside. And that was one of the problems that we had."[39]

The enterprises of The East provided not only financial stability to the overall institution but also offered vital community services that served as models for what is and was possible in terms of institution building and self-reliance. The East attempted to put into practice the idea that a community should control its life-sustaining institutions and benefit from them. Yet, its success has more to do with the lessons learned rather than members of The East collectively benefitting from these unsustainable ventures.

 Kujichagulia

Uhuru Sasa Shule (Freedom Now School)

> We must transfer our concerns from starting temporary schools to the development of permanent institutions of learning for our nation's becoming.
>
> JITU K. WEUSI, *Black Books Bulletin*

Background: Antecedents of Uhuru Sasa Shule

The contemporary African-centered school movement "traces its beginnings to three distinct sources. . . . Malcolm X's black nationalism and later the cultural nationalist theory of Maulana Karenga, outgrowths of the Freedom School efforts of the Civil Rights movement, and the efforts of the Council of Independent Black Institution (CIBI)."[1] Additionally, the Black student and Black studies movements in historically white institutions in particular, and the Black Power, Consciousness and Arts movements provided elements that African-centered schools drew upon as well as challenged. As a critique, organizers and designers of these schools and cultural centers questioned the reality of an "independent" African-centered institution on a white campus as it related to the Black studies movement and thus sought to establish such institutions in urban communities. The organizational impetus for the African-centered school movement can be traced to a number of conferences that facilitated the early development of independent African educational institutions. The four Black Power conferences (1966, Washington, D.C.; 1967, Newark, N.J.; 1968, Philadelphia, Pa.; 1969, Bermuda, an international meeting) set the tone for the later efforts that followed.

In essence, these conferences provided a platform, a meeting ground, and a background "against which the Black world [had] become more politically astute. [Further, it] . . . provided the forum out of which Black people from all walks of life [had] begun to develop the skills to manage their own liberation and survival."² Jitu K. Weusi, a participant, described the second National Conference on Black Power as a "momentous and historic event for all Black Americans. . . . [The nightmare of integration had] officially died and was buried at this conference. The dream that was born at this convention was the idea of Black nationhood (here in North America) and self-determination for Black people."³

Efforts that followed include the formation of the National Association of African American Education (NAAAE), under the leadership of Preston Wilcox, which had its first meeting in June 1968, in Chicago, Illinois. At this meeting, the following issues were engaged: "Higher education, blackening the curriculum, black educators, black students, school and black community, [and] materials of instruction. When it met again in August 1968 in St. Louis, it followed through on the above themes but in the context of nation building."⁴ During the period of August 20–24, 1969, the NAAAE conducted its first-anniversary meeting in the form of a five-day Black Communiversity, which congregated in Atlanta, Georgia. The university format was utilized "to afford Black people an opportunity to learn-by-doing; to learn from each other (not 'I teach' but 'We learn') and to provide a laboratory for addressing in a systematic way the survival prerequisites for Black people." The underlying thrust of the meeting was to "draw upon the collective competence of those assembled—in a reasoned (and feeling) manner—to design ways and means to discharge the responsibility of their birthright, i.e., the obligation to perceive it to be their absolute duty to help create a better life for and with the Black community."⁵

The following year, the California Association for Afro-American Education (CAAAE) and Nairobi College jointly sponsored the Workshop on the Independent Black Institution (August 17–19, 1970) in East Palo Alto, California. At that workshop, fifty persons representing more than twenty Independent Black Institutions (IBIs) met at Nairobi College to (1) review and analyze developing models for the IBI; (2) set up a functional network for communication purposes; and (3) develop a working plan for establishing a nationwide system of IBIs.[6] At the first Congress of African Peoples, convened in Atlanta, Georgia, September 3–7, 1970, two reports were produced from the working session on Independent Black Educational Institutions (IBEIs) of the Council on Education and Black Students workshop chaired by Preston Wilcox.

The eleven conference workshops all placed an emphasis upon the development of institutions.[7] The first report, edited by Preston Wilcox, was entitled "Workshop on Education and Black Students, Congress of African People, Summary Report." At the working session on IBEIs, within the workshop chaired by Wilcox, there were two schools of thought: One wanted to continue to pursue community control of public schools (arguing that most African children were in public schools), while the other wanted to either establish new IBIs or strengthen existing ones. The latter strategy received the most attention.[8] The second report, edited by Frank Satterwhite, took on the task of writing a manual on how to set up an IBEI, which was one of the major recommendations make by the IBI workshop of the Congress of African People meeting. In 1971, that report was published as a booklet titled *Planning an Independent Black Educational Institution*. Satterwhite stated the purpose of the publication as follows:

> What we have attempted to do is to combine the knowledge gained from existing independent institutions [that] have confronted and are presently confronting the myriad of problems implicit in establishing African social structures. Our experiences have shown that when maximum consideration is given to the topics presented herein, problems inherent in the establishment of an independent educational institution may be minimized.[9]

In April 1972, the African-American Teachers Association (ATA), a vanguard in the philosophy of community control of schools, with a membership of over six hundred teachers, sponsored a New York City convention for Black teachers. The two major purposes of the convention were to (1) establish a school controlled by the ATA; and (2) concretize a strategy and plan of action to protect Black teachers' and students' rights in the public school system.[10] At this meeting, Weusi, John Churchville, and others already involved in building independent institutions became frustrated by the group's inability to develop a consensus around a plan of action. This, in turn, resulted in a major proposal coming from the independent Black schools workshop that a Council of Independent Black Institutions (CIBI) should be created.[11] As a result, on Sunday April 23, 1972, under the guidance of Weusi, representatives from several independent Black schools located in the Philadelphia and New York City areas met to pool resources and ideas. After a planning session held in Philadelphia in May 1972, the national founding meeting of the CIBI took place in Frogmore, South Carolina, at the Penn Community Service Center, from June 29 to July 3, 1972.

In addition to these conferences, concrete efforts at the community level furthered the development and advancement of the reality of viable and sustainable independent Black educational institutions. Thus, before the formation of the CIBI, newly established institutions, such Uhuru Sasa Shule, were already in the formative stages of development and expansion. One might argue, "It was through the struggle for self-determination by Black people in the Bedford-Stuyvesant section of Brooklyn that [The East] emerged as a natural stage in development."[12] Yet, "[n]obody can really say that [the designers of The East] had any blueprint of what [The East or Uhuru Sasa Shule] would be or how it [would] affect [their] lives when [they] started."[13]

The Structure of Uhuru Sasa Shule

During February 1970, Uhuru Sasa Shule (Freedom Now School) emerged as the primary institutional component of The East. It was a nationalist enterprise built upon the knowledge and practical application of the *Nguzo Saba*. Its mission was the development of skills and thinking necessary for nationhood and liberation from the dominant political and cultural thought and behaviors. In other words, the aim of Uhuru Sasa was to create a "new" African personality in America in order for Africans to build and create in their best interest. As such, Uhuru Sasa sought to create educational programs structured to meet the needs of not only the general student population but also the families and broader communities of those students. It began as an evening school for the youth of the African American Student Association (ASA) and other high school students. Not until April 1970 did the elementary school come into being, followed by the primary and secondary levels in the fall. The daycare center, known as Imani Child Development Center, began somewhere around 1972. Therefore, the organizational structure of Uhuru Sasa Shule consisted of the (1) Imani Child Development Center (Level A); (2) Primary (Levels B–C), Elementary (Levels D–G), and Secondary schools (Levels H–K); and (3) the Evening School of Knowledge.[14] The policymaking body of the formal structure consisted of a student-, teacher-, and parent-governing council. This council, which began in March 1970, concerned itself with matters such as fund-raising, complaints about teachers, delinquent tuition payments, budgeting, and curriculum. Parents were "given a careful orientation to the programs, purposes and goals of the school and [had to] attend seminars held once a month."[15] Moreover, Uhuru Sasa held that if parents were to play major roles in the development of the institution, they had to make the sacrifices necessary for reeducation and commitment through their participation in the parent council, bimonthly lecture series (for parents), and the Evening School of Knowledge.

The Uhuru Sasa headmaster was responsible for the daily supervision of the school, but his activities were under the direct supervision of the parent council, to whom he would submit regular reports. Additionally, there was a guidance unit, created by the parent council and composed of teachers and students, to serve families having difficulties and set the criteria for expected behavior and academic performance. The major qualifications necessary to teach at the school were dedication and the ability to learn how to teach in an African-centered environment and through the corresponding approaches to learning and teaching. Attendance at bimonthly meetings amongst all *walimu* (teachers), weekly-level meetings with the *mkuu* (headmaster or teachers' supervisor) and one parent-council meeting on a rotating basis were required of all teachers. One of many unique aspects of the school was that teachers were on twenty-four-hour call! Consequently, "there [was] continuous communication and parents and teachers [counseled] other parents and [assisted in] their homes whenever they [needed] to have a family discussion on the progress of a student."[16]

Initially there was a great deal of teacher turnover. However, once the teachers began to commit themselves to the school's philosophy of nation building and self-reliance, the staff became more stable, even though some degree of turnover continued. As members of a family-based and sustained institution, parents were expected to contribute to the operation of the school through either a small tuition fee or the provision of services. Those who could not afford the cost of tuition donated their service or work to the school, and both students and teachers maintained the facility, thus consolidating resources by not needing to hire a maintenance staff. In the first full year of the school, the tuition fees were (1) for the primary school: ten dollars a week for the first child, five dollars for the second, and no tuition for additional members of the same family; (2) for the elementary school: forty dollars a month for the first child, twenty dollars for the second, and no tuition for additional members of the same family; (3) for the secondary school: twenty dollars a month per student; and (4) in the Evening School of Knowledge: a five-dollar registration fee per student. Tuition was to be paid in advance on a weekly or biweekly basis; tuition delinquency was considered just cause for students being asked to leave the school. Services such as door-to-door transportation, available to all students except those of the Imani Child Development Center, were provided at an additional cost. Monthly transportation cards were given to those students who paid the appropriate fee.

The basic financial needs of the school were offset by revenue generated from the other institutions or enterprises of The East, in addition to the cultural and political fund-raising events. This approach followed The East's attempt to put into practice the concepts of extended-family living and cooperative economics. In fact, the "principles taught in Uhuru Sasa [were] put to work in the everyday operation of The East."[17] The *Nguzo Saba* permeated the organizational structure of The East and Uhuru Sasa, including the Imani Child Development Center. This underpinning assisted in the institutionalization of the school's strong emphasis on African identity, purpose, and direction.[18]

The Imani Child Development Center

The Imani Child Development Center, according to one of the founding women, started out as "a place for sisters to leave their children while they were on duty at The East."[19] Sources reveal the names of only three directors: Aminisha Black (1972–73), Wambui Thabiti (1974–77), and Nassoma Jumatatu (1980–83).[20] These and other women of the organization "were concerned about the environment in which their children [and their] future would spend their hours."[21] The primary impetus for the child development center was the emerging families that developed from relationships consummated at The East or the new mothers who came in contact with the institution. Thus, The East Sisterhood primarily organized and operated the child development center.[22] Sources point out the "name Imani [was] taken from the seventh [principle] of the Nguzo Saba . . . which means '[f]aith.' The name was chosen as an ever-present reminder of the [f]aith we [Africans] must have in ourselves—'the ability to care for our own' and the [f]aith that a Black mother must have when she leaves her child."[23]

Although this educational component of Uhuru Sasa was born out of the immediate needs of The East family, it soon grew to include young African-descended children of other families, ranging from nine months to three years of age. The older students were "taught numbers, alphabets, [and] shapes" in addition to being given "activities which [taught] self-reliance (putting on garments, buttoning, lacing, etc.)." The "younger children (6 months–1½ years) [were] engaged in play that [taught] manipulative" as well as verbal skills within the context of appropriate affective development.[24] Parents were expected to be actively involved in not only the evaluation of Imani and ongoing fund-raising committees but to participate in weekend trips, *Karibu* (welcome) Days, in which parents would visit and spend the day, and workshops presented by the Imani staff. The staff believed that curriculum was the strategy by which one fulfills the goals of education (see appendix E for Imani curriculum and daily schedule). The seven educational goals of Imani were:

1. To enable children to further develop and strengthen their motor skills;

2. To have children devise strategies for getting something they want;

3. To enable children to become aware of their nutritional needs;

4. To enable children to respect their bodies, strengthen their minds, and acquire the skills to learn how to learn;

5. To enable children to develop their creative skills (through reading, writing, computation, and analysis);

6. To enable children to develop positive self-images through knowledge of their rich African culture and traditions; and

7. To enable children to discipline their heads, minds, and bodies through practical application.

Activities for *watoto* (children) aged nine to thirteen months old were geared toward allowing them to explore their environment, making discoveries about the space around them, and learning how to use their bodies to solve problems. The activities would always be accompanied by descriptions of what was occurring. These descriptions would help formulate the child's vocabulary. Although the child was expected to learn to complete tasks and use skills a certain way, the way in which he or she did so was never considered wrong. Instead, the child was shown another way of learning how to perform the expected task. Thus, an attempt was made to avoid the use of constant "no" and "don't," which were considered to be inhibiting. In terms of social value instruction, children were expected to share through the giving of toys or, when possible, food to other children. At story time, they shared and practiced songs. Simple images reflective of African culture and tradition were emphasized throughout the learning areas.

The Imani staff expected that the movements of *watoto* fourteen to eighteen months old would become less awkward and begin to appear smoother through fascination with experiment and discovery (such as through water and dirt play). The fact that substances do unpredictable and sometimes interesting things when manipulated was held to always stir a child's curiosity. Spontaneous curiosity about the nature of things was greatly encouraged. In addition, it was held that from a baby's point of view, unfamiliar objects were made to be investigated (such as pulling apart beads that can be put back together and opening and closing doors). Supervision was necessary but with minimum interference from an adult. The child needed to be encouraged in his or her independence and made to feel proud of his or her new skills. Furthermore, adults were to allow him or her to use newly acquired skills and to offer praise accordingly.

Specific activities heightened the children's motor, verbal, communication, observational, and social interaction skills. Those activities included, but were not limited to, coloring using large crayons and paper, playing on low slides, climbing onto stools and boxes, and sand/dirt play with pans, handles (of various objects), and spoons. Imani staff believed that self-confidence and self-reliance should be developed in children through action and thus promoted activity (i.e., the children should be the ones doing) rather than passive observation through imitative play, music boxes, singing rhymes, and listening to records with bells and whistles. Children were given a variety of picture books and were encouraged to categorize them into similar groups. In doing so, they learned about organization as it related to what things are used for; what different people do; the awareness of clean-up and mess-up processes (putting toys away); and where objects are kept.

For *watoto* nineteen to twenty-three months of age, the Imani staff focused their curriculum content on what they termed "African heritage" as both guide and substance. Hence, motor skills, communication, social practice (i.e., the *Nguzo Saba*), story time and role-playing, nutrition, and verbal communication would be based on principles or values that an African "hero" personified for an allotted two-week period of instruction. Next to the respective African figure's name were motivational keys—that is, symbols, images, or phrases that invoke the intended principles that the personality represented in the child's consciousness. Those figures, with their motivational keys in parentheses, included Hannibal (elephants), Mansa Musa (shields, camels, and horses), Harriet Tubman (trees with people hidden with rifles behind them), Marcus Garvey (flag, boat, and hat), Rosa Parks and Martin Luther King (bus), George Washington Carver (peanuts), and Malcolm X (glasses). In the final two weeks of instruction, all eight of these personalities were reviewed, and children were given a simple verbal test for recognition and a motor skills test. They were expected to master a variety of skills, including the ability to recognize and point to body parts when named; identify basic geometric shapes and colors; distinguish self from others (in group pictures); group up to five objects by shape and color; understand the concept of and demonstrating *over, under, up, down,* and *across;* and, when shown items and their random removal, recognize any changes made and tell the difference.

For those *watoto* two to three years of age, staff expected them to develop organizational skills (daily routines, environment); understand that pictures and images represent objects and people, and that names (words) represent things; understand language and use it to communicate; develop specific motor skills; develop a sense of self, family, and world; gain and develop self-confidence; and solve problems. In addition, children were expect to master observational skills, a sense of self, language, problem solving, and gross motor skills. Auditory development content dealt with interpreting sounds, hearing and reproducing sounds, and learning new melodies and songs of phonic sounds. Olfactory skill development examined sensation through comparison and contrast of odors and included park explorations, which provided an occasion to smell plants, and matching pictures with the appropriate items through smell. Taste sensation engaged the students through tasting certain foods, comparing those tastes, and examining what effects healthy and nonhealthy foods have on the body in pursuit of an understanding of wholesome and healthy diets.

The Imani staff held that through talking to children, including their communication with each other, the *Nguzo Saba* must be consistently stressed. Their actions and those of the children must be about unity, self-determination, collective work, cooperative economics, purpose, creativity, and faith. A child's identity, place, and responsibility in family and community were expressed in verbal communication, during story time, and in social interactions. The driving question was, "How can we teach our children to show respect and kindness for all forms of life and to respect every role played by living creatures?" It was concluded that adults must allow children to experiment and make mistakes, to an extent, in order to find solutions and provide increased and varied experiences. All of these expectations were prompted by the staff's "desire for [their] children to have an early conditioned awareness of Africa" and, by extension, themselves. The last section of the curriculum addressed what constitutes one's family and its members. A prominent quote by the late Dr. John Henrik Clarke, in June 1968, formed part of the documentary evidence for Imani and is presented here as a summation to the ideational focus of its curriculum and pedagogy: "Heritage is how a people have used their talent to create a history that gives them memories that they can respect and which they can use to command the respect of other people. The ultimate purpose of heritage and heritage teaching is to use a people's talent to develop an awareness and pride in themselves so that they can become a better instrument for living together with other people. This sense of identity is the stimulation for people's honest and creative efforts. A people's relationship to their heritage is the same as the relationship of a child to its mother."[25]

Imani Child Development Extension

Given the structure and practice of extended-family living at The East, the Imani Child Development Center also established an "extension" that provided activities for children up to the age of nine during meetings or events. Functions took place at either the armory or at The East; tentative or reserved space at The East building included Yusef Iman's office and the third-floor hallway. The extension was staffed by all East family members. The method of assigning responsibilities began with a list of all family members, followed by polling those members so as to assign persons to work (usually) one day out of the week at the extension. As meetings or events became known, East family members were notified. The extension was in operation from Monday through Saturday, staffed by no more than seven persons each day. Some outdoor activities included rope jumping, ball games, and races, while indoor activities focused on story telling, Kuumba (creativity) charades, hand-clapping games, blocks, and other games.

The Theoretical Basis of Uhuru Sasa Shule

The ideational orientation of the Imani Child Development Center was no different in substance from that of Uhuru Sasa Shule. In fact, Imani was the ground floor upon which Uhuru Sasa would continue to develop the child. The learning and learning theories at Uhuru Sasa Shule were linked to the ideology and existence of independent schools. The school believed that African-descended children, if given a medium to express their nationalism or cultural integrity, would obtain a more positive learning experience and perform accordingly. Wambui Thabiti, former director of Imani and teacher, commented that the "major difference between [Uhuru] Sasa and other schools [was] their starting children at 3 years of age and a cultural and historical study of the origins of Black people along with the academic program."[26] Discipline and adherence to structure and respect for the traditional wisdom of elders was emphasized throughout the educational programs. In fact, everyone was expected to stand at *angulia* (attention) to the elders entering the building or a room, unless told otherwise. Both teachers and students were expected to "be the sample and the example" (i.e., live the example and lead by it); demonstrate preparedness and promptness; exercise appropriate cleanliness, nutrition, and hygiene; adhere to school policies; study, study, study! The notion was held that if the teacher reached the child at a personal level and related to him or her as such, the learning process would then be progressively advanced. Thus, parents were given copies of their children's work along with discussions of their progress and behavior. Learning through repetition and imitation are considered strong mechanisms for internalizing the host of concepts being explored.

From the onset, Uhuru Sasa set as its educational goal "the knowledge and application of the: Umoja (unity); Kujichagulia (self-determination); Ujima (collective work and responsibility); Ujamaa (cooperative economics); Nia (purpose); Kuumba (creativity); and Imani (faith)."[27] In fact, in the latter years, each subject was directly involved with one of the seven principles. Thus, for example, *Umoja* was a marker of the morning ceremonies; *Kujichagulia* for martial arts; *Ujima* for lunch; *Ujamaa* for vocational and physical education; *Nia* for math, science, language arts, and history; *Kuumba* for the humanities; and *Imani* for the closing ceremonies (i.e., pledge, songs, inspirational words, announcements).[28]

The Teaching Strategies of Uhuru Sasa Shule

The ideological principles of Uhuru Sasa were reflected in the development of the methodologies for instruction, which required extensive teacher training, because formal credentials were less relevant and, in most instances, were considered a hindrance to the school's purpose. The skills and commitment that a person brought to the school were more appreciated. Besides the tasks of keeping records of attendance and report cards, an Uhuru Sasa teacher's plan book included the subjects taught; identity, purpose, and direction (i.e., the ideological orientation through which the lessons are conveyed); schedules of meetings and activities; list of *walimu* names, addresses, and phone numbers; and a list of educational references and resources. Each Uhuru Sasa classroom had a red, black, and green flag (developed by Marcus Garvey); the *Nguzo Saba;* an Ankh; picture files; maps of Africa, the world, the United States, Brooklyn, and areas of The East; *Weusi Alfabeti* books (The Black Alphabet); cleaning items (e.g., broom, rags, a dust pan, and trash cans); height measurers; weather terms, seasons, and days of the week in both Kiswahili and English; a collage of African historical figures; and science and library corners. Most supplies, such as pencil sharpeners, were also found.

The above materials were presented to provide a mental picture of a typical Uhuru Sasa classroom and teacher and, by extension, the varied means by which the curriculum was transmitted to students. The educational environment and pedagogy of Uhuru Sasa was the outcome more so of its intense teacher-development efforts rather than a by-product of any single teacher. Mandatory teacher-training sessions were conducted every week—sometimes four times a week—throughout the school year, including each Saturday; a three-week training course was held during the summer and a one-week session in the winter. Selected students were also taught the skills necessary for effective teaching. The first teacher-training workshop was instituted in April 1970; the three-week course was sponsored by and delivered through the Teacher Training Institute (TTI) of CIBI. The first TTI was designed by "John Churchville, [then] director of the Freedom Library Day School in Philadelphia, [and was] constructed as a vehicle to stimulate teachers who wanted to equip and perfect themselves as educators of Black youth. The first two Institutes (1972 and 1973) were held in Philadelphia, in 1974 and 1975 in Brooklyn. The Uhuru Sasa School was the host institution."[29]

The aim of TTI was "to develop highly skilled, sensitive and politicized Afrikan teachers."[30] Among the topics typically covered during TTI, those that took precedence included classroom instruction, African child development, protocol and discipline, historiography, interdisciplinary cognitive skills, curricula design, and administration and parent education. As a result of consistent teacher development, the teaching strategies of Uhuru Sasa focused on ideology, methodology, and subject matter, with the intent being the merger of these aspects into the lesson plan. In many respects, emphasis was placed on disciplined character and total concentration on the tasks assigned; television viewing was greatly discouraged. The children were reminded of the rules and expectations, which were also reinforced beyond the planned lesson, and which even included how to walk the stairway (i.e., quietly, quickly, and safely). In regard to discipline, Uhuru Sasa was known for its measures, which derived from the teachers' belief that "We must be firm but with love [and thus reserve] . . . the right to use corrective discipline wherever necessary."[31] Bear in mind that many of the teachers were also parents of students who attended the school. Uhuru Sasa contended that instructional innovations could stimulate language growth and mathematical (logic) ability. Consequently, a tool such as the Cuisenaire-Gattegno system was an approach to mathematics used at certain levels.

The mathematical approach used a box of wooden or plastic cubic Cuisenaire rods of different colors ranging from one to ten centimeters in length. The rods were used initially in play activity, and as the child began to discover different relationships for himself or herself, the teacher began to concentrate on use of the rods to embellish cognitive growth. A typical strategy would begin with the teacher holding up two different sizes and colors of rods, such as a red rod valued at two and an orange rod valued at five, and the operation would be addition. The problem and solution resembled this: red rod (two) and orange rod (five) equals red plus orange (seven). The child gave an answer. The strategy was repeated until the correct color values were learned. The child received consistent reinforcement of positive responses that lacked excessive verbal exchanges.

Similar to the Cuisenaire rod method, reading activities were pursued under a language method based on colors. On the walls of each classroom were charts containing a color-coded letter for each sound in both Kiswahili and English. After learning the sounds and their color association, the children would then blend sounds to formulate words. If the learning task was to develop children's reading-readiness skills, the teacher would provide the rules and instructions and use a pointer without commenting verbally during the activity. Emphasis was placed on the conservation of energy so that the child could think clearly before responding. The teacher would encourage a correct response by having the child repeat letters and their color-coded sounds. If, for example, a child had an incorrect letter in a word, he or she would be asked, what is the "brown" sound? What is the "yellow" sound? Now can you combine these two? This approach was intended to take advantage of the child's "natural" learning style based on an analysis of his or her ability to learn to speak, which had been equated with the mathematical concept of algebra. As such, Uhuru Sasa sought to "develop mathematicians and thinkers who will be able to clearly draw relationships to symbolic meanings in the world; therefore, [Uhuru Sasa had] instituted a number of instructional innovations to stimulate language growth and mathematical ability."[32]

The Curriculum of Uhuru Sasa Shule

The curriculum was regarded as a contributor to consciousness by instilling values, identity, and a historical sensibility through African history, geography, and cultural life; African experiences in the Americas and Caribbean; Black aesthetical expressions of art, music, dance, drama, and poetry; school and class as a family concept; and by speaking Kiswahili and using African terms and expressions in dress, ceremonies, rituals, pledges, songs, and symbols to reaffirm desired goals at various times in the school day. In other words, the curriculum should create the capacity and ability to do, that is, to take control of all aspects of one's life by virtue of having developed adequate concepts, skills, and perspectives. It was comprehensive in scope and demanded concentrated effort from both the teacher and child.[33] Each division or level of Uhuru Sasa had a body of knowledge and skills specifically designed to meet the needs of the students involved.[34]

The curriculum addressed the specific skills of language and concept development, creative arts, and problem solving, reading, writing, math, and practical skills. In language development, the goal of expressive and receptive competencies in verbal communication was pursued with the idea that English was a tool to be learned in all its facets so as to use the language effectively, and Kiswahili was a language used to reaffirm the (cultural) identity of the students. Through the means of classification, serialization, contrasts, and temporal relationships, concept development dealt with the child's ability to develop an organized way to see and comprehend the world. The goal was the development of an African world outlook that would be able to make appropriate sense of information gathered and used. In creative arts, Uhuru Sasa used African music and dance as "high spiritual ceremonies" that required great care and discipline, while the general arts were integrated into all areas of instruction. Here, the goal was the development of adequate discipline and the unfolding of creativity (and care) as prerequisites to experiencing the meaning of the music and dance. The child's ability to use the environment in ways that allowed him or her to reach desired goals was the essence of solving problems, whether academic or interactional and affective. Competencies in written language were the goal of both reading and writing, though both skills necessitated prerequisites through hands awareness, concepts of space (spatial) and direction, and small motor skill development. In addition to the Cuisenaire-Gattegno method, Uhuru Sasa used traditional math approaches that taught counting by rote, math symbols, and concepts of number value and size. Practical skills included daily tasks and significant real-life acts that a child encounters in the course of living life through his or her culture, and thus physical development stressed the discovery and comprehension of some of the things needed to build a nation (e.g., food, shelter, clothing) and develop it (see appendix E).

As a result of the belief that the curriculum should contribute to the capacity and ability to do, there was the attempt to provide practical life skills, particularly, those expressive of African cultural continuity.

> Uhuru Sasa further expanded this [practical life skill] concept to "industrial Kuumba" (creativity) and [h]ome industry starting at the

beginning level of sequential development. These activities [would] be performed at home at the child's leisure and [were] designed to foster skills of self-reliance and respect for the ability to use talents and resources creatively. . . . [They included] activities such as carpentry, sanding, varnishing, painting, food preparation, setting the table, sewing, washing, cleaning. Emphasis [was] on neatness, completion of a task, pride in one's work, and respect for tools. The belief [was] that through Industrial Kuumba, the child [would] be prepared to improve his [or her] surroundings, to leave the world in better condition than when he or she inherited it.[35]

Uhuru Sasa's conviction that "small children who are allowed to do meaningful (adult-type) work in their homes, schools, and communities begin to see themselves as capable persons" was quite evident through the levels and goals of the curriculum.[36] This perspective also underpinned all structures of the school, including the Evening School of Knowledge, which was an extension of what occurred at The East and Uhuru Sasa. Many persons who enrolled in the evening school classes would later become a part of The East and its family. The school was a community, family, and living institution.[37]

The Uhuru Sasa family-unit system enabled students to move from one family unit to the next upon demonstration of satisfactory academic progress. This structure allowed for the closeness and communal spirit developed within the context of family. In fact, the practice of calling parents, making homes visits, having students spend nights or weekends at a teacher's home, and the planning and implementation of family outings was anything but a singular event. Clearly, the families and staff of Uhuru Sasa believed "that students cannot be taught family unity and unity of a people *(umoja)* without having experienced or lived it in some form."[38] In the early years, the school was divided into groups according to age and gender. Although the girls and boys were taught in distinct classrooms, the teachers coordinated their lesson plans so that all the children received the necessary content, depending on age and level of readiness.

In the early years of the school, the primary students, for example, were divided into six groups according to age and gender. Those groups were (a) Damu Wachanga (Young bloods), three- and four-year-old boys;

(b) Ibo Dada (Ibo sisters), three- and four-year-old girls; (c) Bantu, four- and five-year-old boys; (d) Congolese, four- and five-year-old girls; (e) Ashanti Warriors, six- and seven-year-old boys; and (f) Ashanti Dada (Ashanti sisters), six- and seven-year-old year old girls.[39] The attire for boys consisted of a *kufi* (cap), *dashiki* (loose-fitting shirt), and pants; the girls wore a *lappa*, that is, a loose-fitting piece (or pieces) of African print hemmed at the bottom and top and wrapped around the body, and a *buba* (full top garment often with embroidery or designs). As early as 1977, the school was divided up into eleven levels and seven curricula domains for the purpose of curriculum development. While the levels were developed by age, the designers were also cognizant that age was not the sole reason for promotion within the school. The African nations for which the various divisions or classes were named included Abyssinia, Ethiopia, Kush, and Nubia at the primary level; Ta-Merry, Sais, Kemet, Sudan, Egypt, and Nile at the elementary level; and Azania, Namibia, and Zimbabwe at the secondary level.[40]

By 1980, however, the classes consisted of students of both gender and were organized in accordance to age and specific African nations: Ethiopia (ages three and four); Kush (ages five and six); Benin (ages seven and eight); Namibia (ages nine and ten); and Zimbabwe (ages eleven through thirteen). During the 1980s, the curriculum consisted of language arts, math, science, social studies, political science, and the humanities, which included songs, folklore, poetry, drama, dance, music, martial arts, woodwork, and Spanish. The reasons for this shift in the content and structure of Uhuru Sasa will become evident in the subsequent discussion of some of the school's historical developments. The school's daily schedule and subject areas seemed to have remained the same during the 1980s.

8:00–8:50 A.M.	*Umoja:* Morning ceremonies, breakfast, and martial arts
8:50–9:00 A.M.	Pledge and song
9:00–9:45 A.M.	*Nia:* Math
9:45–10:30 A.M.	*Nia:* Language arts
10:30–11:15 A.M.	*Nia:* History, social studies, geography, political education (Weusi studies)

11:15 A.M.–12:00 noon	*Nia:* Science
12:00–1:00 P.M.	*Ujima:* Lunch
1:00–1:45 P.M.	*Kuumba:* Humanities
1:45–3:00 P.M.	*Kujichagulia:* Martial arts
3:00–3:45 P.M.	*Ujamaa:* Vocational and physical education
3:45–4:00 P.M.	*Imani:* Closing ceremonies, which included the pledge, songs, notices and announcements, and inspirational words.[41]

The Evening School of Knowledge

The Evening School of Knowledge began in the fall 1970, in conjunction with the full-time program of Uhuru Sasa. The major distinction between the Evening School and other components of Uhuru Sasa was that is was not age-specific, although it placed emphasis on attracting adult and elder persons from the community. The Evening School allowed for those working in the daytime to be recipients of a quality education, in addition to learning what their children learned if their children were enrolled in Uhuru Sasa. The courses offered resembled a "communiversity" (i.e., a university structure rooted in and for the community's development). Throughout its existence, the name of the school changed from the Evening School of Knowledge to the Evening School of Uhuru Sasa to The East Evening School. Nonetheless, the mission of the school and the quality of the courses offered, for the most part, remained the same.

On Monday, courses on Kiswahili, Black music theory, effective Black writing, history, and Black revolution were taught. Courses geared toward achieving the high school equivalency diploma were also available. On Tuesday, the courses consisted of the history and culture of Africa, photography, art, electronics workshops, and a Black film festival. On Wednesday, the classes on Kiswahili and those necessary to earn a high school equivalency diploma continued alongside courses on office practices, gun safety, first aid, and nation building in addition to a Black woman's seminar and a jam session with notable jazz musicians. On Thursday, the art, photography, and electronics workshops continued along with classes on food science and body health, Yorùbá language, and sewing African clothing.

On Friday, there was only "the new African man" workshop, which did not last long; this workshop was a product of the male orientation and influence at The East during the early 1970s. On Saturday, courses offered included African dance and drumming, self-defense, teacher-training workshop, economics and the African world, and African literature. Lastly, Sunday's program consisted of courses on Yorùbá culture, Black religious thought, a lecture series, a Black soul session (drama, plays, poetry), and the universal temple of thought (for people of all faiths).[42] To summarize, the contents of the Evening School structure and courses endured with minor changes largely in format, schedule, and instructors.

Historical Developments in the Life of Uhuru Sasa Shule

A group of eight teachers from the African-American Teachers Association (ATA) made a commitment to the youth who had been expelled or suspended from the public high school to become volunteer teachers and educate them from Monday to Thursday, 3:30 P.M. to 9:30 P.M. This was the beginning of Uhuru Sasa Shule as an evening school on February 1, 1970. By June 1970, Uhuru Sasa had approximately sixty high school students and fifteen elementary school students.[43] In the fall of 1970, the school began with 170 students; by the end of the school year it had approximately two hundred students who were taught by fifteen teachers—ten full-time and five part-time.[44] In 1971, Jitu Weusi wrote, "When [Uhuru Sasa Shule] began in February 1970, it was based on a philosophy which was a reaction to white institutions. In September 1970, [we] were equipped with a Black ideology (education for self-reliance and nationhood) and a reason for our existence. The concept of an independent Black school is one that has developed as we have groped to establish our revolutionary 'institutions.'"[45]

With this philosophy the school population grew, developments in the infrastructure began to take on more form, and, by 1972, an internal inventory and assessment of the school and The East organization's strengths and shortcomings were completed.[46] In the latter part of 1972, Uhuru Sasa became one of the founding institutional members of CIBI, with Jitu Weusi as its national executive officer. Consequently, Uhuru Sasa became the site of numerous educational conferences and conventions, forums, and teacher-training institutes. In the same year, the student population increased by fifty from 1970 with an overall enrollment of 120 preschool, one hundred elementary, and thirty secondary students.[47] With the contrasting factors of growth and limited space, the school could only admit a certain number of students; thus, after applications were handed in, there was an interview process administered by the parent council.

For the life of the school (specifically, throughout the 1970s) the aforementioned numbers of students remained consistent, notwithstanding some intervals of increase and decrease. Uhuru Sasa resided in school district thirteen (Central Brooklyn community). Although it did not seek accreditation from the New York City Board of Education, it did request and receive a provisional charter on May 26, 1972, by the Board of Regents of the University of New York State.[48] Yet, this was regarded as a mistake, as it was believed that being chartered also meant incorporation and brought on legal and tax-related problems.[49] After receiving the provisional

13. *From right to left:* Kasisi Jitu Weusi, Toola (Edgar Booker), and Maliki (George Robinson). Photograph by Osei Terry Chandler. Used with permission.

charter for only the primary and elementary schools of Uhuru Sasa, the institution became incorporated as the Freedom Now School, Inc., a nonprofit education corporation.

This provisional charter, according to Jitu Weusi, was sought for two reasons: (1) for the financial benefits accredited nonpublic schools receive from New York State; and (2) when students transferred they would not be penalized for attending the Uhuru Sasa. Weusi notes, however, that "the accreditation of any institution has got to come from the people and that the people accredit it by their involvement; by taking active steps to put their children in the school and [becoming] a part of the school; and by their sanction of what the school is doing."[50] He maintains that this has always been the first and most important level of accreditation. Following this line of thought, in 1973, a community of independent Black schools in Brooklyn were organized to form the "Brooklyn Family Schools" in the spirit of collectivity and accountability (to each other). Schools were "organized for the purpose of providing positive education for Black children . . . [while] functioning as a familyhood, looking toward Uhuru Sasa as a positive example."[51] The Brooklyn Family Schools consisted of Uhuru Sasa, Weusi Shule (now Johnson Preparatory), Al Karim Family School, Shule ya Mapinduzi, and Robert Conner Memorial. Uhuru Sasa held seven-week-long summer day camps in Brooklyn, Bronx, Queens, Manhattan (particularly Harlem), and Staten Island, which attracted students from the Brooklyn Family Schools and other educational institutions.

In 1974, Uhuru Sasa enrolled 250 students and employed forty-five full-time and six part-time members of the teaching staff. By 1976, the school's sixth year of operation, the parent council, in seeking to enlarge the "teaching facilities which will include a Science Laboratory and Library," began an "Our Building Fund Drive" to renovate a newly acquired two-story building located at 1310 Atlantic Avenue.[52] Before moving to this location, the elementary and secondary schools were located at 1281 Bedford Avenue. At the Atlantic Avenue location, there was a confrontation with the Long Island Railroad (LIRR) who, as a part of their renovation, wanted to build a staircase coming down on the side of the street where the new Uhuru Sasa building was located. After LIRR construction workers dug four large craters on the school's property, a combined picket line and demonstration of over five hundred people took place around the proposed railroad station.[53]

On account of the demonstration, the LIRR "promised to cover the holes with asphalt and find an alternative" location; that same year Uhuru Sasa moved to the Sumner Avenue armory, seemingly as a result of not securing the space at 1310 Atlantic Avenue. Between 1970 and 1976, Uhuru Sasa remained at The East facility; during 1976, the school fluctuated between the Atlantic Avenue location and The East building, then relocated to the Sumner Avenue armory on Marcus Garvey Boulevard. According to a former teacher, with an enrollment of 325 students, Uhuru Sasa "was forced to move in 1976 from the two buildings it was occupying on Bedford Avenue and on Claver Place, to the enormous Sumner Avenue armory. The school [rented] approximately one half of the facility from the city's Department of Real Estate for $500 per month."[54] The armory had been the possession of the federal government until 1970. Thereafter, the New York City Board of Education took ownership of it, followed by The East in 1976, which resulted in half of the facility being used by The East and the other by a fire department. In September 1976, Jitu Weusi resigned as chairperson of CIBI. High amongst his reasons was the "need to do some study and observation and to examine from afar just what CIBI was and how it could have a real impact upon the education of Black youth in America."[55] His other concerns included the transient and irresponsible membership and rampant opportunism.

Two years later, Weusi's and Uhuru Sasa's relationship with CIBI became questionable in light of some of Weusi's actions and the uncertainty of CIBI's significance to Uhuru Sasa. The minutes of a CIBI Central Committee meeting (April 1978) suggest that Weusi's decision to turn a regional science fair at Uhuru Sasa, where projects would be selected for the CIBI national science fair, into "the national Uhuru Sasa educational conference" was driven by his political aspirations. Some members of the Central Committee expressed the opinion that Weusi was attempting to sabotage the relationship between Uhuru Sasa and CIBI in light of the fact that he "was outvoted in his push for Uhuru Sasa to leave CIBI by The East family who decided to remain in CIBI." Moreover, it was expressed that the "general East family realized [the change to a national conference] only gradually and due to the large turnover in staff and the family, few remaining people recognized CIBI as significant in terms of conference conflict or East [i]nvolvement." Certainly, such conflict or the source of it "would eventually force CIBI to kick Uhuru Sasa off CIBI Central Committee."[56]

Consequently, a motion was passed to have a "resolution" meeting in June in Chicago between Haki Madhubuti, Hannibal Afrik, Jitu Weusi, Kofi Lomotey, and Kalamu ya Salaam at a time mutually agreeable to all. The tentative agenda was centered around (1) clarity on the institutional relationship between Uhuru Sasa and CIBI; (2) on what level Uhuru Sasa will remain in CIBI, especially as it relates to institutional involvement and national responsibility; and (3) final contact or attempt to clearly understand past dynamics and future dynamics between Jitu, Hannibal, Kofi, and Kalamu. During the early parts of the Central Committee meeting, April 22–23, 1978, it was motioned that "Uhuru Sasa be given [the] office of secretary/treasurer, tentative upon Uhuru Sasa as an organization accepting the responsibility."[57] Uhuru Sasa's representative, Tamisha Afrika, seconded this motion and, without any discussion, it was unanimously voted on in the affirmative.

In August 1978, Jitu Weusi relinquished his duties as director of The East organization and headmaster of Uhuru Sasa. Subsequently, he became the chairman of the Black Community Congress, a founding member of the Black United Front, and also he pursued a superintendent position in school district 16 (Bedford-Stuyvesant).[58] At the time of his departure, it was reported that Uhuru Sasa had "a student body of over 400 students 3 to 17 years of age and is currently awaiting a permanent charter and diploma granting privileges to be bestowed by the New York State Board of Regents and State Education Department."[59] In August 1978, Dr. E. Curtis Alexander assumed the role of Uhuru Sasa's headmaster, while Adeyemi Bandele accepted the responsibility of directing The East organization.

Within a year or so, Dr. Alexander either left on his own accord or was ousted from his position as headmaster. One of the factors contributing to his removal was the fact that he had "phased out all of the school's teachers hired under the previous administration and replaced them with college-educated persons."[60] The initial actions of Dr. Alexander support

14. Malika Iman, one of Yusef Iman's daughters, and Adeyemi Bandele in front of The East complex on Claver Place. Photograph by Osei Terry Chandler. Used with permission.

this claim. Upon arriving at Uhuru Sasa, he commented, "we were not greeted by a staff of 'teachers' who were committed to taking the struggle for 'quality' Black education to a 'higher level' as perceived by us; therefore, it was necessary for some staff to commit what [Paulo] Freire calls Class Suicide." Furthermore, he fashioned the curriculum in such a way that it did "not offer Weusi or Black Studies" because this was contradictory to the educational program, and he demanded that teachers successfully complete a college-level teaching course in order to maintain their employment.[61] On April 25, 1980, Uhuru Sasa was removed from the CIBI Central Committee and demoted from its responsibilities of National Public Relations and Fundraising Office to serve as a supportive member, taking on the responsibilities formerly assigned to Uhuru Sasa.[62] Uhuru Sasa, as represented by Sister Ibura, was present as this meeting. The decisions made at the April 25 meeting were the result of Uhuru Sasa, as the CIBI East Coast Regional Convener, not calling any regional meetings, and neither completing responsibilities outlined nor returning phone calls from the National Executive Office. Although the Uhuru Sasa representative offered a proposal that expressed Uhuru Sasa's desire to remain on the CIBI Central Committee, with a commitment to complete all assigned work except the responsibilities of fund-raiser, the committee voted unanimously to remove them from the body.[63]

Jumibia Nyahuma, then headmaster of Uhuru Sasa, sent a letter dated April 24, 1980, to the national executive officer of CIBI explaining that there were numerous reasons why Uhuru Sasa was not able to carry out its function, including his own lack of communication and poor approach to work. The reasons were that (1) the armory, which Uhuru Sasa used, was up for auction; (2) the school was hit with a ten-thousand-dollar electric bill, in which the utility company (Con Edison) got a judge to reverse the Public Service Commission's decision of only paying fifteen hundred dollars to making full payment. The lights were then shut off until the school was able to work out a payment plan with Con Edison; and (3) Jumibia's return to school to finish his degree, coupled with his personal problem.[64] Jumibia soon left the position, and in August 1980, Lubaba Ahmed became the headmistress of Uhuru Sasa, eventually succeeded by Rashida Kierstedt.[65] At this point, in 1983, the school only accommodated children aged three to fourteen (kindergarten to eighth grade). Unclear, however, is who took the responsibility of heading the school, if this was the case, until its demise. Before the decline of Uhuru Sasa, the last-known attended CIBI function was the conference on parent involvement in the "Independent Black School," October 12, 1985, which was sponsored by Afrikan People's Action School in Trenton, New Jersey.[66]

One source claims Uhuru Sasa "closed its doors in 1984, [as] a result of constant political and financial struggles."[67] Jitu Weusi asserts that The East—it is unclear whether this is inclusive of Uhuru Sasa or related to the structure at 10 Claver Place—officially closed its doors in September 1985.[68] Segun Shabaka argues that, in actuality, the folding of the school occurred in 1986, and the closing of the cultural center coincided with the loss of the armory in the summer 1987.[69]

Though there is no real consensus on the actual date of the school's demise, what is more significant is the loss of such an institution to the

African-based community in general and to youth in particular. Many of the persons and families recalled the love and discipline, large family atmosphere, committed teachers, and examples set by elders, the identity development, and the political and cultural consciousness developed through the institution. These reflections clearly paint a picture that suggests African-descended families are the only ones capable of providing a cultural context for their children's development, not solely because they are the children of those families, but also because they are the continuation of the people and the libratory work which they are a part.

In January 1999, Daphine Bailey, a former teacher at Uhuru Sasa Shule, carried on the work of the *shule* by establishing the Imani Day School Computer Campus. Its mission is to provide kindergarten to third-grade students with "positive attitudes toward learning, with respect for self, family, tradition and leadership, in a Pan-African academic environment."[70] According to the founder, students receive a strong academic and cultural foundation through a full-day program and after-school classes and activities reminiscent of Uhuru Sasa. On Uhuru Sasa Shule, Kofi Lomotey, past executive officer of CIBI, recalls: "During [the late 1960s and early 1970s] . . . that institution provided an inspiration for literally thousands of Africans around the country, and even in the Caribbean, and maybe to a lesser extent in Africa. That was the flagship in terms of what we could do in [the area] of independent education—so that was [a] tremendous loss [when Uhuru Sasa closed]. We have flagships now, but at that point it was Uhuru Sasa [Shule]."[71]

5 Kuumba

The International African Arts Festival

> For five summer days, the [International African Arts Festival] transforms the athletic field at Boys and Girls High School in Central Brooklyn into a massive celebration of the cultures of the African diaspora. Nearly seventy thousand people, linked by a heritage rooted in the African motherland, converge in a joyful expression of spiritual connection, communal responsibility and cultural pride.
>
> AFRICAN STREET FESTIVAL ANNUAL REPORT, 1995

In 1971, few could have possibly envisioned that the summer "block party" on 10 Claver Place would develop into an annual festival with the scope and depth of what has become the International African Arts Festival. As the joint venture of The East and Uhuru Sasa Shule, the event began as an end-of-school-year ceremony designed by the parents of Uhuru Sasa to acknowledge their children's achievements. The intention of the parents was that the ceremony should have appropriate meaning and, consequently, reflect their love and thanks for the sustained efforts of their children. Today, what used to be a block party and graduation ceremony now has the distinction of being one of the most anticipated cultural extravaganzas in Brooklyn, New York State, and across this country. The event has hosted more than sixty thousand Africans residing in various parts of the world in the safe, culturally affirming, and communal environment. The festival ritualistically honors its place of conception each year by beginning the event, usually on Saturday, with a parade that starts around 11 A.M. at 10 Claver Place, between Putnam and Jefferson avenues.

A parade of floats, drummers, stilt walkers, children, marching bands, drill teams, and a flag presentation of African nations advances up Fulton Street to the festival grounds. This procession usually involves thousands of parade participants and spectators. The event changed from the Afrikan Street Carnival to the African Street Festival to the International African Arts Festival. The name changes were indicative of a reexamination of the perception, structure, and approach to the event. Specifically, "The name change [underscored] the Festival's standing in the global community and the scope of activities presented at the event."[1] This chapter tells the story of the festival's growth and expansion, challenges, and vision for years to come.

Formative Years of the Afrikan Street Carnival

A 1978 statement published by the Afrikan Street Carnival coordinators indicated, "The Afrikan Street Carnival began in 1973 as an open-house fundraising event for the Uhuru Sasa School."[2] Other sources, however, point out that what was then the Afrikan Street Carnival "began as a one day affair in 1971 as part of a commencement exercise at the Uhuru Sasa School. . . . The response was so overwhelming that the following year it was extended to a three day weekend and began to take on a life its own."[3] During the initial one-day affair, parents developed a ceremony to acknowledge the hard work of the students and, in so doing, "presented" themselves to the students through the creative expressions of song, poetry, arts and crafts, games, food, and music. Yet in 1971, the graduation ceremony was not formally (or informally) referred to as a carnival. Based upon positive feedback on the ceremony, the idea of a "street carnival" the following year was supported. "It was in late June in 1972 when the staff of the Uhuru Sasa School, which was then functioning out of 10 Claver Place, decided to have a three day carnival as part of the school closing program and fundraising project."[4]

Basir Mchawi, former editor of *Black News*, recounts that the carnival had two related foundations: "The original idea was to have an event to mark the end of the school year at Uhuru Sasa. . . . The other foundation piece of the original Afrikan Street Carnival was to start the summer off on a positive note for the entire community with special emphasis on the youth."[5] The carnival also served as an occasion or a fund-raising outlet for The East. The growth that would facilitate the event was not without its share of local confrontations. Perhaps the benchmark of those confrontations, especially in the formative years of the event, was the conflict that erupted with the St. Peter Claver Catholic Church, located across the street from The East facility. Kwesi Mensah Wali recalls, "As the [carnival] grew, the conflict of interest began to boil" between The East and the Catholic church.[6]

One speculation is that the conflict was because of the projected sounds of the carnival stage, lodged in front of The East, into the church. However, according to Jitu Weusi, when the festival grew to the point where the streets were overcrowded, it was "then the Catholic Church [began] their vendetta to undermine [the] festival."[7] It is true that by 1974 the carnival had outgrown its two-block radius and now extended to and used parts of Jefferson Avenue between Claver Place and Franklin Avenue. The specific reasons behind the church's opposition to the carnival remain unclear. What is clear, however, is in 1975, "with the support of the local police department . . . St. Peter Claver Catholic Church, a white-controlled church with a [Black] membership, opposed the carnival."[8] The opposition demanded that the carnival be held elsewhere, since no permit would be granted. The East was determined that the carnival would, in fact, go on and run for seven days. In the ensuing standoff, a special task force of the mayor intervened and "decided that it would be wise if permits were in fact granted and the carnival held."[9] Thereafter, the carnival ran for four days instead of seven.

The nature of the confrontation with the church was not germane to the carnival alone but was a unique expression of how some persons responded to the activities of The East and its members. Speaking of the attitudes of persons who had initial contact with The East, Kwesi Mensah Wali recollects, "We were outcasts, called crazy by some of our family members and community because we identified ourselves as Africans with a Pan-African ideology. Today, those ideas don't seem so strange to most Africans of the diaspora."[10] Notwithstanding these various forms of oppositions, there was also a need for the carnival, in particular, to expand its geographical boundaries in order to accommodate the rapid growth. Accordingly, Segun Shabaka, carnival coordinator, announced in 1977 that in order to "meet the growing demand and take the Afrikan Street Carnival into phase two, which is involvement and internationalization, The East/Uhuru Sasa will be holding its 6th annual Afrikan Street Carnival at Boys and Girls High School field."[11]

The transition to Boys and Girls High School initiated, though not immediately, a number of other significant developments. For one, there was a shift from last-minute planning to actually planning for the event a few months in advance, sometimes beginning as early as January for the event in June. In 1985, with the election of Wali as chairman, event organizers began to consider the full use of the infield which, two years later, was taken over along with the asphalt track surrounding the infield. By 1993, the event had branched out onto the streets. In addition to the event becoming an administrative year-round operation, the staff and coordinators had also to reexamine what they were really doing in the context of the purpose and meaning the event and the notion of "carnival." This moment of reexamination prompted the organizers of the Afrikan Street Carnival to change its name and structure and their approach to the annual event.

In 1986, the transformation of the Afrikan Street Carnival to the African Street Festival coincided with structural changes that took the form of a board of directors chaired by Wali. Other changes include creative color designs and images on promotional materials, in contrast to the text layout of prior years, and the theme and African phraseology concepts, such as the celebration of Marcus Garvey's centennial in 1987 and the use of Sankofa in 1988.[12] Other themes included "We Want to Work" (1975), "Tradition and Reason" (1983), "Simumyue—We Are One" (1990), "Ayéraye—You Will Live Forever" (1994), and "Siyinqaba—We Are a Unique Culture" (1997). These African phrases were used in the festival, as Wali explains, "to project some of these bits and pieces of African wisdom and knowledge, so the theme is usually something that's going to attempt to inspire some individual.... [In addition,] it's a way of communicating something about Africa that may not have been known by the masses."[13]

15. A scene from the first African Street Festival held at 10 Claver Place in front of The East complex. Photograph by Osei Terry Chandler. Used with permission.

Developments of the International African Arts Festival

In the development of the carnival to a festival, the organizers realized that what they were doing, in actuality, was not a carnival in the traditional sense. In other words, when a person thinks of a carnival, given the demographics of Brooklyn's global African population, an average person might come to expect something similar to what occurs in Trinidad, since the common perception of "carnival" was costumes, music, dance, and other related elements. The organizers thus became aware that they were doing more than a carnival or creating carnival type of atmosphere. "So [with] the change, it seemed very natural that the change [from carnival] would go to festival, because it was [a] more festive kind of a situation." According to Mzee Moyo, Chief of Operations, the name change occurred in the event's "growth and development and . . . it came out of a Pan-African [worldview] . . . [since] The East/Uhuru Sasa is a Pan-African philosophy. So if we are dealing with a Pan-African philosophy, it's not just something local, it's more on a national, international [level]. So that's where we decided that we needed to broaden the scope and deal with it from an international perspective."[14]

Furthermore, the inaccuracies conveyed in the term "street," as in African Street Festival, compelled some to think of and, perhaps, to visualize a street-oriented event such as a block party. Consequently, the festival was being seen as a block party, which only reinforced the need for a name that could encapsulate and describe the enormousness of what was taking place. The result was the International African Arts Festival. Wali recounts that festival organizers "thought of naming it the 'African World Festival' but decided on 'International African Arts Festival' to give it a worldly flavor."[15]

As with The East, "the heart of festival's philosophy [were] the seven principles of Kwanzaa and Kawaida, which subscribe to African traditions.... The Nguzo Saba ... [was] the basis for each year's festival theme. The theme [was] a phrase in an African language which [was] paired with original artwork for presentation on festival's programs, posters, and t-shirts."[16] The *Nguzo Saba* are at the core of the Kawaida philosophy and practice. According to Segun Shabaka, member of the National Association of Kawaida Organizations (NAKO), "Kawaida, which is an on-going synthesis of the best of nationalist, Pan-Africanist and socialist thought and practice, seeks to resurrect African life and community by the creation, recreation and recirculation of the best of African and African American culture; e.g., views and values."[17] Beginning in 1977, NAKO organized annual symposiums on culture, community, and struggle at the Boys and Girls High School auditorium during the festival.

The name change to the International African Arts Festival in 1996 coincided with the twenty-fifth anniversary of the festival and the year in which it received 501(c)(3) tax-exempt status. The move to refine the structure of the organization appeared to have been motivated by tax-exempt status requirements, which enabled organizers to receive state funding. The festival's pursuit of state funding, under the pretext of a viable arts organization performing a significant function in the African-based community, began somewhere between 1986 and 1987. However, festival organizers, according to a 1995 annual report, maintained that the festival had "remained primarily self-supporting for 25 years."[18] As it relates to funding and the festival's views on monetary sources, Wali recounts that "[w]e've found that the name 'African' makes a big difference [to] a lot of people across the board. . . . And when it comes to the funding aspect they would just close the book [if it said African]. But by the same token, we're not about to sell our souls . . . [and] the African had to remain just like the Benin mask had to remain as part of the logo."[19] Throughout the 1970s, the event made the modest transition from being free of charge to requiring a minimal fee, but the festival did not make any significant adjustments in relation to the changes in the national and local economy. Still, in recent times, some have thought the organizers of the festival to be financially well off. In the words of Wali,

> Many people think that we at the festival make millions . . . if you were to go outside and talk to folks about our economic status, and I am talking about personal [income]. Mzee [Moyo] is the Chief of Operations, I am the chairman of the board and artistic director and they see the two of us as two of the richest guys in Brooklyn. . . . If the festival paid my salary, I would be here in shorts, literally. . . . Security costs money; restrooms, field lights, stage lights, sound, artists and entertainers [cost money]. People don't see expense, they see income. We do what we do because we believe in the mission and we believe in the love of our people. This is a [family] sacrifice that we make. Most people don't have a clue why we do what we do or how.[20]

Within the past seven to ten years, organizers have started "to focus on the paying population," which, for Mzee Moyo, would be more or less a figure of fifty thousand with a moderate average attendance of sixty-five thousand.[21] The primary structure of the contemporary festival consists of a talent search, scholarship program, Ankh awards, and the children's and evening programs, all of which are informed by mission of the festival, which is to advance the preservation and continuity of African cultural expressions through exposure in the African-based community in America. Therefore, the purpose of the festival "is to preserve and perpetuate African cultural traditions and to unify, renew and empower the brothers and sisters who attend." The primary driving force behind the festival is family—the local, national, and global African family. Every aspect of it seeks to strengthen the spirit of family through shared experiences that are wholesome and uplifting (see appendix F for programmatic content of the festival).[22]

The festival's talent search began in 1985 as a platform for aspiring performers, and its goal was "to form a long-term supportive relationship with aspiring artists."[23] Its scholarship program was designed for college-bound high school seniors, while the Ankh award was presented each year to persons from the African-based community for their outstanding contribution to perpetuate African culture and traditions through dedicated service and righteous conduct.[24] The children's program introduced the youth to the music, dance, art, and various aspects of African life and practice in addition to promoting a sense of tradition in the children themselves. The evening entertainment program was designed for all members of the family and was presented in a warm, relaxed, and safe

16. International African Arts Festival promotional collage, 1998.

environment; the festival "is known for its cleanliness and safety because people conduct themselves as they would during any family event."[25]

A goal of the festival has always been fostering a sense of ownership of the festival on the part of the community. To "encourage these feelings, the planning committee continuously listens to and acts on community opinions and suggestions. This open-eared approach often is reflected in decisions about event logistics, program formats and performers."[26] It is clear that organizers of the festival, in the words of Mzee Moyo, view the role of the event as "presenting what we do—making it available—so that people can see how they can interact with other Africans and see that they are African. In other words, we lay out the playing field and we try to make that presentation. But the main thing is making that presentation so that when people come . . . [they] feel a closeness, [they] feel free, [and they] don't feel threatened."[27] Yet, if the festival is an intergenerational celebration hinged on the construct of familyhood, how are the tasks of organizing the festival and maintaining its values transmitted in the development or future of the event?

The response: The festival is like a work in motion. It involves on-the-job training in the attempt to transmit the responsibilities; according to festival organizers, this is a difficult task owing to the fact that the same conditions of where, how, and when the festival began do not exist. However, there are current attempts to identify young people who have developed an interest and, thereafter, having them involved to the point where they can begin to make a sound commitment. This recruitment process includes inviting more interested persons to meetings and enabling thems to observe how the festival is structured and operated while incorporating their ideas. Likewise, there is the feeling that it is "not an easy task passing on the baton, because first of all you have to know how to pass the baton . . . [and in passing] the baton, there's got to be a rhythm and that rhythm has to be in the person that's receiving as well as the person that's passing."[28] In the intent and act of organizers passing on the baton, they are still in the process of learning how to transmit their responsibilities to ensure the recipients are competent and creative enough to carry out festival's mission.

In the eyes of the organizers, the future and vision of the International African Arts Festival is pictured as something never-ending and that, by necessity, requires continuous hard work and persons committed to the established tradition. Yet, this tradition seems to be constant as the flow of a river but always changing in form and presentation. In the words of festival organizers, "We have to be able to deal with change, but also maintain our integrity and at the same time maintain the spirit of the festival—that's the key. So that's where the young people could come—to bring in some fresh and new ideas—but there's a certain basis that you want to keep, so that it stays very, very focused."[29] Additionally, one of the other challenges is how the new location will affect the nature and structure of the event, given its growth and expansion.

What is clear at this point is that festival organizers do not want to go outside of the African-based community or to consider the festival as a commodity to be sold to another audience under the auspices of generating revenue. Nonetheless, the question of how to maintain this tradition and avoid commercialization is one of the most serious challenges that organizers are facing. At one point, the idea of using the Boys and Girls High School field as the base and then branching out onto the streets in various directions existed and, perhaps, is no longer being entertained, given that in 2004, the festival was held at the Commodore Barry Park in downtown Brooklyn.[30] In terms of institutional continuity, the question must be asked why the festival is still in existence (and viable) and not The East, when both have coexisted and developed together through the agency of members who invested time and energy in both operations. The idea here is not to compare the two entities, but rather to search for possible (fundamental) lessons that might be drawn from the core organization and one of its extensions that became an institution in and of itself.

Basir Mchawi's observations are insightful here. He wrote, "the evolution then from Afrikan Street Carnival to African Street Festival to the new International African Arts Festival [was] consistent with the vision, growth and development of The East organization and the smaller institutions that formed under The East umbrella."[31] If there was a consistency in the vision, growth, and development of The East and the evolution of the festival, why is The East not in existence? The critical juncture that distinguished it from the festival, as the latter is an ideological continuation of the former, was when the festival became an "adaptive entity" by periodically addressing the questions of "who are we?" and "what is our purpose?" The process of self-examination prompted the necessary and manageable internal transformations among a core group of organizers that sought to (re)clarify the festival's mission and refine these transformations within a particular vision. This process allowed the festival to adapt to the changing nuances of its urban and sociopolitical environment, while holding steadfast to its core values and traditions.

One significant lesson drawn is that an impediment to institutional development occurs when core values are not internally (re)examined in the context of their full meaning, utility, and adaptability toward the institution's growth without compromising its mission. Traditions or core values are both stable and dynamic, much like culture, and can contribute to an institution's development or demise if they remain either too loosely constituted or too rigid. Given that institutions do not yield power nor provide life to themselves, it is the members that do so and, thus, the examination must begin within and with the membership if they are to be dynamic agents of their own development. Many of the shortcomings that self-determining institutions incur could be greatly minimized through a continual, dual self-examination and reaffirmation process in the areas of mission, core values, and strategic goals. In other words, the cases of the International African Arts Festival and The East suggest that effective institutional transformations and longevity come through the personal transformations of those institutional members periodically engaged in self-assessment and (ritualized) reaffirmation processes.

6 Imani

The Challenge of Continuity and The East Legacy

> The commitment to creating a world order that is consistent with our cultural identity is not unique to this generation. Indeed it has characterized the resistance and rebuilding efforts of our people since our first encounter and awareness of the avarice driven morality and inhumanity of the Arab and European imperialists. The option of nationbuilding is the continuation of a three millennium war to maintain the sanctity of our souls, the sanity of our minds, and the integrity of our cultural/historical reality.
>
> KWAME AGYEI AKOTO, *Nationbuilding*

Nationality, Socialization, and African Descendants

It is nearly impossible to speak of an African or African-descended nationality in North America devoid of concerns of culture, socialization, and institution building as a requirement of self-determination.[1] The ideology of Black nationalism in the United States has been dormant if not fragmented in some historical periods. As a cultural and political thrust, however, its presence has provided much of the content and context for a number of sociopolitical and cultural movements for genuine self-sufficiency and self-determination. In essence, nationalism for Africans and their progeny has been and strives to be a contributory, albeit contested framework toward reconstituting identity and peoplehood in an intrusive and ongoing sociohistorical context of denial, shame, and negation. Even though the analyses contained in several texts on Black nationalism may conclude otherwise, an examination of the relational concepts of Black cultural nationalism, nationhood, and nation building and their synergetic connection to an African-descended cultural identity and nationality strongly suggests that cultural nationalism is concerned not only (or most importantly) with culture, but with the politics of life and living in pragmatic, ideational, and spiritual terms. The nationalist tendency among Africans captured and transshipped to North America can be traced to the logic of resistance as a natural response to the system of enslavement and white political and cultural hegemony.

Among writers of the history of Africans in America, few would argue that resistance against hegemony does not occupy a central space in the contemporary African-descended narrative. Cheek writes that resistance is "a matter of the spirit, and it was a spirit that burned fiercely in [African-descended] people."[2] The reality of being African or of African descent in an anti-African social order and ideological context, and the acceptance of this reality, may very well provide a resolution through the agencies of family and community, spirit, and culture to the ambiguity that surrounds African cultural identity in the United States. Thus, to advance a sense of self and community in an environment that is hostile to such advancement is a testimony to the African spirit and its humanity. The human spirit, in this context, seeks not only to resurrect and reconstruct itself; it also seeks self-consciousness. Therefore, culture building may be impeded, but it does not stop. Where the phenomenon of cultural hegemony exists, that is, the need "to force the [dominated] to relinquish internal control (independence) in order to accept external control (dependence)," the impetus for counter-resistance is an inevitable reality.[3] In this respect, Black nationalism challenges the power relations within the existing social order as well as imbues African and African-descended people with the requisite cultural clarity and the imperatives of self-development.

For The East, the bonding agent that held the organization ideologically and pragmatically whole was an investment in Black nationalist theory and practice, particularly as expressed by the cultural value system articulated in the *Nguzo Saba*. Through weekly political education classes, members devoured and debated nationalist concepts and case studies, and many became steadfast to the nationalist ideas of Marcus Garvey and Omowale (Malcolm X).[4] A key instructional text of The East was E. A.

Essien-Udom's *Black Nationalism: A Search for an Identity in America*. The relative consistency between theory, practice, and principle made The East a living, breathing manifestation of what the organization advocated. Thus, Omowale personified one of the finest examples of Black nationalist thought and practice among The East members. His efforts at the community, national, and international levels were exemplified to some extent at The East. "In the political realm, The East played a major role in attempting to transform the politics of Central Brooklyn. . . . [As such,] The East was always at the political forefront locally, nationally and internationally."[5] The experiences of The East were bounded both by a Black nationalist tradition and by the historical complexities of nationalist thought and praxis.

The East seemed to have clearly understood the necessity and praxis of pan-Africanism through the life of its institutional components. During its existence, the *Black News* publication circulated from Austin, Texas, to Australia, and Uhuru Sasa students traveled to and studied in various countries. The East operated a land-cooperative project in Guyana and institutionalized specific areas of indigenous development initiatives as seen in Ghana and Tanzania at the time of their respective political independence. The East also supported a number of African liberation movements, especially through its ability to give representatives a platform to dialogue with the African-descended community in North America about the nature of such struggles. To The East, nationhood meant primarily a strong sense of community amongst Africans and a relational accountability to the principles that augmented and sustained the integrity of that composite communal unit. Substantive manifestations of nationhood could be seen in the institution and enterprises of The East. One might look, for example, at the Uhuru Sasa Shule complex, which included the Imani Child Development Center and the Evening School of Knowledge. Uhuru Sasa was a comprehensive model of education from birth to adult to elderhood that could indeed be reproduced, especially through the international scope and efforts of CIBI.[6]

Black News, published monthly, informed and was informed by the African diasporic community. In an age of technological sophistication, the control and currency of information and images has to be contested, considering the power knowledge has to inform (or misinform), shape thought, and propel action. Hence, the necessity and implication of not having a *Black News* publication of some sort seems quite clear to members of the African-descended community who do not control the images they consume, the ways in which they are depicted, and how they receive decision-forming information. Lastly, when we examine the International African Arts Festival, which matured from a city block celebration to an annual event that attracts well over seventy thousand local and global peoples of African descent, the pan-Africanist praxis is also quite evident. The festival functions not only as a meeting ground for many African and African diasporic communities but also as a ground for the building of consciousness and family, and a recommitment to culture and community.

In many ways, The East sought to practice the principles of being a cultural nation through its Brooklyn-based institutions. As Jitu K. Weusi stated in conversation, "We practiced nation building where we were and moved on."[7] On one hand, this statement simply meant a person could not give what she or he did not have; on the other hand, it meant that meaningful theory must be grounded in and derive from praxis. The expectations associated with doing *kazi* (work) were extraordinary. Somewhere in 1970s, the concise ideological statement, "Black was necessary, but not sufficient," circulated widely as well as the saying, "Kazi is the Blackest of all." "Interpreted," explained Weusi, "[the latter phrase] means if you are so Black, [let's] see how much work you can do for the Black cause [i.e., the struggle toward self-determination]."[8] These concise sayings encapsulated, in a very real sense, the commitments and aspirations of some East members who (literally) gave their life and effort toward the building of an African cultural nation. The commitments were surpassed by only the sacrifices members made around family and children, time and energy, and fiscal and other resources.

As a result of the nation-building vigor manifest at The East, the emphasis on and respect for work among the young and old, men and women is an often disregarded dimension, as if the process and objectives of nation building can be actualized without protracted labor. The idea was that everyone works, bearing in mind that developing a social and political consciousness as well as a controlled physical space also required intensive efforts that were viewed as familial imperatives in the process of building a "nation." Ideology can sometimes be a straitjacket to development. The East, however, found such rigidity unproductive and narrow in scope. Its doors, consequently, were open to all African persons regardless of their ideological disposition, relative religious orientation, or cultural consciousness. Of course, this kind of openness came with consequences such as interlopers, agent provocateurs, and individuals with personal baggage that, at times, had the potential of disrupting the order established at The East. However, the genuine willingness to develop in concert with those African and African-descended persons whose intentions outweighed their political consciousness or personal development allowed The East to grow and develop successful enterprises.

The East Legacy: Implications for Understanding Cultural Nationalism

Considering The East as a viable reference in institutional and nationalistic development among people of African descent, one can argue the central challenges of African or African-descended life in North America (and elsewhere) are those of family and identity. More precisely, the challenges of unambiguously reclaiming their cultural ancestry and projecting that reality within the constellation of family, community, and nation. Community institutions, like The East, are entities whose survival and development are contingent upon the interchange between the institution and its community. The institution is conceptualized here as independent and interdependent in that it is a distinct feature as well as an interconnected part of the community. In regard to their structural characteristics, institutions differ in complexity based upon the number and kinds of both the components involved and the constraining and facilitating conditions linking the components. The functioning of each component is controlled or managed by a collective state. Furthermore, institutions are always in a process of transformation; although some components will change while other defining ones remain the same, minor changes will effect the total operation.

Changes or minute inputs into dynamic institutions can create major changes, and because of such changes predictability becomes very limited. In the natural world, "fractional changes in degrees of temperature on the ocean surface turn tropical storms into hurricanes."[9] In the life of an institution, a change in leadership or in one or more components can enhance or disrupt the entire multifaceted operation, with little if any room for forecasting the outcome of such changes. Likewise, human behavior, in the context of sociocultural organizations, is unpredictable; unless such persons are committed to growing with institutional purpose and mission, their transformations could either contribute to the development or be the detriment of the institution. Recent studies in organizational theory suggest a significant correlation between organizational development or success and adaptability. These research efforts reveal that adaptability is a central operating principle for success; to be adaptive, organizations must unambiguously respond to two essential questions: Who are we? What is our purpose?[10] According to one report, "The essence of adaptability is the ability to change form while staying true to core identity. This presumes that there is clarity and consensus regarding core purposes. The willingness to struggle and continually refine 'who we are' is one hallmark of the adaptive [institution]."[11] I take the position that institutional development—like human development—consists of transformations or developments that occur in life cycles.

An example of such an institutional development is The East, which went through the three fundamental and overlapping phases or cycles: emergence (to fulfill a specific mission), ascendance (point of maximum efficiency), and transcendence (ceasing to exist in its original form). The emergence phase corresponded to the conception of the organization out of the conditions and consciousness of the architects and supporters, who forged their material and immaterial resources to give birth to The East idea and structure. The ascendance phase was marked by points of maximum efficiency and was associated with levels of developmental and expansive productivity consistent with the mission and stated (or unstated) objectives of the organization and its adjoining institutions. In the transcendence phase, the term "transcendence" is used not to connote finality but the cyclical development of the organization, whereby it took on new form that was akin to the process of becoming an ancestor. When someone becomes an ancestor, it is held (generally among Africans) that the person does not die but rather takes on another form in the reality of the immaterial (spirit) domain, and that this transcendence is a natural stage in human development. In physics, the idea is the same: Matter cannot be destroyed, only reconstituted into another or new form.

The pattern of emergence, ascendance, and transcendence is also based on the truism that energy, as the life of an organism or organization, can never be destroyed but only reconstituted into a new form. According to this perspective, the existence of an institution is contingent upon the very need(s) or purpose(s) that called it into existence. In this context and that of nation(alist) building, The East's immediate antecedents include Marcus Garvey's UNIA and African Communities League and the efforts and ideas of Martin Delany, Harriet Tubman, Edward Blyden, Ida B. Wells, Bishop Henry McNeal Turner, David Walker, Nat Turner, Omowale (Malcolm X), and countless others. In other words, if this nation(alist) building tradition is a family lineage, The East was merely a child or representative.

The East is worthy not only of examination but also of emulation because cultural community centers and organizations have long served as focal points or as anchoring family-based formations in the history of African descendants in North America. These cultural centers are institutions that serve both core and peripheral purposes. At the core, they facilitate the functions of families where there is no consistent tradition of culturally focused and healthy family development. They also operate in the capacity of "liberated territories" wherein these families can develop and expand. The necessity of functioning as liberated territories also adheres to the peripheral demands of the institution, because the development and expansion of an African-centered mind and spirit in the present social and political arrangement is tantamount to intentionally committing arson in a fire station.[12] As such, cultural community centers help to build as well as rely upon committed families guided by purpose and the principles of self-determination. These family-based institutions have had the capacity to overlap into larger family units and networks of culturally focused communities across national and transnational landscapes.

When institutions consist of committed families, they not only facilitate family and nation development through substantive relationships and efforts but also may well define or give shape to the vision of the communities in which they exist. Imbued with cultural clarity and commitment, these communities have the primary mission of accomplishing their ancestral mandate toward the realization of genuine self-sufficiency and self-determination. This has been largely the (unfulfilled) object and projection of African cultural and institutional building in North America.

The necessity of establishing African-centered institutions does not supersede the establishment of African-centered communities; those institutions must be natural outgrowths of such communities. As appropriate extensions of family and facilitators of family development, institutions are not the goal but rather the means to nationalist and transnationalist goals as they relate to the concurrent development of a global African consciousness and communitarian sensibility. Holistic community development requires multilayered institutions that speak to the entire life cycle of a people but are informed and sustained by family units. The family is ultimately the principal institution responsible for ensuring the communities' functionality, development, and continuity. In this context, The East experience represents a concerted effort in nation(alist) building, a family and institutional building strategy, and a vision of African-centered community life and development in North America. The task of nation(alist) building is an intentional and continual process, and those persons and institutions that have committed themselves to this task must be assessed not necessarily in terms of success or failure, but in terms of their contributions to this process.

Furthermore, this process is not a step-by-step procedure but the focused and conscious application of collective resources, energies, and skills to the task of liberating, maintaining, and developing the psychic and physical space Africans and African-descended peoples identify as theirs. Africans in North America reside in a social order wherein the terrain of their minds is a contested area. Therefore, this "contested area" is a life and death struggle to maintain and develop a sense of sanity whereby their psyche becomes a territory unoccupied by, in Ayi Kwei Armah's words, the predator's and destroyer's thoughts and images.[13] The assaults of white images and cultural thought are relentless and, by necessity, efforts to be defensive as well as offensive must also be unyielding. The founders of The East saw that African-descended youth of the community were becoming causalities in this assault and, knowing the terrain of public schooling and that those public schools were advocates for the American state and its vested interests, opted for institution building. This was the motive for establishing Uhuru Sasa Shule, the primary component of The East, which sought to insulate the minds and spirits of the youth from such assaults as well as to develop these youths to be principled examples of self-determination and self-reliance.

The students and staff at Uhuru Sasa Shule were involved in all the operations and the activities of The East. Therefore, The East became a training ground that would contribute to the "nation" becoming. The land base or territory that usually accompanies the definition of nationhood existed in the form of The East building and where its institutional components resided, and the understanding was that the skills needed to liberate and develop such a space should be obtained through some form of practice. Thus, for example, trips to and residence in Guyana provided some of the adults a semblance of hands-on training (for the nation becoming) in working with the land and subsisting without the amenities or gadgets that Western culture offers. Likewise, the preschool children of Uhuru Sasa were provided with practical skills involving daily tasks of real-life situations. "These activities [were] . . . designed to foster skills of self-reliance and respect for the ability to use talents and resources creatively. [They included] activities such as carpentry, sanding, varnishing, painting, food preparation, setting the table, sewing, washing, cleaning." Additionally, emphasis was placed on neatness, completion of tasks, pride in one's work, and a respect for tools. Uhuru Sasa held the belief that education should contribute to consciousness by instilling values and an African cultural and historical identity in addition to creating the capacity and ability to "do" and develop the adequate concepts, skills, and perspectives. Uhuru Sasa believed that "small children who are allowed to do meaningful (adult-type) work in their homes, schools, and communities begin to see themselves as capable persons."[14] The learning experiences of all levels of Uhuru Sasa embodied this outlook. Furthermore, the context in which learning occurred, as many interviewed East members recalled, was one of love and discipline, a large family atmosphere, committed teachers, examples set by elders, identity development, and political and cultural consciousness.

Recent research on the notion of "school culture" in the realm of public schooling informs us that "strong cultures provide the internal cohesion that makes it easier for teachers to teach; students to learn; and for parents and administrators and others to contribute to the instructional process."[15] At best, these findings only confirm, for those who need the validation, why designers of African-centered schools place great emphasis on the vitality of African culture, and the character of the socialization process and its connection to self-determination and institution building. Further research into effective schooling has also pointed out that effective schools are those that have a built a system of belief, supported by cultural forms that give meaning to the process of education. The perspective that emerges out of these studies and The East experience is that culturally competent African-descended educators are best capable of providing for African-descended students not solely because of "cultural synchronization," but more importantly because these students are a continuation of the work and people that preceded them. Although members of The East did not make all the necessary provisions for its continuity, they did create and allow for the establishment of a number of existing institutions and organized activities. Among them is Ujamaa Institute, Little Sun People, Weusi Shule (Johnson Preparatory), Zidi Kuwa, Shule ya Mapenduzi, Imani Day School Computer Campus, Black Veterans for Social Justice, and other educational and social enterprises.[16]

As one of the early independent community schools in the late 1960s, Uhuru Sasa Shule provided a methodology for educational institution building for a number of African-centered and privately run schools that exist today. Similarly, the operations of The East provided not only financial stability for the institution but also vital community services that served as models for what was and is possible in terms of building sustainable institutions in the African- descended community and in the pragmatism of self-reliance. The idea that a community should control and operate its institutions and businesses and benefit from them was certainly put into practice at The East. The activities that emerged as institutional combustions provide insight into how cultural nationalist thought and praxis can exist in the life of a community and the fullness that such a political and cultural philosophy can provide. The specific lessons derived from the operations of The East are found in the need for effective business planning and management, the development of skill-based competencies, and vision and consistency in ventures that are vital to family and community development. Consistent with these lessons are those provided by East members in the leadership of the organization, which are a part of the present East family.

The legacy of The East, as articulated by Jitu Weusi, is presented here from an essay entitled "The East Legacy" to serve the purpose of providing a reflective analysis that was internal in origination. Weusi's main points were as follows:

1. Collective Leadership: No one person can build and sustain an institution. Any institution that is going to mold and shape our people's lives today must be developed collectively. If any individual is sincere in helping our people, he/she must realize that when individuals join together as a group and learn to assume the roles of both leader and follower they empower the effort. Thus, future successes of our movement will be born[e] out of the efforts of collective leadership.

2. Meaningful [and Critical] African Consciousness: Information about African history and struggles over the past five hundred years is voluminous and requires an intellectual army to engage in research and discussion. To maintain contemporary African consciousness regarding day-to-day affairs requires a full-time staff. If we say that our people and their history and accomplishments are important, we cannot provide a superficial standard of consciousness. We must struggle constantly to maintain as much consciousness as possible for our people. We need more publications, more research, more programs, films, videos, and other vehicles of information and education. We must fight for Black studies and anything that can arouse the awareness of our oppressed peoples.

3. Hard Work/Respect for Work: There is a tendency among some segments of our population to look disdainfully at the concept of work. In the study of our people's survival over the past five hundred years, hard

work and respect for good work have provided enormous dividends. We cannot lose this ethos. If we are going to build a community of the future that will amplify and surpass all the past efforts, we need to change our outlook toward work. At The East, there was a saying, "Kazi is the Blackest of all" (Kazi is Kiswahili for work). Interpreted, it means if you are so Black, let's see how much work you can do for the Black cause.

4. Economic Nationalism: Being a part of an independent institution like The East afforded one the opportunity to see how potent the economics of two hundred families working together toward the same goals could be. At this time in the history of the U. S., Black economic behavior is very important. We must build and patronize stores and businesses that keep dollars in our community. We must own the property in our communities. The next great frontier for the Black struggle will be around economic issues. Our understanding of economic nationalism and how it can be used as a weapon in our total struggle for freedom is a valuable asset.

5. Appreciation of our Culture: Culture is defined as a people's "Way of Life." For many years, many of our people seemed to despise our way of life. At The East, members gained an appreciation and respect for our culture, which was based on communalism. East members appreciated the bonds of friendship and family that we built. East members appreciated the challenges that working with our people and communities presented. Constant renewal and re-energizing for our culture is needed. Constant assurance of ourselves so we can retain our roots and sense of peoplehood is also needed. We must never lose sight of the valuable role that culture plays in our struggle for liberation.[17]

The profundity of Jitu Weusi's analysis is that it addresses the implications of The East experience from the perspective of an integral East member, in ways reflective of the overall analysis I have presented thus far. Based on The East experience, a collective that seeks to build an institution must honestly engage itself in a serious process of bringing resolution to internal conflicts (interpersonal and collective) and establishing means to effectively anticipate and resolve future conflict. In addition, a collective must do the required research, first beginning with a self-examination of the collective's skills, resources, and knowledge, and then examining what similar efforts preceded them and what has to be done to either build upon the antecedents or start anew. The research should be conducted in the form of continual and honest assessments, including the making of wise decisions through consensus and, if not possible, through a system that considers the input of those committed to the purpose and mission of the institution. Lastly, the collective must also be able to operate an institution as a business entity, in consideration of its purpose and mission, and actively engage in immediate and long-term planning.

In addition, provisions must be made to own a building or land space, determine the guiding principles underpinning the institution, and anchor the structure in a spiritual-cultural system of values and beliefs that is either overarching, pan-Africanist in orientation, or speaks to the collective's specific cultural reality. For self-determining institutions, development is not solely a question of adaptability; designers and developers of such institutions have to approach this task fully cognizant of the temporal and spiritual realities that influence their very existence. Moreover, the designers and developers must consist of women and men, from youth to elders, engaged in and committed to the developmental process. The foundational rituals, symbols, and core values of an institution must be rooted in a system that enables members to relate to one another in a healthy manner. This sense of rootedness would, therefore, provide order, stability, and meaning to core elements of the institution in addition to clarifying its identity and mission.

The East experience in nation(alist) building contributed greatly to the lives of its members and the cultural and political life of Brooklyn and the larger African diasporic community. The institution, an influential example of the practice of the *Nguzo Saba* and the Kawaida philosophy, pioneered in the areas of building self-determining institutions, providing prototypical models, and educating thousands of African-descended children and adults. As Segun Shabaka recalls, "[The East was a] major spreader of Black people learning to look and appreciate African, African American, African diasporan culture in its best and we tapped into that, spread it, and networked with people around the world."[18] Also, these developments and activities did not occur in a vacuum at 10 Claver Place in Brooklyn but were part of the encapsulating phenomena of the Black Power, Black Consciousness, and Black Arts period and a transnational network of key institutions and groups of people. Subsequently, most of The East's energies went into institutional development for the benefit of the immediate and larger African-based community. Notwithstanding uncertainties in the formation of the organization, the architects were determined to contribute to the nationalistic development of African and African-descended people in North America and elsewhere. In doing so, they contributed to our understanding of the pragmatism of cultural nationalism and institution building, and a fuller meaning of the intersections of nationalism, education, economic self-sufficiency, the arts, and organizational culture in the late twentieth century.

Epilogue

The East Family at Present

Although The East no longer exists as an institution with an attendant physical structure, its family continues and is reaffirmed through the means of an annual newsletter published by The East family committee and a Kwanzaa reunion. The newsletter is a significant binding instrument in that it shares information on (1) the family's college students and graduates; (2) births and marriages; and (3) relocations and announcements; it also contains sections such as "tribute to our ancestors" and "road to success." Its section on networking is a compilation of businesses owned or operated by East family members, including Awareness Communication Bookstore, Kente Productions, Little Sun People Learning Center, Little Black Genius Kamitic Academy, and Revolution International Entertainment. Other businesses range from real estate to baking services to dance companies.

The East Family Kwanzaa Reunion began in 1989. Since then, the gathering has become a tradition that provides a communal space for the children, adults, and elders of The East. The newsletter is distributed at the reunion, and scholarships for youth of the families, ranging from elementary school students to college students, are awarded. The East family committee coordinates these activities. Although I am unaware of the selection process for committee members, all current members are women. The annual programs put forth by the committee include poetry, a fashion show, thoughts and words of inspiration, a Karamu (feast), and family togetherness.

From their own words, it is clear that the members of The East family are "committed to keeping The East legacy alive because we know that our years at The East under the leadership of Kasisi Jitu Weusi, were a significant part of our lives. We take pride in looking at our young adults who are the children of The East sisterhood and brotherhood.... As parents, we take pride in saluting them. Our only regret is that there is not a cultural and educational center for people of African descent for our grandchildren to continue the tradition." Although the latter statement is accurate, some traditions of Uhuru Sasa continue within the second and third generations of the families. For example, "Three year old Dakari, son of Makini Weusi, leads the Weusi family daily with the *sifa* [praises or prayer] at the dinner table. He also sings Praise the Red, Black and Green. He is the third generation of this family to follow these traditions."[1]

During the 1998 Kwanzaa celebrations, I had the opportunity to attend the annual East family and friends Kwanzaa Reunion. Although this was no substitute for what took place at The East, there was a strong sense of family, community, and continuity of certain East traditions. The young adults, by way of illustration, formed two lines at one point and began marches and drills and the singing of songs that were reminiscent of Uhuru Sasa. Even though some of the children of these adults were not afforded the opportunity to attend Uhuru Sasa, they actively participated in these exercises until it became a little overwhelming. The fashion show was an excellent display of expressive culture that really got those in attendance going. Yet, there was a significant moment where Jumibia Nyahuma, who began teaching at Uhuru Sasa as a teenager, delivered words of inspiration and a charge to the youth. Likewise, a young person of the Mashariki family conveyed similar words of responsibility and thanks to the adults and elders in the room. This was, indeed, an intergenerational conversation that in some ways attempted to transmit cultural knowledge and experiences of value from one generation to the next. Two elders, Mama Kuumba Coard and Mzee Moyo, have joined their ancestors since the publication of the book's first edition. Deservingly so, they form part of its dedication.

APPENDIXES

NOTES

BIBLIOGRAPHY

INDEX

Appendix A
The Mashariki and Required Reading Lists[1]

Mashariki Reading List

Level One

The Kitabu (Imamu Halisi)
The Quotable Karenga (James Mtume and Clyde Halisi)
Black Value System (Amiri Baraka)

Level Two

Axioms of Kwame Nkrumah (Kwame Nkrumah)
Quotations from Chairman Mao Zedong (Chairman Mao Zedong)
Malcolm X on Afro-American History (Malcolm X)

Level Three

Building Revolutionary Ujamaa and Pan-Africanism (Honorable Shabazz)
Dope: An Agent of Chemical Warfare (Herman Ferguson)
Education for Self-Reliance (Julius Nyerere)

Level Four

On Contradictions (Chairman Mao Zedong)
Garvey, Lumumba and Malcolm (Shawna Maglangbayan)
From Plan to Planet (Haki Madhabuti)
The Philosophy and Opinions of Marcus Garvey (Amy J. Garvey)

Level Five

Neo-Colonialism: Last Stage of Imperialism (Kwame Nkrumah)
Black Revolutionary Story of Padmore, Black and White Book (James Boggs)
African Religions and Culture (Edward W. Blyden)
How Europe Underdeveloped Africa (Walter Rodney)
Political Leaders as Representatives of the Culture (Sekou A. Toure)
Man and Socialism in Cuba (Che Guevera)

Level Six

Art of War (Sun Tzu)
Notes on Military Warfare (Chairman Mao Zedong)
Consciencism (Kwame Nkrumah)
Diet, Nutrition, and Exercise (Dr. Sealy)
Ujamaa (Julius Nyerere)

Required Reading List

History

Malcolm X on Afro-American History (Malcolm X)
Before the Mayflower (Lerone Bennett)
Black Man of the Nile and His Family (Dr. Yosef Ben-Jochannan)

Pan-Africanism

Pan-Africanism History (author unknown)
Neo-Colonialism: Last Stage of Imperialism (Kwame Nkrumah)
The Philosophy and Opinions of Marcus Garvey (Amy J. Garvey)

Biography

Harriet Tubman (author unknown)
Ghana: An Autobiography of Kwame Nkrumah (Kwame Nkrumah)
The Autobiography of Malcolm X (Malcolm X with Alex Haley)

Metaphysics

The Pleasantries of the Incredible Mulla-Nasrudin (Idries Shah)
The Way of the Sufi, part 1 (Idries Shah)
The Sufi Message, vol. 1 (Hadzart Inyat Khan)

Drama

The Slave and the Toilet (Leroi Jones/Amiri Baraka)

Politics

Wretched of the Earth (Frantz Fanon)
The Enemy (Felix Greene)
The Dialectical Method, 3 volumes (author unknown)

Economics

Man, Money, and Goals: A Fundamental Book on Economics (author unknown)
Black Economics Development (William F. Haddad)
The Economics of Africa (Peter Robson and D. A. Lury)

Appendix B

Letter from Jitu Weusi to Amiri Baraka, December 12, 1973 (Transcribed from the original letter)[1]

TO: Imamu Amiri Baraka, Chairman
Congress of Afrikan People

FROM: Kasisi Jitu Weusi, Director, *The East* Family
Brooklyn Chapter Congress of Afrikan People

SUBJECT: CLARIFICATION OF INTERNAL DIFFERENCES AS THEY AFFECT THE FUNCTIONING OF THIS CHAPTER AS AN INTEGRAL PART OF THE CONGRESS OF AFRIKAN PEOPLE

Appreciating what has been said and if we understand things correctly, we representatives of *The East* Cadre deem it absolutely necessary that for purposes of the future progress of C.A.P. and the movement of Afrikan people that we examine whatever internal differences that exist at this present time between National office C.A.P. (CFUN) and Brooklyn C.A.P. (East). We have over the past two and half years attempted to cement an alliance with the CFUN organization under the leadership and wisdom of Chairman Imamu Baraka. This alliance has been based on our complete devotion to the ideology of revolutionary Black Nationalism, the practice of Pan Afrikanism and principles of brotherhood and comradeship embodied in the Nguzo Saba and our mutual respect and understanding for the philosophy of Kawaida (Afrikan tradition and reason). This alliance seemed almost a natural union as we looked around and sought the help and companionship of other Black institutions headed in a similar direction. Certainly we have been felt and learned much from this alliance and we have been indeed very proud to attach the level of our development and progress to the growth of a progressive national organization, the Congress of Afrikan People. However, as we have ventured down the road of peace and progress, numerous misunderstandings, rumors, opinions and assumed facts have blocked the path to the total and complete Unity that must be established between organizations if we are to complete the arduous task of "Revolution" for the Black masses in our lifetime. We therefore present the following points for discussion, not in a spirit of dissension and divisiveness but in the disposition of Unity and Struggle. We hope we can have an open discussion that observes only the principle of Truth as a watchword.

QUESTIONS

1. In the interpretation of the doctrine of Kawaida and correct positions on Black Revolutionary Struggle within the United States, must all C.A.P. organizations submit to views held by the Chairman? Are there any other valid thinkers in the arena of Revolutionary Black Nationalism?

2. Is it the objective of the Chairman to make all C.A.P. organizations "carbon copies" of the CFUN organization? Are there any things other Cadre groups can bring to the C.A.P. and contribute to the national body? (Except products)

3. Are the terms, "Unity without Uniformity" and "Operational Unity," formerly code words for Umoja, used by the Chairman no longer applicable to our struggle?

4. Does the Chairman see the present state of leadership within the C.A.P. developing into a personality cult with the Chairman having the *only* influence on member organizations?

5. Why have most of the operational tentacles of the C.A.P. been relocated within the NewArk (Treasury, Delegate Reception, Afrikan Printing Coop., United Nations Representation, Newspaper) chapter?

6. Whatever became of the effort to clarify the concept of the "Extended Family"? This point was briefly mentioned at the cadre session of the C.A.P. but has not been heard from since.

7. How and under what circumstances has *Black News* been given the status of a "magazine," when it was adopted at the June meeting of C.A.P. that *Black News* carrying the section Fundisha would be the *official* voice of C.A.P.?

8. How can we consider participation in an economic union when at the present time there are *absolutely no* types of goods/services being exchanged between the National office (NewArk) and the Brooklyn Chapter *(The East)?* Not

only aren't there any trade agreements between these two organizations but there appears to be outright aversion. Several people have been assured that *"The East is not a Kawaida organization"* and that "things taught at *The East* are completely different from what is taught in NewArk." With these views presently held, is economic union possible or desirable?

9. Why are beginning cadres in the Bronx and Manhattan relating to the NewArk Chapter and not to the local chapter? Would it not be peculiar if chapters in New Jersey started coming to Brooklyn for classes, instructions, directions, etc.?

10. The National office (CFUN) has a reputation for its cold and distant greeting and treatment of Brother Cadre from *The East*. This has largely remained unexplained to us. *The East* Family has still maintained a role of friendship and brotherhood with Kasisi Nakawa. Is this seen as a defiance of the National office (CFUN) or the personal wishes of the Chairman?

11. What is the purpose of the extended bureaucracy that exists at the NewArk office (National) that serves as a deterrent toward good relationship and effective communications? (Calls often disconnected, people held on for long periods, while they await answers, simple questions are not answered)

12. Are there real differences or extended criticisms that Chairman has of our organization/family? Is it possible that the Brooklyn Chapter can be viewed by the Chairman's office with mutual respect and acceptance or will we be merely "tolerated"?

13. Does the Chairman see the Brooklyn Chapter as an obstacle to the national direction of C.A.P. now being charted? If this question is answered affirmatively, is it possible for the two organizations to have an alliance outside of the Congress of Afrikan People?

Appendix C

The East Brotherhood Code Committee (Transcribed from the original document)[1]

Introduction

> The nation—like a seed in a Sisters womb.
> Forming taking shape growing
> It will be.

We know this with the same assurance we place in the rising and setting of the sun or the change of seasons. We will be a full grown nation. Just as a child looks upon its parents to see its future, we see our traditional greatness and know our destiny.

Four hundred years from captivity and enslavement we ask the New African Man to come and be us. The Old/New African Man. We throw off the tired nigger shells that try to contain the energy and beauty of what we really are (get back negro/nigger ways—Black folks is growin now.) We try to walk a new path guided by Kawaida. A hard path to walk this new one. Judgment is poor when we lack sufficient righteous experience. To help us, we provide a basic code of behavior to assist the Doctrine and make it more concrete.

We are Black Men. Leaders teacher warriors workers poets the majority creative force in the universe. Dig us. The many forms and names of what we are: Sunni Ali John Coltrane Chaka Imamu Baraka Nat Turner Amenhotep Maulana Karenga

> The Black Man
> Magician for a new age
> Priestly transformer and raiser of the dead
> We are the Old/New African Man

We think shrewdly and act swiftly and decisively realizing that politics is simply the means for obtaining, maintaining, and using power. We are the catalysts and builders of the Black Nation within us. The forgers and shapers of generations to come. The guidance, wisdom and understanding of a new world in human form. Lover/leader and always disciplined. These are some of the qualities we seek to develop as we develop the Nation we are all part of.

> Sifa Ote Ina Mtu Weusi
> All Praises Is Due the Black Man
> Brother Quentin L. Basir

The Brotherhood Code

> Brotherhood Code Committee
> Quentin, Kwesi, Karriem, Rondu

Mental

1. We are advocates of the Doctrine of Kawaida and strive to grow and develop by its guidance.
2. We *value* our leaders.
3. Brothers must always be prepared to represent the organization.

Agitate—we must expose the system as corrupt and unworkable using Black Nationalism and The Spiritual Doctrine of Kawaida as our guide.

Educate—We must rationally and clearly present the framework of Black alternatives by applying the Nguzo Saba.

Organize—On the basis of these alternatives, we must begin to build Nation structures (institutions).

4. Each Brother by bettering himself betters the organization. In order to survive we must constantly study and train. We must work towards the highest level of discipline in order to restore our people to their traditional greatness.
5. We must become examples so that our achievements become inspirational. We must leave legacies.
6. We must move to gain more technical Nation building and maintaining skills. When we say Nation we do not mean "underdeveloped" or "second rate."
7. We must actively seek to guide the younger Brothers and Sisters of the Mashariki, realizing, that one day, they will take our place.
8. We must be patient and understanding in moving to win the minds of our people not yet committed to Black Nationalism or the Spiritual Doctrine of Kawaida.

9. We will never misuse the Spiritual Doctrine of Kawaida to meet some personal need.

Physical

1. Brothers are responsible for their appearance at all times. We are reflections of [The East] and should mirror its values. When on [East] business we should be particularly careful about our dress because the first impression we make on others will be a visual one. Clothing should be clean unless a particular function warrants kazi in which soiled clothing is preferable.

2. We should wear African clothing as much as possible because this is both traditional and reasonable.

3. Talisimus should be worn at the Mashariki, when representing [The East] family among other African people, and at any other time we wish as long as the symbol is not endangered.

4. We should take good care of our bodies realizing that it is the only one we have. There are no replacements or replacement parts. Proper hygiene is essential to our every day functioning.

5. All Brothers must observe dietary rules so that our functions are not hampered by illness. When we are weak, the Nation shares our weakness.

6. All Brothers must actively participate in self-defense. If our bodies are weapons, we will never be unarmed.

7. Brothers must never be in a position where our judgment is impaired by some drug (alcohol, tobacco, marijuana, heroin).

8. When business is to be taken care of, a business-like attitude should prevail.

9. Brothers should be in attendance at all required meetings at the correct time. Specifics regarding the number of meetings required will be made available.

10. There is no exemption from kazi because of position or past accomplishments. We do not accept comfort corruption within the organization.

11. Brothers placed in leadership positions are responsible to see that all expected work is finished. Leadership is also responsible to see that all Brothers and Sisters placed under their command know what functions they are to fulfill.

12. We wish to make [The East] secure. A uniformed security force, trained and disciplined will be formed. All Brothers will have a uniform consisting of a red cloth dashiki, black pants, combat boots, and a green [East] arm patch (to be designed).

13. We are responsible for the collective welfare. For instance we see that Sisters get home safely.

14. We do not duck work. We take initiative in doing things. We do not have to be told what to do.

15. We will never gossip or take part in petty arguments. We reject all actions that seek to divide us.

16. A committee should be formed to judge code infractions and to set up a uniform system of punishments.

Spiritual

Spirituality is an intense emotional appreciation for the highest values of man which are positive to human life and development, that is to say, those values which most promote life and development such as the *Nguzo Saba*. Spirituality gives us the strength to carry on our struggle. The spiritual can give us control over our bodies and minds. If we can apply the Black spirituality that is within us all to our advantage, we will function much better. We must develop our spiritual selves because it is the spirit that gives us the power and Imani to act correctly. The seventh principle of the *Nguzo Saba* is the one that binds the other six together. Without Imani, to talk of any of the other six principles would be hard. Just as the *Nguzo Saba* are [sic] a totality, we must move to become the *total* Blackman. Our spirituality must be developed just as well as our mental and physical selves. To talk of any one aspect in complete isolation (mental, physical, or spiritual) is not a realistic view. Here are some basic ideas that may help our spiritual development.

1. We struggle always, realizing that Blackness is a 25 hour a day job. When we deal in Blackness, we deal in spirituality.

2. We pledge our total devotion to our Black Nation and will employ any righteous means necessary to achieve our goal of Nationhood.

3. Just as we feed and develop our bodies and our minds, we must feed and develop our spirits. We must become familiar with *our* basic spiritual thought. The spirit is the backbone for moving to greater understanding. We must become in tune with our inner selves.

4. We must be honest both with others and with ourselves.

5. We must be sincere for as Hazrat Khan says "sincerity is the principle thing in life."

6. The spiritual ministry of the organization must begin to disseminate food for our spirits and give us the vehicle in which we can develop.

7. By our actions we must aspire to unity with the Creator. It is no coincidence that our ancestors often functioned from theocratic structures (Read *The Book of*

the Dead.) Spirituality and politics are not necessarily contradictory. Our new politics is a spiritual thing, dealing with the highest values.

Social-Moral

1. Brothers should greet everyone who comes into the Mashariki in a pleasant and warm manner.
2. We give praise where praise is due.
3. We function with each other in the spirit and reality of Umoja.
4. We believe in Ujamaa and the concept of the extended family. We must put this belief into practice.
5. Although we believe in Ujima, each Brother is responsible for his well-being and the well-being of his family. Each small unit is another aspect of the organization. If each small unit is functional, the larger unit will be a success [for] as Maulana Karenga says: "A house is so important because it is the smallest example of how the Nation works."
6. Brothers must be sensitive to the needs of Sisters. We must strive to perfect the workings of the household.
7. Brothers in leadership positions must make their households examples for others to learn from.
8. All Brothers should be actively involved with a Sister who seeks or has the potential for growth as related to our Doctrine.
9. We are not players or creepers but Blackman, therefore we should not seek to play or creep. Playing creates bad feelings and bad images.
10. We cannot misuse or abuse Brothers and Sisters outside of the Mashariki family structure. We believe as Brother Stokely said that "every Negro is a potential Blackman."

        Asante sana,
        The Brotherhood Code Committee

Appendix B

The East Collective, Family, and Supporters Responsibilities (Transcribed from the original document)

East Collective

Responsibilities of Collective to Organization

Highest level of dedication through participation in all areas of work requested. This collective is responsible for electing leadership and ratifying its policies when necessary. Members of this collective must be prepared:

A. To, if necessary, get involved in the organization's external activities (BUF, BCC, forums, holidays, memorials, concerts, rallies and other communities events).

B. To participate in the political educational workshops (study, examination, theory & practice, and must support Akiba Mkuu Bookstore, Imani Daycare, and Uhuru Sasa).

C. To be a member and do all shopping at the Uhuru Food Coop.

D. To be responsible for twenty-five *Black News* per issue.

E. To attend monthly familyhood, Karamu, and monthly collective meetings.

F. If outside employment must make an Ujamaa contribution (based on their need and salary).

G. To be on twenty-four-hour call.

Responsibilities of Organization to Collective

The organization is responsible for providing:

A. Cooperative buying.

B. Educational institutions for members and family.

C. Place to buy educational materials (bookstore).

D. Forums.

E. Cultural and political programs (educational and entertainment); 50 percent discount for nonworkers and a 75 percent discount for workers.

F. Child care center (day) (at Imani rates).

G. An official communication organ (*Black News*).

H. Counseling (family and personal).

I. Person to perform ceremonies (wedding, naming, etc.).

J. Funerals.

K. Self-development classes (martial arts, drama, dance, etc.).

L. Catering service (low-cost).

M. Typesetting, layout, and publishing services (low-cost).

N. Speakers Bureau (low-cost).

O. Agricultural training in the Cooperative Republic of Guyana.

P. Training in work areas.

Q. Collective retreats (twice yearly).

R. Group security.

S. Family collective given first choice on inside and outside positions.

T. Service Bureau (housing, loans, credit union, pension, emergency funding).

East Family

Responsibilities of Member to Organization

This body consists of all paid staff. Members of this body have not yet developed the level of participation necessary to be in the collective. In addition to full-time/part-time employment members of this body:

A. Must adhere to organizational standards and departmental policies

B. Must undergo orientation sessions

C. Must attend monthly familyhood [meetings]

D. Must be member of Uhuru Food Coop

E. Must be responsible for ten *Black News* per issue

F. Must be responsible for two tickets to three major fund-raisers of the organization/shule

G. Have the option to participate in political education

H. Must pay organizational taxes

Responsibilities of Organization to Member

The East organization was responsible for providing:
   A. Cooperative buying.
   B. Educational institutions.
   C. Place to buy educational material (bookstore).
   D. Forums.
   E. Cultural and political programs (educational/entertainment); 25 percent discount.
   F. Child care center (day) (at Imani rates).
   G. An official communication organ (Black News).
   H. Counseling services—low-cost; 25 percent discount.
   I. Catering services—low-cost; 25 percent discount.
   J. Typesetting, layout, publishing—low-cost; 25 percent discount.
   K. Training in work areas.
   L. Person to perform ceremonies—low-cost; 25 percent discount.

East Supporters

Responsibilities of Member to Organization

This body consist of brothers and sisters outside of The East collective and East family who are interested in supporting the goals and ideals of the organization through services and/or finances. Members of this body:
   A. Must be a member of Uhuru Food Cooperative.
   B. Must be responsible for two tickets or more to three major fund-raisers.
   C. Must be willing to support the organization in any way they can (i.e., flyers, materials, donations, etc.).
   D. Encouraged to service the organization for at least ten hours per month through: (a) home assignment; (b) departmental assignment; and (c) other.
   E. Must be responsible for at least seven *Black News* or more plus postage per issue.
   F. Must make $5.00 or more yearly contribution—Jan. to Dec.

Responsibilities of Organization to Member

The East organizational services are available:

A. Cooperative buying.

B. Educational institutions for member and family.

C. Place to buy educational material (bookstore) and forums.

D. Cultural and political programs (educational/entertainment); 5 percent discount.

E. Childcare center.

F. An official communication organ (*Black News*).

G. Counseling (family and personal); 5 percent discount.

H. Person to perform ceremonies; 5 percent discount.

I. Speaker Bureau, films; 5 percent discount.

J. Catering Service; 5 percent discount.

K. Typesetting, layout, and publishing services; 5 percent discount.

Appendix E

Uhuru Sasa Shule Protocol, Calendar, Curriculum, Daily Schedules, Praises, Pledges, and Songs (Edited by author)

Uhuru Sasa Shule Protocol

The protocol, particularly during the later years, adhered to at all times by headmaster/headmistress, teachers, students and staffs appear below. Most of the African terms employed derive from the Kiswahili language of East Africa.

Rules of Diplomatic Etiquette

    1. Identity: manners, morals, and code of African image through traditional reason.
    2. Direction: character-building through self-discipline.
    3. Purpose: to stress unity and strength through order.

March and Drill Commands (Usalamu)—Afrikan Drill (Tambura)

Ungulia: Attention
Pumzika: Parade rest
Nje: At ease
Kundini to songea: Left face
Kundini ya songea: Right face
Geuka songea: About face
Mbele songea: Forward march
Acha: Halt

Manners

Tafadhali: Please
Asante Sana: Thank you very much
Sikitu: You are welcome
Nisamehe: Excuse me
Baba: Father
Mama: Mother

    1. Protocol predicts well-thought-out actions as it relates to greetings, manners, praises, deeds, classroom, *kutano* (assembly), trips, and *choo* (bathroom).

    2. All teachers *(walimu)* are addressed as Mama (female) and Baba (male) because they are reflections of parents who are the students' first teachers.

    3. Standard procedure: *Angulia* (at attention) while standing, sitting, greeting someone, speaking, lining up, during drills, while singing, and marching.

    4. Personal: Be beautiful at all times in appearance and attitude. Body and clothing must be clean, neat, and modest—Sisters are not to wear pants (except in gym, etc.) and brothers are not to wear sneakers (except in gym).

    5. Decorum: Always to be polite, patient, and positive in speech and action.

    6. Names and titles: All *wanafunzi* (students) address each other with "brother" or "sister." For example, Brother Oba, Sister Ayo.

Uhuru Sasa Shule Calendar

The Uhuru Sasa Shule school year is divided into four terms of fall (September 27–December 30), winter (January 17–April 1), spring (April 18–June 25) and summer (July 11–September 2). The calendar is punctuated by several important days of observance. In November (Black Solidarity Day, the first Monday; Veterans Day, November 11), December (assassination of Fred Hampton, December 4), winter break (December 22 to January 4) and Kwanzaa (December 26 to January 1), January (Dr. Martin Luther King, Jr., birthday, January 15), February (assassination of Malcolm X, February 21; birthday of Frederick Douglass and Black History Month), March (Sharpville Massacre in South Africa; East's New [Sun] Year, March 21), April (assassination of Dr. Martin Luther King, Jr., and Bobby Hutton, April 3 and 6), spring break (April 13 to 24), May (Birthday of Malcolm X, May 19; African Liberation Day, last Saturday in May), August (Marcus Garvey's birthday, August 17).

Table E.1. Uhuru Sasa curriculum design

School	Level	Age
Imani Child Development Center	A	9 mos.–3 yrs.
Uhuru Sasa (primary)	B	3–4
Uhuru Sasa (primary)	C	4–6
Uhuru Sasa (elementary)	D	6–7
Uhuru Sasa (elementary)	E	8–9
Uhuru Sasa (elementary)	F	10–11
Uhuru Sasa (elementary)	G	12–13
Uhuru Sasa (secondary)	H	14
Uhuru Sasa (secondary)	I	15
Uhuru Sasa (secondary)	J	16
Uhuru Sasa (secondary)	K	17

Imani Child Development Curriculum: A Summation

Entering Imani–initiation ceremony: When a new child came into Imani (and at the beginning of September), all the *watoto* (children) would sing the "Name Song" and kiss them on both cheeks.

Kuzaliwa (birthdays): There were monthly *kuzaliwa* celebrations and all *watoto* with birthdays in the same month would have their birthday celebrated on one chosen day.

Advancement to oldest group ceremony: Each student brought in two pieces of fruit. The *mwalimu* (teacher) then lit the seven candles associated with Kwanzaa, while students would sing an *Nguzo Saba* song and "Praise the Red, the Black, and the Green," after placing the fruits in a special basket. Afterward, the pledge would be said along with inspirational words from the *mwalimu*. The *mwalimu* would then take the *watoto* and the basket of fruits into another section of the room where the older *watoto* were waiting. The basket of fruits would be placed on the floor with everyone forming a circle around it. The older *watoto* sang and danced with songs of "Welcome My Brothers and Sisters," while the younger *watoto* passed out the fruits.

Imani graduation ceremony (held in June for 3-year-olds): After preparations, the *watoto* made the invitations for the parents who would be invited, the younger *watoto* made gifts for the graduates and the graduates made something to leave in the Imani Child Development Center. With the ceremony itself, students would march and drill, carrying empty baskets, and then place the baskets in the center of the room. Thereafter, the pledge and songs would be recited, with the *watoto* seated in a circle. Each graduate would be called upon to share words of inspiration, followed by a presentation of gifts to Imani, while the graduates sang, "Asante to Imani." The Imani *watoto* would place their gifts in the baskets and sing "We Have Done Black Things Today." Afterward, the graduates would make a "pilgrimage" down the hall to visit their new classroom along with their parents. While the *watoto* and their parents were on their visit, food was being set up, awaiting their return. The feast would commence as the *watoto* gave the graduates their gifts.

The primary categories for activities performed at Imani were motor skills; verbal communication; African heritage; social interaction (social value exchange—*Nguzo Saba*); nutrition; story time; and observational skills. According to the Imani staff, this curriculum guide stemmed from African heritage. For example, the motor skills, communication, social practice (i.e., *Nguzo Saba*), story time and role playing, nutrition, and verbal communication would be based on a "hero" that week. As such, if the studies were centered on Hannibal, elephants would be involved as identifiers. For Harriet Tubman, it would be trees with people hiding behind them with rifles; for George Washington Carver, it would be peanuts; and for Malcolm X, it would be glasses. Therefore, a lesson plan centered on Marcus Garvey involved a discussion about Marcus Garvey's hat, its shapes, the singing of a song named after him, and discussions about the Umoja, Kujichagulia, and Ujima needed to build a ship. In addition, students would create a large red, black, and green flag for the child development center.

Table E.2. Uhuru Sasa Shule curricular domains

Language arts	Reading comprehension; spelling; grammar; penmanship; creative writing; research skills; library skills; speech; debating
Social studies	African history; world history; U.S. history; African-American history; Third-World history & culture; economics; Kiswahili; current events
Math	Arithmetic; computation; computer math; problem solving; language of math; symbols; math projects; business math; geometry; algebra; trigonometry
Science	Air, gas, & water; weather; biology; anatomy; earth science; chemistry; applied science; machines; animal life; plant life
Work body development	Self-reliance; gymnastics; physical fitness; completion of task; manual dexterity; march & drill; self-defense; weaponry; work project
Creativity (Kuumba)	Drawing; painting; arts & crafts; singing; sewing; music; photography; acting & recitation
Family affairs	Hygiene, home economics, sex education; male & female roles

Daily Schedules

Imani Child Development Center (ages 9 months to 3 years old)

7:30–9:00 A.M.	Arrival and creative playtime.
9:00–9:45 A.M.	Breakfast.
9:45–10:15 A.M.	Clean up and potty, *choo* (bathroom) diapers.
10:15–11:15 A.M.	Planned learning activities (beginning with pledge and song).
11:15–11:30 A.M.	Preparation for nap and potty.
11:30–1:30 P.M.	Naps.
1:30–2:45 P.M.	*Sifa* (praises/prayers), lunch and clean up.
2:45–3:00 P.M.	Potty.
3:00–4:00 P.M.	Planned learning activities.
4:00–4:30 P.M.	Pledge, song, preparation for home.
4:30–6:15 P.M.	Tutoring for older *watoto* (children) and creative playtime for others. Fees are charged for services after 6:15 P.M.

Primary School (ages 3 to 7 years old)[1]

8:30–9:30 A.M.	Arrival of *wanafunzi* (students) and creative playtime: a correct and positive start determines the course of the school day, making the morning activities of utmost importance. Calisthenics: a healthy body is as important as a developed mind. The *wanafunzi* do exercises that are invigorating and that are challenging.
	Songs: there are a variety of Black songs that the *wanafunzi* sing in the morning that bring a good feeling to the air and teach political or cultural lessons as well.
9:30–10:00 A.M.	Breakfast: consists of hot cereal or muffins, juice or fruit.
10:00–10:15 A.M.	Opening Exercises (e.g., pledge, song): during these exercises the *wanafunzi* should receive their inspiration and purpose for the day. Everything is done in Umoja (unity). *Wanafunzi* are called on to say something inspirational, something that will perpetrate in their mind's alliance with Black people and our struggle for freedom. The *wanafunzi* all pull together by saying seven *harambees*. *Harambee* means, "let's all pull together." In Umoja, a pledge of dedication is made to the Liberation Flag, followed by the singing of "Praise the Red, the Black, and the Green," which reinforces faith in Blackness.
10:15–11:00 A.M.	Political Education, Current Events: academic learning reinforced by political awareness makes for well-rounded and more complete brothers and sisters. Our *wanafunzi* are provided with a historical base from an African perspective. They receive in their education an understanding of what the [role of the] African [in America] has been and what our role should be in terms of ending our oppression and building for ourselves. *Wanafunzi* are kept abreast of political events that affect Black people, which adds to their understanding of the past, present, and future of African people everywhere.
11:00–12:00 noon	Communication Skills: this time is used to strengthen communication skills, which includes reading, writing, phonetics, speaking and listening (following instructions). The importance of these skills is also given attention at preschool level.

12:00–12:45 P.M.	Lunch: mealtime is very important. Inspirational words and *harambees* are said again to point out to the *wanafunzi* that eating is serious business. The meal itself is void of meat, milk, and excessive sweets. This minimizes the chances of *wanafunzi* turning up sick and helps to keep them alert and bright. The meals do include fresh fruits and vegetables, fruit juices, and other items that vary from day to day (such as fresh salad, whole wheat bread sandwiches, soup, etc.). *Sifa* (praises/prayers) are said before each meal.
12:45–1:00 P.M.	Post-lunch Activity: this time period gives the *wanafunzi* the opportunity to relate to each other in a more relaxed atmosphere and get to know each other while their food gets a chance to digest properly. It also helps develop the concepts of self-help and Ujima (collective work and responsibility) as the *wanafunzi* deal with post lunch and classroom chores.
1:00–2:00 P.M.	Nap and Rest Time: keeping the body in good shape requires *rest* as well as activity. During rest period the *wanafunzi* take a break in their full day to rest and are properly refreshed and ready to deal with the rest of the day's activities when the rest period is over.
2:00–3:00 P.M.	Mathematics—Algebricks: the importance of mathematics is also realized at Uhuru Sasa.[2] The *wanafunzi* are taught mathematics by the use of algebricks, which enables our young brothers and sisters to deal with algebraic concepts that are dealt with (or mis-dealt with) in the enemy school system at the junior high school level. Algebricks substitute lengths and colors for numbers, enabling the brothers and sisters to see and touch mathematics.
3:00–4:00 P.M.	Physical Activities, Arts and Crafts, Black Story Hour: self-defense and other activities to strengthen the body are learned and practiced. Arts and crafts include drawing, pottery, and other innovative ideas that are relevant and that bring out the Kuumba (creativity) of the *wanafunzi* and *mwalimu* (teacher). African tales and other Black stories are read at this final hour of the *shule* [school] day.
4:00–4:15 P.M.	Closing Exercises: a closing pledge is made to the Liberation Flag and the song "We Have Done Black Things Today" is

	sung. These exercises help give the [*wanafunzi*] the feeling that their day had a purpose, that being Black is a full time job and what they learn should be practiced at home.
4:15–5:45 P.M.	*wanafunzi* Depart: During this time while the *wanafunzi* are waiting to be picked up, classrooms are cleaned up and made ready for the next day.

Elementary School (ages 8–14)[3]

8:30–9:00 A.M.	Arrival, breakfast, morning exercises.
9:00–10:00 A.M.	Physical Education: self-defense, drill, marching, first aid, and hygiene.
10:00–11:00 A.M.	Communications: grammar, reading, spelling, penmanship, and vocabulary.
11:00–12:00	Nation-building skills: history, current events, civics, geography, and political education.
12:00–1:00 P.M.	Lunch.
1:00–2:00 P.M.	Music, art, reading, library hour, drama, and Kiswahili.
2:00–3:00 P.M.	Math.
3:00–4:00 P.M.	Science; departure (4:00 P.M.)

Uhuru Sasa Secondary School Program (ages 14–18)[4]

Academic
First Session (September 27 to December 31): (a) Math (rods); (b) Biology; (c) Communications (reading and listening); (d) African History (pre-1500 A.D.); and (e) Third-World Thought (study of relevant ideologies).
Second Session (January 17 to April 1): (a) Math (practical applications); (b) Communications (writing and talking); (c) Caribbean History; (d) Chemistry; and (e) African Thought (study of present-day Africans).
Third Session (April 18 to June 25): (a) Math (business and industrial); (b) Physics; (c) Communications (newspaper and periodical analysis); (d) History of Africans in North America; and (e) New African Thought (ideologies of the future).

Recreational
    1. Personal (use of special creative talents) and Group: (a) Parties (special theme); (b) Self-defense; and (c) Team sports (e.g., basketball, track).

Social

1. Propagandizing in the Community: (a) Making parties and dances (with ideas) and (b) Sponsoring functions (that include the broader community).

2. Trips: Short- and long-distant trips.

3. Internal (among themselves): Applying principles of African socialism.

Vocational

1. Participation in the Overall Functioning of The East: (a) Uhuru Sasa School (teacher training); (b) Black News; (c) [East] Kitchen; (d) Tamu Sweet-East; and (e) Kununuana.

2. Assignment to specific business people (for purpose of learning trade).

Evening School of Knowledge: A 1979 Schedule and Course Description[5]

Monday: nutrition, photography, patrol (7:00 P.M.), and first aid (8:00 P.M.).

Nutrition: study of foods and their value to the body.

Photography: elementary photography, basic camera usage and care.

First aid: basic preventive techniques and life saving techniques.

Tuesday: yoga (7:00 P.M.)

Yoga for beginners and intermediates. Postures, breathing techniques, and elementary mediation techniques.

Wednesday: patrol and political education (7:00 P.M.).

Political education: history with political analysis.

Thursday: martial arts (7:00 P.M.).

Martial arts: self-defense techniques for beginners and intermediates.

Friday: speech, poetry and writers, gun safety, radio communications, and arts and crafts (7:00 P.M.); movement and drama (8:00 P.M.).

Speech: development of vocal powers, projection, etc.

Poetry and writers workshop: basic writing techniques to encourage the expression of your creativity through writing.

Gun safety: safe and proper handling, cleaning, and storing of guns.

Radio communications: introduction to the technology of radio communications.

Arts and crafts: learn the creative use of common ordinary items to create beautiful and useful articles.

Movement: body movement and exercises to develop grace and mobility and better control of our physical bodies.

Drama: acting techniques and skills geared to bring out the ability that is innate in all of us.

Saturday: Kiswahili and mind and thought power (1:00 P.M.); children's theater (from 1:00–3:00 P.M.).

Kiswahili: learn elementary conversational Kiswahili, the African language first adopted for use by Black people in America.

Mind and thought power for daily living: Discover the power of the mind and learn how to develop your own mind power and put it to practical use to improve your life.

Children's theater: develop the creative, imaginative spontaneity of children for use in meaningful daily life activities or on stage.

Uhuru Sasa Shule Praises, Pledges, and Songs

Sifa (praises/prayers)

Sifa zote kwa Mumba (all praises due to the Creator)
Sifa zote kwa weusi jamaa (all praises due to the Black family)
Sifa zote kwa Imani watoto (all praises due to Imani children)
Asante sana (thank you very much)

Uhuru Sasa Pledge

For the fruition of Black power, for the triumph of Black nationhood, I pledge to my Afrikan Nation, and to the building of a better people, and a better world, my total devotion, my total resources, and the total power of my mortal life.

We are the first and last, the alpha and the omega
We pledge to THINK BLACK, SPEAK BLACK
BUY BLACK, PRAY BLACK
LOVE BLACK, LIVE BLACK AND BE BLACK
Because we are Black.
We will do Black things today
To assure us of a Black tomorrow.

Praise the Red, the Black, and the Green

Praise the red, the black, and the green,
Brothers and sisters are being redeemed.
Open up your eyes and see, we're on our way to being free.
Because red is for the blood that we shed,
Black is for the race, that's us, green is for the land uh huh . . .
So the Black man can take his rightful place.
Praise the red, the black, and the green,
brothers and sisters are being redeemed.
Open up your eyes and see, we're on our way to being free.

We Have Done Black Things Today

We have done Black things today and
we will do Black things again tomorrow.
We have done Black things today and
we will do Black things again tomorrow.
Will you? Yes I will. Will you? Yes I will. Will youuuuuuu?
One more time (repeat) . . .
Asante sana (thank you very much).

Uhuru Sasa Song

I see that look of surprise in your eyes . . . Yeah, yeah
I know you wonder . . . Yeah, yeah
From where that thunder
You see us now we're Black and we're proud
I said Uhuru Sasa . . . Freedom now, Freedom Now!

Appendix F
Programmatic Content of the International African Arts Festival

Mission Statement

The International African Arts Festival is recognized as a national annual event that attracts participants and visitors from across the country and around the world. The mission of the International African Arts Festival is to advance the ideologies of cultural preservation and pride through the perpetuation of a medium of exposure and expression in the African descended community. In addition, the purpose of the festival "is to preserve and perpetuate African cultural traditions and to unify, renew, and empower the brothers and sisters who attend. The festival provides visitors the opportunity to give thanks, to contribute to their community's economic development and to encourage their children to carry on the quest for knowledge of self." As such, the primary driving force behind the International African Arts Festival is family—immediate, extended, community, and global. Every aspect of the festival seeks to strengthen the family spirit through shared experiences that are wholesome and uplifting.[1]

The International African Arts Festival uniquely provides a means for African descendants to fuse their diverse cultural and social backgrounds. Through personal interface and exchange of goods and artifacts in the African Marketplace, the International African Arts Festival promotes economic support and self-reliance for community-based businesses and merchants. In fact, the five-day festival employs more than three hundred people, including the famous African Marketplace that holds "over 300 merchants and small business people who utilize [the] event as an opportunity to introduce new products, strengthen business ties and services while developing marketing and networking strategies."[2] The African Marketplace is segmented by way of African nations, such as Nigeria, Uganda, Kenya, Ghana, Mali, and Zimbabwe.

Talent Search

The International African Arts Festival's Talent Search began in 1985 as a platform for aspiring performers. It features, annually, singers, dancers, comedians, actors, musicians, rappers, marching bands, poets, and steppers. The goal of the Talent Search, as articulated by the festival organizers, "is to form a long term supportive relationship with aspiring artists." The ensuing relationship is attempted to be further nurtured through a process in which the first-place winners are asked to return the following year and to pass the kente cloth crown, a prize given to first-place winners, on to the new winner(s). The following year they return as paid performers.[3] This exciting segment of the International African Arts Festival was devised to showcase the untapped reservoir of talent that exists among youth, whether single acts or groups, between the ages of twelve and twenty-one, in the African descended community through exposure to an appreciative audience. It is also a vehicle through which we may include and involve the youth of our community in a positive and uplifting community activity designed to emphasize our likenesses rather than our differences. The festival's commitment to showcase both professional and amateur talent in a cultural setting, allows the audience and the performers to be reunited through a common bond of shared experiences. Auditions for the Talent Search are held, annually, from mid-May through early June and cover all five boroughs of New York City.

Scholarship Program

Convinced that self-reliance is the key to self-improvement, the International African Arts Festival seeks to motivate, inspire, and assist the youth of the African descended community through sponsorship of a scholarship program designed to encourage knowledge and achievement. This program provides a unique opportunity for youth who, because of economic restrictions, would otherwise be limited in their ability to pursue excellence in a chosen field of endeavor. The Scholarship Awards are only for college-bound high school seniors.

Ankh Award

The International African Arts Festival further complements its mission by paying tribute to those whose lives in the African descended community exemplify the standards and tradition of African cultural heritage through presentation of the Ankh Award. This award is presented each year to the person or persons from the African descended community whose outstanding contributions perpetuate African culture and heritage through dedicated service and teachings.[4] The Ankh Award, which represents a symbol of life and lifetime achievement, is the highest honor the International African Arts Festival can bestow.

Children's Program

The Children's Program of the International African Arts Festival exists to enhance self-awareness, self-identity, and self-fulfillment through exposure to the richness of culture as its exists in the African descended community. This program introduces children of African descent to the music, dance, art, and diversity of their African heritage in addition to promoting a sense of tradition in the African descended child. For children, the festival activities include the petting zoo, games, puppeteers, dance and art workshops, and storytelling hours by African "griots" who provide a sense of tradition and continuity for the children. In African culture, festivals are a celebration of life, growth, learning, and knowledge. It is a time when everyone comes together to share their joys, sorrows, and other experiences. The International African Arts Festival provides an opportunity for the children of the African descended community to become active participants in this tradition rather than onlookers. It also serves as a source of pride and enrichment for children within a culturally diverse community. Children who participate in the International African Arts Festival socialize, interact, network, and develop long-lasting supportive friendships with other children who are developing African consciousness.

The Evening Program

The International African Arts Festival's Evening Program is often called a "family reunion" because it is where people from all segments of the community come together to enjoy the richness and diversity of their culture as people who share a common heritage. It is through this program that the International African Arts Festival fulfills its primary mission of advancing the ideologies of cultural preservation and pride. Featuring a wide variety of family entertainment including some of the world's most renowned performing artists, the International African Arts Festival takes pride in promoting family unity through the presentation of entertainment that showcases the architects and interpreters of the many art forms inherent within the African descended community. In the best tradition of the African experience, this entertainment is appropriate for all members of the family and is presented in a warm, relaxed, safe environment. Throughout the history of the festival, there has never been an incidence of violence during this annual celebration. In fact, the "Festival is known for its cleanliness and safety because people conduct themselves as they would during any family event. This communal attitude, combined with twenty-four-hour maintenance and security staffs, handicap accessibility, and signed translation of many events, ensures a high level of enjoyment for all visitors." In addition to all the programming that occurs on festival grounds, the festival's Media Square, which began in 1995, "provides exposure for print and broadcast media that target African, African American and Carribean audiences."[5] The International African Arts Festival's Evening Program works in conjunction with all other festival events to provide constructive activity in a community where the average resident cannot afford to travel or attend the many high-priced activities held throughout the city during that time of year. The festival has been held in the Commodore Barry Park in downtown Brooklyn since 2004.

Notes

Introduction

1. *African Street Festival Souvenir Journal* (Brooklyn, N.Y.: The East, 1978), 1.

2. Mwalimu J. Shujaa, "Education and Schooling: You Can Have One without the Other," in *Too Much Schooling, Too Little Education: A Paradox of Black Life in White Societies*, ed. Mwalimu Shujaa (Trenton, N.J.: Africa World Press, 1994), 14–15.

3. For a discussion on the "bio-genetic rope," see K. K. B. Fu-Kiau's *Self-Healing Power and Therapy* (New York: Vantage Press, 1993), 78.

4. C. J. Munford quoted in James Turner, "Black Nationalism: The Inevitable Response," *Black World* 20, no. 3 (1971): 7. See Sterling Stuckey's *Slave Culture: Nationalist Theory and the Foundations of Black America* (New York: Oxford Univ. Press, 1987). He has a very insightful discussion on the cohesiveness of enslaved African identities, values, and pan-African concerns.

5. Kwame A. Akoto, *Nationbuilding: Theory and Practice in Afrikan-Centered Education* (Washington, D.C.: Pan-Afrikan World Institute, 1992), 69. Nationhood, ultimately, is not solely or most importantly a matter of social definition. See John N. Paden, "African Concepts of Nationhood," in *The African Experience*, vol. 1, eds. John N. Paden and Edward W. Soja (Evanston, Ill.: Northwestern Univ. Press, 1970), 404.

6. See John T. McCartney, *Black Power Ideologies: An Essay in African-American Political Thought* (Philadelphia: Temple Univ. Press, 1992); William L. Van Deburg, *New Day in Babylon: The Black Power Movement and American Culture, 1965–1975* (Chicago: Univ. of Chicago Press, 1992); and Peniel E. Joseph, ed., *The Black Power Movement: Rethinking the Civil Rights–Black Power Movement* (New York: Routledge, 2006).

7. See Akoto, *Nationbuilding*.

8. Ibid., vi; Harold Cruse, *The Crisis of the Negro Intellectual* (New York: Quill, 1984 [1967]), 421.

1. Ujima: Context and Community Control

1. Carol Camp Yeakey, "The Public School Monopoly: Confronting Major National Policy Issues," in *Visible Now: Blacks in Private Schools*, ed. Diana T. Slaughter and Deborah J. Johnson (Westport, Conn.: Greenwood Press, 1988), 297.

2. See Harold Connolly, "Blacks in Brooklyn from 1900 to 1960" (Ph.D. diss., New York Univ., 1973); Robert J. Swan, "Did Brooklyn (N.Y.) Blacks Have Unusual Control over Their Schools? Period I: 1815–1845," *Afro-Americans in New York Life and History* 7, no. 2 (1983): 25; Carleton Mabee, "Brooklyn's Black Public Schools: Why Did Blacks Have Unusual Control over Them?" *The Journal of Long Island History* 11, no. 2 (1975): 23.

3. Connolly, "Blacks in Brooklyn," 16.

4. Swan, "Did Brooklyn," 28.

5. Dominic Nwasike, "Weeksville: The Story of a Black Community," *Negro History Bulletin* 43, no. 3 (1980): 66.

6. Ibid., 67.

7. Swan, "Did Brooklyn," 35, 67.

8. Connolly, "Blacks in Brooklyn," 68, 52, 21.

9. Carleton Mabee, *Black Education in New York State: From Colonial to Modern Times* (Syracuse, N.Y.: Syracuse Univ. Press, 1979), 3, 6.

10. Ibid., 21.

11. Lance McCready, "Community Control of Schools," in *Encyclopedia of African-American Education*, eds. Faustine C. Jones-Wilson et al. (Westport, Conn.: Greenwood Press, 1996), 110.

12. Ibid.; Mabee, "Black Public Schools," 29.

13. Mabee, *Black Education*, 66–67.

14. Ibid., 51–52; Mabee, "Black Public Schools," 25 (emphasis added).

15. Swan, "Did Brooklyn," 33.

16. Ibid., 32, 26, 27.

17. Mabee, *Black Education*, 101. Swan notes, "The black community preferred teachers of their own race to set an example for the children.... During the period of black control, blacks only employed blacks." See Swan, "Did Brooklyn," 39.

18. Mabee, "Black Public Schools," 31.

19. Mabee, *Black Education*, 239, 261, 283.

20. Connolly, "Blacks in Brooklyn," 249–50.

21. For a perspective on the history of Brownsville, see Alter F. Landesman, *Brownsville: The Birth, Development and Passing of a Jewish Community in New York* (New York: Bloch Publishing Company, 1969).

22. Komozi Woodard, *A Nation Within a Nation: Amiri Baraka (LeRoi Jones) & Black Power Politics* (Chapel Hill: The Univ. of North Carolina Press, 1999), 30.

23. Connolly, "Blacks in Brooklyn," 271, 345.

24. James J. Doughty, "A Historical Analysis of Black Education, Focusing on the Contemporary Independent Black School Movement" (Ph.D. diss., The Ohio State Univ., 1973), 84.

25. *Black Power Conference Reports* (New York: Afram Associates, 1970), 15.

26. Doughty, "Historical Analysis," 86.

27. Ibid., 85; Naomi Levine, *Ocean Hill–Brownsville: Schools in Crisis, a Case History* (New York: Popular Library, 1969), 12–13.

28. Doughty, "Historical Analysis," 86; *Black Power Conference Reports*, 16.

29. Clayborne Carson et al., eds., *The Eyes on the Prize Civil Rights Reader* (New York: Penguin Books, 1991), 336; James E. Blackwell, *The Black Community: Diversity and Unity* (New York: Harper and Row Publishers, 1975), 123; Levine, *Ocean Hill–Brownsville*, 12–13.

30. Jitu K. Weusi, personal communication, 1998.

31. Louis Kushnick, "Race, Class and Power: The New York Decentralization Controversy," in *Black Communities and Urban Development in America 1720–1990*, ed. Kenneth L. Kusmer (New York: Garland Publishing, 1991), 7:287–88.

32. Dan A. Lewis and Kathryn Nakagawa, *Race and Educational Reform in the American Metropolis: A Study of School Decentralization* (New York: SUNY Press, 1995), 41.

33. Ibid., 41–42.

34. Levine, *Ocean Hill–Brownsville*, 13.

35. Martin Mayer, "The Full and Sometimes Very Surprising Story of Ocean Hill, the Teachers' Union and the Teacher Strikes of 1968," in *Black Protest in the Sixties*, eds. August Meier, John Bracey, Jr., and Elliott Rudwick (New York: Markus Wiener, 1991), 170–72.

36. Levine, *Ocean Hill–Brownsville*, 16, 17.

37. Kushnick, "Race, Class and Power," 289.

38. Dora Pantell and Edwin Greenidge, *If Not Now, When? The Many Meanings of Black Power* (New York: Dell Publishing, 1969), 97.

39. The Mayor's Advisory Panel on Decentralization plan to decentralize the schools in New York City recommended the creation of thirty to sixty autonomous local school boards. Each was to have power over budget, curriculum, and personnel, and to be composed of six elected parent representatives and five representatives appointed by the mayor from a list submitted by community groups. The plan also suggested that state licensing qualifications suffice for teachers and supervisors in the districts. The Bundy Plan received a myriad of heated reactions: Alfred A. Giardino, president of the board of education and a dissenting member of the Bundy panel, called the plan too much too soon; the CSA condemned it; and the UFT attacked it and called it a "balkanization" of the schools.

40. Maurice R. Berube and Marilyn Gittill, eds., *Confrontation at Ocean Hill–Brownsville: The New York School Strike of 1968* (New York: Praeger Publishers, 1969), 14.

41. Jitu K. Weusi, interview, July 25, 1998.

42. Robert J. Braun, *Teachers and Power: The Story of the American Federation of Teachers* (New York: Simon and Schuster, 1972), 239, 15.

43. Mayer, "Surprising Story of Ocean Hill," 178.

44. Kushnick, "Race, Class and Power," 287.

45. Braun, *Teachers and Power*, 240.

46. Ibid., 242, 241.

47. Carson, *Eyes on the Prize*, 100.
48. Kushnick, "Race, Class and Power," 291.
49. Ibid., 294.
50. Braun, *Teachers and Power*, 216–17.
51. Rhody McCoy, "Why Have an Ocean Hill–Brownsville," in *What Black Educators are Saying*, ed. Nathan Wright (New York: Hawthorn Books, 1970), 255.
52. Braun, *Teachers and Power*, 68.
53. Albert Vann, "The Agency Shop," in *What Black Educators are Saying*, 234.
54. J. K. Weusi, personal communication, 1998.
55. Mwalimu J. Shujaa and Hannibal T. Afrik, "School Desegregation, the Politics of Culture, and the Council of Independent Black Institutions," in *Beyond Desegregation: The Politics of Quality in African American Schooling*, ed. Mwalimu Shujaa (Thousand Oaks, Calif.: Corwin Press, 1997), 254.
56. Leslie Campbell [Jitu K. Weusi], "The Difference," in *What Black Educators are Saying*, 26. "Negro" is meant to be belittling.
57. Braun, *Teachers and Power*, 14–15 (emphasis added).
58. Sara Slack, "Franklin Kids Were Mad at Everybody," *The New York Amsterdam News*, Oct. 5, 1968, 1.
59. Braun, *Teachers and Power*, 11.
60. James Turner, "The Sociology of Black Nationalism," *The Black Scholar* 1, no. 2 (1969): 26.
61. Asa G. Hilliard III, *The Maroons Within Us* (Baltimore, Md.: Black Classic Press, 1995), 8.
62. K. Kia B. Fu-Kiau and A. M. Lukondo-Wamba, *Kindezi: The Kôngo Art of Babysitting* (New York: Vantage Press, 1988), 40.
63. The use of the term "African" and its meaning in a global context is best described by Kwame Nkrumah in his *Class Struggle in Africa* (1970): "All peoples of African descent, whether they live in North America or South America, the Caribbean, or in any other part of the world are Africans and belong to the African nation" (87).
64. Mwalimu J. Shujaa, "Introduction to Part I," in *Too Much Schooling*, 9–10.
65. Charles H. Wesley, *Prince Hall: Life and Legacy* (Washington, D.C.: The United Supreme Council Southern Jurisdiction, Prince Hall Affiliation, 1977), 26–27.
66. James Anderson, *The Education of Blacks in the South, 1860–1935* (Chapel Hill, N.C.: The Univ. of North Carolina Press, 1988), 12.
67. Ibid., 3–4.
68. Evelyn Brooks Higginbotham, *Righteous Discontent: The Women's Movement in the Black Baptist Church, 1880–1920* (Cambridge, Mass.: Harvard Univ. Press, 1993), 54.
69. Shujaa and Afrik, "School Desegregation," 260.
70. Ibid., 266, 260.

71. Shujaa, "Education and Schooling," 33.

72. Mwalimu J. Shujaa, "Afrocentric Transformation and Parental Choice in African American Independent Schools," *Journal of Negro Education* 61, no. 2 (1992): 157. Also see Joan D. Ratteray, "Independent Neighborhood Schools: A Framework for the Education of African Americans," ibid., 141–42.

73. Shujaa, "Introduction to Part I," 22.

74. Tunde Adeleke, *UnAfrican Americans: Nineteenth Century Black Nationalism and the Civilizing Mission* (Lexington: The Univ. Press of Kentucky, 1998), 150.

75. Ibid., 15.

76. Council of Independent Black Institutions [CIBI], *Members' Handbook* (Buffalo, N.Y.: CIBI, 1998), 10, 15.

77. Leslie Campbell [Jitu K. Weusi], "The Black Teacher and Black Power," in *What Black Educators are Saying*, 23–24.

78. Kofi Lomotey, interview, June 16, 1998.

2. Nia: The Birth of The East Organization

1. The spelling of *Afrikan* with a "k" derives from the Kiswahili language.

2. J. K. Weusi, interview, July 25, 1998.

3. Woodard, *A Nation Within a Nation*, 7.

4. Imani Publications, "The East: A Model of Nationhood," *Imani* 5, no. 2 (1971): 30.

5. J. K. Weusi, interview, July 25, 1998. Jitu admits that throughout the constant harassment and demonizing portrayals, it was the youth that bolstered and carried him through this period. Most of his peers, including some who were very close to him, kept a healthy distance.

6. Jumibia Nyahuma, interview, July 26, 1998.

7. J. K. Weusi, interview, July 25, 1998.

8. Nyahuma, interview; The East Program and Curriculum of Uhuru Sasa Shule (Brooklyn, N.Y.: The East, 1971), 5.

9. Imani Publications, "The East," 30.

10. J. K. Weusi, interview, July 25, 1998; *Black News* 1, no. 21 (1970): 10.

11. *Black News* 1, no. 21 (1970): 11.

12. Imani Publications, "The East," 35.

13. Monica Surfaro, "The East, A Black Culture and Education Center, Brings Bit of Africa to Brooklyn," *New York Times*, Aug. 17, 1977, 78.

14. Jitu K. Weusi, interview, Aug. 1, 1998.

15. Martha Bright, interview, June 12, 1998.

16. J. K. Weusi, interview, Aug. 1, 1998.

17. Ibid.

18. Adeyemi Al-Muqaddim, "A Time to Build Again," *Black News* 3, no. 14 (1976): 13.

19. Jitu K. Weusi, "Return to the Soil: Cooperative," *Black News* 3, no. 3 (1975): 11. For more details on the plans for the cooperative farm in Guyana, sponsored by Uhuru Sasa and Al-Karim Schools, see pages 11–13.

20. Ibid., 11, 12.

21. J. K. Weusi, interview, Aug. 1, 1998.

22. "Special Guyana Section," *Black News* 3, no. 20 (1977): 9.

23. J. K. Weusi, interview, Aug. 1, 1998.

24. The East Program and Curriculum of Uhuru Sasa Shule, 12.

25. Jitu K. Weusi, *A Message from a Black Teacher* (Brooklyn, N.Y.: East Publications, 1973), 11.

26. "Around the Far East," *Black News* 1, no. 27 (1971): 13.

27. Bright, interview; John Watusi Branch, interview, Aug. 18, 1998; J. K. Weusi, interview, July 25, 1998.

28. "Kasisi Yusef Iman: The Pictorial Biography of a Great Renaissance Man" (unpublished manuscript courtesy of the Khadijah and Lumumba Bandele Papers), 59.

29. Big Black, "Around Our Way," *Black News* 1, no. 41 (1972): 15

30. Jitu K. Weusi, "Around Our Way," *Black News* 2, no. 17 (1974): 14.

31. Woodard, *A Nation Within a Nation*, 109; Amiri Baraka, *The Autobiography of LeRoi Jones* (New York: Freundlich Book, 1984), 274.

32. Woodard, *A Nation Within a Nation*, 120.

33. See Madeleine Coleman, *Black Children Just Keep on Growing* (Washington, D.C.: Black Child Development Institute, 1977), 47, for a chart on Baraka's structure of CFUN. CFUN's structure derived from Maulana Karenga's US Organization.

34. Maulana Ron Karenga, *Kawaida Theory: An Introductory Outline* (Inglewood, Calif.: Kawaida Publications, 1980), 15.

35. Scot Ngozi Brown, "US and the Origins of Simba Wachanga: An Interview with Wesley Kabaila," *Umoja Sasa* 8, no. 2 (1996): 15. *Umoja Sasa* is a student publication published through Ujamaa Residential College, Cornell Univ.. For a detailed study of the US Organization, see Scot Brown's *Fighting for US: Maulana Karenga, the US Organization, and Black Cultural Nationalism* (New York: New York Univ. Press, 2003).

36. Clyde Halisi, *Kitabu: Beginning Concepts in Kawaida* (Los Angeles: US Organization, 1973), 4.

37. "An Interview with Dr. M. R. Karenga, Creator of Kwanzaa," *Black News* 4, no. 23 (1982): 22, 7.

38. Brown, "Simba Wachanga," 14.

39. "Interview with Karenga," 7.

40. Ibid., 13.

41. Baraka, *Autobiography*, 255, 226.

42. Ibid., 166; Amiri Baraka, *The Autobiography of LeRoi Jones*, rev. ed. (Chicago: Lawrence Hill, 1997), 404.

43. Baraka, *Autobiography*, rev. ed., 292.

44. Brown, "Simba Wachanga," 24.

45. Halisi, *Kitabu*, 8, 20.

46. "Interview with Karenga," 21.

47. Recall that the prototypical response by an advocate was: "If I have said anything of beauty, or anything of value, all praise is due to Maulana . . . [or Imamu as result of Baraka's revision] and only the mistakes have been mine."

48. J. K. Weusi, interview, July 25, 1998.

49. Woodard, *A Nation Within a Nation*, 168–69, 185, 220.

50. Baraka, *Autobiography*, rev. ed., 290.

51. "Preparation for Our Meeting on Sunday," East memorandum, Dec. 9, 1973.

52. Baraka, *Autobiography*, rev. ed., 306; Joseph F. Sullivan, "Baraka Drops 'Racism' For Socialism of Marx," *New York Times*, Dec. 27, 1974, 1; Amiri Baraka, "Individualism Brings Two Resignations from the Congress of African People," *Unity and Struggle* (1975): 7, 8. For one of the most divisive reports that came with Baraka's defection from the nationalist ranks with his embracing of Marxist, Leninist, and Maoist theories, see Charlayne Hunter's "Black Intellectuals Divided Over Ideological Direction," *New York Times*, Apr. 29, 1975, 1, 57.

53. Baraka, *Autobiography*, rev. ed., 306; see Amiri Baraka's "Kawaida: National Liberation and Socialism" (n.d., n.p.). As a result of feeling betrayed by African-descended elected officials, such as Kenneth Gibson of Newark, and "experiencing a profound crisis in faith, Imamu Baraka and the Congress of African People began to consider the theories of socialism more seriously, and at the end of the process they embraced Marxism." See Woodard, *A Nation Within a Nation*, 224.

54. "New York State Black Assembly Communication Network," Feb. 24, 1975 (press release courtesy of Preston Wilcox and the Afram Archives). This charge was only one of five serious charges brought against Amiri Baraka and CAP.

55. J. K. Weusi, interview, July 25, 1998.

56. Job Mashariki, interview, Aug. 16, 1998; Aminisha Black, interview, Aug. 12, 1998.

57. *Mashariki* means "East" in Kiswahili, that is, a compass point. The term was adopted as the organization's name.

58. Minutes of Balozi Wazee meeting, Sept. 26, 1972 (courtesy of the Salik Mwando Papers). The Super Simbas were also generically referred to as a "youth group" without gender specificity.

59. Minutes of Balozi Wazee meeting, Nov. 28, 1971 (courtesy of the Salik Mwando Papers).

60. Minutes of Balozi Wazee meeting, Jan. 30, 1972 (courtesy of the Salik Mwando Papers). The italicized word "bad" is underlined in the original document.

61. Minutes of Balozi Wazee meeting, Feb. 13, 1972 (courtesy of the Salik Mwando Papers).

62. "East Brotherhood Code Committee" (courtesy of the Salik Mwando Papers), 1–2.

63. Ibid., 3.

64. Ibid., 2–5.

65. Ibid., 4.

66. Balozi Wazee minutes, Nov. 28, 1971.

67. Balozi Wazee minutes, Sept. 26 1972.

68. "The East Sisterhood," *Black News* 2, no. 16 (1974): 11.

69. Balozi Wazee minutes, Nov. 28, 1971.

70. *Black News* 2, no. 14 (1974): 27; ibid., no. 18 (1974): 12.

71. Minutes of East Brotherhood Meeting, Nov. 22, n.d. (unpublished one-sheet document in author's possession). The East Brotherhood also developed policy statements that advocated, "Brothers must be sensitive to the needs of Sisters. We must strive to perfect the workings of the household. . . . We are not players or creepers but Black men, therefore we should not seek to play or creep. Playing creates bad feelings and bad images" (East Brotherhood Code Committee, 2–5).

72. Balozi Wazee minutes, Nov. 28, 1971.

73. "The Principles and Institution of Baba Umoja" (unpublished document in author's possession), 1.

74. "East Brotherhood Code Committee," 3.

75. "Mashariki Dress Code: Directive I" (courtesy of the Salik Mwando Papers).

76. "East Brotherhood Code Committee," 3.

77. J. K. Weusi, interview, July 25, 1998.

78. "East Brotherhood Code Committee," 5.

79. According to The East, this matter was never clarified, since a number of East members, as well as US Organization members, practiced polygyny and Amiri Baraka's CFUN did not (see appendix B). The reason Baraka did not engage in such relationships, even though he attempted to, was due to his second wife, Amina Baraka, who was a staunch advocate against such living arrangements.

80. J. K. Weusi, interview, July 25 and Aug. 1, 1998; Basir Mchawi, interview, Aug. 18, 1998.

81. J. K. Weusi, interview, July 25 and Aug. 1, 1998; Basir Mchawi, interview, Aug. 18, 1998.

82. James Williams, interview, June 26, 1998; Okolo Buyu, interview, Aug. 19, 1998; Abimbola Wali and Martha Bright, "The East Sisterhood: An Institution Beyond Walls," paper presented at the annual Council of Independent Black Institutions conference, Fort Valley State Univ., Nov. 15–16 2002, 6.

83. Khadijah Bandele, interview, Aug. 21, 1998.

84. Black, interview. Aminisha Black was known as Aminisha Weusi. In Kiswahili, *weusi* means "black."

85. Mchawi, interview.

86. Gladstone Modele Clarke, interview, Mar. 10, 1999.

87. Wali and Bright, "The East Sisterhood," 12.

88. Ibid., 2, 4–5.

89. Fela Barclift, interview, June 30, 1998; Lumumba Bandele, interview, Aug. 7, 1998.

90. Lumumba Bandele, interview; Buyu, interview.

91. Lumumba Bandele, interview.

92. Black, interview.

93. Sobonfu Some, *The Spirit of Intimacy* (New York: William Morrow and Company, 1999), 38.

94. Barclift, interview.

95. Clarke, interview.

96. Black, interview.

97. Uhuru Sasa Shule, *The Parent Handbook* (Brooklyn, N.Y.: The East, 1980), 4.

98. Aminisha Weusi, "Evaluation Report," June 22, 1977 (unpublished evaluation report courtesy of the Aminisha Black Papers), 3.

99. Ibid.

100. Mchawi, interview.

101. Mashariki, interview; Matthew Holmes, interview, July 14, 1998.

102. Bright, interview.

103. Weusi, "Evaluation Report," 3.

104. Mchawi, interview; Weusi, "Evaluation Report," 3.

105. Imani Publications, "The East," 10; Holmes, interview.

106. Weusi, "Evaluation Report," 1.

107. Ibid., 1–2.

108. Mzee Moyo, interview, Aug. 17, 1998.

109. Weusi, "Evaluation Report," 4.

110. Ibid.; Mashariki, interview.

111. Salik Mwando, interview, Nov. 5, 1998.

112. Nyahuma, interview.

113. *Black News* 1, no. 21 (1970): 11.

114. Moyo, interview; Buyu, interview. The names of members also began to reflect respective pursuits.

115. Ideological classes were means to inculcate members into the specific ideological orientation of an organization and to see and experience reality from its ideological position. For The East, political education classes transmitted not only the specific ideological orientation of the organization but sought to reeducate and encourage study in order to

build a commitment or bring awareness to the nationalist Pan-Africanist movement and its historical developments and ideational figures among the larger community. Political education classes were the hallmark of nationalist organizations in the late 1960s and 1970s. In fact, their existence determined the caliber or quality of the organization. That is to say: All substantive and thorough nationalist organizations had political education classes.

116. Okolo Buyu noted that The East did not want to become a religious institution or "religion," as some regarded the Kawaida philosophy of Maulana Karenga, which may explain why The East was not or chose not to be rooted in a particular African "religious" system.

117. Purpose and Standards Committee, letter, Dec. 3, 1978 (courtesy of the Aminisha Black Papers).

118. Basir Mchawi saw the move to the armory as a costly mistake of The East. See *Black News* 4, no. 22 (1982): 39.

119. Mchawi, interview; Segun Shabaka, interview, Mar. 27, 1999.

120. Shabaka, interview.

121. Ibid.

122. Yusef Waliyaya, interview, Aug. 3, 1998.

123. Shabaka, interview.

124. Segun Shabaka suggested that the school closed in 1986 and the Uhuru Cultural Center closed in 1987.

125. Shabaka, interview.

3. Ujamaa: Enterprises of The East

1. "Black News: A Brief History" (unpublished report courtesy of the Salik Mwando Papers), 1.

2. Big Black, "Around Our Way," *Black News* 1, no. 21 (1969): 10.

3. J. K. Weusi, interview, July 25, 1998.

4. "Black News: A Brief History," 2.

5. "Background, Goals, and Personnel" (unpublished *Black News* essay, 1971), 1.

6. James Williams, "Whose Puddle Do I Be Standing In," *Black News* 1, no. 41 (1972): 22. For further details on his position, see "The Power of Hungry Black Nationalists," *Black News* 1, no. 41 (1972): 10; "*Black News* Position on African Nationalism," *Black News* 1, no. 39 (1972): 2.

7. Salik Mwando, interview.

8. Williams, interview.

9. Salik Mwando, interview.

10. Mchawi, interview.

11. Ibid.; Msemaji Weusi, interview, Aug. 20, 1998. Jitu Weusi wrote, "The newspaper, published monthly, was mailed to individuals and organizations in thirty-two states and five

foreign countries, and was our communication link with the outside world." See the *International African Arts Festival 25th Anniversary Souvenir Journal* (Brooklyn, N.Y.: International African Arts Festival, 1996), 14 (hereafter referred to as *25th Anniversary Souvenir Journal*).

12. *Black News* 1, no. 1 (1970): 14.
13. *Black News* 3, no. 15 (1976): 3.
14. Shabaka, interview.
15. Ibid.
16. Shabaka, interview; Msemaji Weusi, interview, Aug. 20 1998.
17. J. K. Weusi, interview, July 25, 1998.
18. Moyo, interview.
19. *Black News* 3, no. 8 (1976): 8.
20. In 1969, Jitu reported, "one of the major sore spots of The East operation has been our kitchen." See *Black News* 1, no. 21 (1969): 11.
21. J. K. Weusi, interview, July 25, 1998.
22. Jitu K. Weusi, "The East Legacy," in *International African Arts Festival Souvenir Journal* (Brooklyn, N.Y.: International African Arts Festival, 1996), 15.
23. Moyo, interview.
24. Adeyemi Al-Maquaddim, *The East Mental Ministry Report* (Brooklyn, N.Y.: The East, 1972), 7.
25. K. Mensah Wali, interview, Aug. 8, 1998; J. K. Weusi, interview, July 25, 1998.
26. Big Black, "Around Our Way," *Black News* 1, no. 28 (1971): 10; Uhuru Sasa Shule, "Institutional Booklet" (Brooklyn, N.Y.: The East, 1971; courtesy of the Salik Mwando Papers), 15.
27. Imani Publications, "The East," 36.
28. K. Mensah Wali, interview, Aug. 8, 1998.
29. East Co-op Food store, "Advertisement," *Black News* 3, no. 4 (1975): 17. Jitu Weusi recalls that the food cooperative was named "Uhuru Food Coop" in 1975 when it became a retail operation. However, the foregoing *Black News* advertisement says, "East Co-op Food store," not Uhuru Food Coop in 1975.
30. Monica Surfaro, "The East, a Black Culture and Education Center, Brings Bit of Africa to Brooklyn," *New York Times*, Aug. 17, 1974, 81.
31. Jitu K. Weusi, "Uhuru Food Coop: We Want Your Business!" *Black News* 4, no. 1 (1978): 21.
32. "Uhuru Food Coop Advertisement," *Black News* 4, no. 4 (1979): 11; J. K. Weusi, interview, July 25, 1998.
33. Moyo, interview.
34. Ibid.
35. J. K. Weusi, interview, July 25, 1998.
36. Mavazi family clothing co-op flyer (n.d.).
37. J. K. Weusi, interview, July 25, 1998.

38. Moyo, interview.
39. Ibid.

4. Kujichagulia: Uhuru Sasa Shule (Freedom Now School)

1. Akoto, *Nationbuilding*, 60.
2. *Black Power Conference Reports* (New York: Afram Associates, 1970), i–ii.
3. Leslie Campbell [Jitu K. Weusi], "The Black Teacher and Black Power," in *What Black Educators are Saying*, ed. Nathan Wright (New York: Hawthorn Books, 1970), 23.
4. Preston Wilcox, "Education for Black Humanism: A Way of Approaching It," in *What Black Educators are Saying*, 9.
5. M. Lee Montgomery, ed., *The Perspectives Gained: Findings of a Five-Day Black University* (New York: National Association for African American Education, 1969), 111–12, 113.
6. Frank J. Satterwhite, *Planning an Independent Black Educational Institution* (New York: Moja Publishing House, 1971), 5.
7. Amiri Baraka, ed., *African Congress: A Documentary of the First Modern Pan-African Congress* (New York: William Morrow and Company, 1972), ix.
8. Shujaa and Afrik, "School Desegregation," 258.
9. Satterwhite, *Planning*, 7.
10. Doughty, "Historical Analysis," 91.
11. Shujaa and Afrik, "School Desegregation," 25; Doughty, "Historical Analysis," 93; see also Uhuru Hotep, "Dedicated to Excellence: An Afrocentric Oral History of the Council of Independent Black Institutions, 1970–2000" (Ph.D. diss., Duquesne Univ., 2001).
12. Imani Publications, "The East," 30.
13. Big Black, "Around Our Way," *Black News* 1, 2 (1970): 10.
14. See appendix E for details regarding the levels of Uhuru Sasa Shule.
15. Imani Publications, "The East," 37.
16. See *Black News* 2, no. 13 (n.d.): 7.
17. Ibid., 35.
18. Madeline Coleman, "Uhuru Sasa Shule," in *Black Children Just Keep on Growing*, 35–40. Permission to use this portion of the publication has been granted by the Black Child Development Institute, Inc., courtesy of Evelyn K. Moore, president and CEO of the institute.
19. Black, interview.
20. The question mark indicates the uncertainty of when Aminisha Black's directorship of Imani ended.
21. "Imani," *Black News* 2, no. 24 (1975): 19.
22. Documents on Imani Child Development Center (courtesy of the Aminisha Black and Khadijah Bandele Papers).
23. "Imani," 19.
24. Ibid.

25. Documents on Imani Child Development Center.
26. "Uhuru Sasa Shule Mwalimu of the Month," *Black News* 3, no. 23 (1978): 16.
27. Uhuru Sasa Shule, "Institutional Booklet," 7.
28. Uhuru Sasa Shule, *Parent Handbook*, 8.
29. "CIBI Perfects Techniques for Teacher Training Institute," *Black News* 3, no. 3 (1975): 6.
30. "5th Annual Teacher Training Institute," *Black News* 3, no. 14 (1976): 19.
31. Uhuru Sasa School programs for academic year 1972–73.
32. Ibid., 13.
33. See appendix E for a detailed overview of Uhuru Sasa's curricula design and contents.
34. Imani Publications, "The East," 38.
35. Coleman, "Uhuru Sasa," 141.
36. Ibid., 143.
37. Kuumba Coard, interview, Nov. 27, 1998.
38. Ibid., 38.
39. Ibid.
40. Gladstone Modele Clarke, "New York Family Schools: Head Start for Black Children?" (masters thesis, Columbia Univ. Graduate School of Journalism, 1979), 25.
41. Uhuru Sasa Shule, *The Parent Handbook*, 8.
42. "Evening School of Knowledge Brochure," *Black News* 1, no. 22 (1970): 17–18.
43. J. K. Weusi, interview, Aug. 1, 1998.
44. Uhuru Sasa Shule, "Institutional Booklet," 8.
45. Ibid., 5.
46. See Al-Maquaddim's *East Mental Ministry Report* for a broader discussion of the topic.
47. Al-Maquaddim, *East Mental Ministry Report*, 3.
48. Copy of Uhuru Sasa's provisional charter courtesy of New York State Education Department, office of the Board of Regents. When a school requests a provisional charter, all the information supplied is projected. After this charter is granted, a school can petition for an absolute charter, which, according to New York State Education Department records, Uhuru Sasa did not file. The provisional charter is only valid for three years. Interestingly, Lesley Jones wrote, "The Uhuru Sasa is an existing corporation working toward full accreditation by the Board of Education." See "Uhuru Sasa Shule Says Family Must Re-Educate," *New York Amsterdam News*, Jan. 15, 1972, B-1. The *Black News*, however, accurately reported, "The shule is accredited by the N.Y. State Education Department but not by the Board of Education." See *Black News* 2, no. 13 (n.d.): 7.
49. Shabaka, interview.
50. J. K. Weusi, interview, Aug. 1, 1998.
51. "Brooklyn Family Schools," *Black News* 3, no. 14 (1976): 18.
52. The Parent Council of the Uhuru Sasa School, "Letter," *Black News* 3, no. 9 (1976): 22.

53. "Don't Railroad Us: The Struggle between Uhuru Sasa School and the Long Island Railroad," *Black News* 3, no. 13 (1976): 13.

54. Clarke, "New York Family Schools," 25.

55. Jitu K. Weusi, "C.I.B.I.: A Critical Evaluation," *Black News* 3, no. 8 (1977): 9.

56. Central Committee Minutes of the Council of Independent Black Institutions, Apr. 22–23, 1978 (courtesy of CIBI archives), 6.

57. Ibid., 7, 4.

58. Aminisha Weusi, "Testimonial Dinner Held for Jitu K. Weusi," *Big Red*, Nov. 19, 1978, 4; Tawwil Abdul Waasi, "Jitu K. Weusi Among Candidates for District 16 Superintendent Job," *Black News* 3, no. 24 (1978): 15. "Jitu, as reported, believed that progressive minded people in the school board would bring about real change in the way schools are run . . . building Uhuru Sasa taught many lessons and has therefore answers to bring to the situation of public schools."

59. Addul-Waasi, "Jitu K. Weusi," 15.

60. Clarke, "New York Family Schools," 28; see E. Curtis Alexander, "Uhuru Sasa 78: The Continuation of a Legacy of Struggle," *Black News* 4, no. 2 (1978): 12.

61. Alexander, "Uhuru Sasa," ibid., 13 (emphasis added), 14–16.

62. Central Committee Minutes of the Council of Independent Black Institutions, Apr. 25, 1980 (courtesy of CIBI archives).

63. Ibid.

64. Jumibia Nyahuma, letter to Kofi Lomotey, Apr. 24, 1980, 1.

65. Uhuru Sasa Shule, *The Parent Handbook*, 2.

66. *Fundisha! Teach! Council of Independent Black Institutions Newsletter* 8, no. 2 (n.d.): 2.

67. Kierna Mayo, "Independents' Day," *City Limits* 22, no. 1 (1997): 20.

68. J. K. Weusi, "The East Legacy," 15.

69. Shabaka, interview.

70. "Innovative, Challenging Program for Day School Students," *Caribbean Life*, Jan. 12, 1999, 44.

71. Lomotey, interview (emphasis added).

5. Kuumba: The International African Arts Festival

1. Greer Smith, "Forward Ever . . . " in *25th Anniversary Souvenir Journal*, 4.

2. *African Street Festival Souvenir Journal* (Brooklyn, N.Y.: The East, 1978), 1.

3. *African Street Festival Souvenir Journal* (Brooklyn, N.Y.: Author, 1990), 5; *African Street Festival Annual Report* (Brooklyn, N.Y.: Author, 1995), 4 (hereafter referred to as *Annual Report* 1995); K. Mensah Wali, interview, Aug. 8, 1998.

4. Segun Shabaka, "The East/Uhuru Sasa's 6th Annual Afrikan Street Carnival," *Black News* 3, no. 18 (1977): 7.

5. Basir Mchawi, "Twenty-Five Years and Counting . . . " in *25th Anniversary Souvenir Journal*, 12.

6. K. Mensah Wali, interview, Aug. 8, 1998.
7. J. K. Weusi, interview, Aug. 1, 1998.
8. Basir Mchawi, "Black News Briefs," *Black News* 3, no. 2 (1975): 6.
9. Ibid., 7.
10. K. Mensah Wali, "Chairman's Message," in *25th Anniversary Souvenir Journal*, 2.
11. Shabaka, "The East/Uhuru Sasa," 7.
12. K. Mensah Wali, interview, Aug. 8, 1998.
13. Quoted in James Campbell, "Festival Fever," in *25th Anniversary Souvenir Journal*, 25.
14. Moyo, interview.
15. K. Mensah Wali, interview, Aug. 8, 1998.
16. *Annual Report* 1995, 4.
17. Segun Shabaka, "National Association of Kawaida Organizations (NAKO): Symposium on Culture, Community and Struggle," in *25th Anniversary Souvenir Journal*, 20.
18. *Annual Report* 1995, 4.
19. K. Mensah Wali, interview, Aug. 8, 1998.
20. Ibid.
21. Ibid.
22. *Annual Report* 1995, 1.
23. Mari Toussaint, "Focus on the African Street Festival Talent Search," in *25th Anniversary Souvenir Journal*, 11.
24. *Annual Report* 1995, 3.
25. Ibid.
26. Ibid., 6.
27. Moyo, interview.
28. Ibid.
29. Ibid.
30. In the year 2000, the festival implemented this idea, and despite low exceptions as a result of its implementation, the event had a very successful outcome. The International African Arts Festival in 2001 was extremely significant since it marked the thirtieth anniversary of the festival. In July 2004, the festival moved to what seems to be its new home: the Commodore Barry Park in downtown Brooklyn between Navy Street and Park Avenue. I attended this event and took notice of the echoing statement, "This will be the permanent home of festival."
31. Mchawi, "Twenty-Five Years and Counting," 14.

6. Imani: The Challenge of Continuity and The East Legacy

1. Amos Wilson, in *Blueprint for Black Power* (New York: Afrikan World InfoSystems, 1998), viewed power as "the ability to do, the ability to be, the ability to prevail.... [Thus,] to be powerless is to be will-less, impotent and lifeless, without effect or influence; to be nothing, of no account" (5).

2. William Cheek, *Black Resistance before the Civil War* (Beverly Hills, Calif.: Glencoe Press, 1970), 1–2.

3. Clovis E. Semmes, *Cultural Hegemony and African American Development* (Westport, Conn.: Praeger, 1992), 2, 3.

4. J. K. Weusi, "The East Legacy," 7. While visiting Nigeria, Malcolm was made an honorary member of the Nigerian Muslim Students' Society, and with the membership he was given the name *Omowale*. In the Yorùbá language, *Omowale* means "the son who has come home." See *The Autobiography of Malcolm X* (New York: Ballantine Books, 1964), 357.

5. Mchawi, "Twenty-Five Years and Counting," 13.

6. Founded in 1972, CIBI is an international umbrella organization for independent African-centered educational institutions. Uhuru Sasa was one of its founding members.

7. Jitu K. Weusi, personal communication, Apr. 25, 1999.

8. J. K. Weusi, "The East Legacy," 17.

9. Robert Garmston and Bruce Wellman, "Adaptive Schools in a Quantum Universe," *Educational Leadership* 52, no. 7 (1995): 10.

10. Ibid., 7.

11. Ibid., 10.

12. Mwalimu J. Shujaa and Nah Dove, "Catch a Fire Without Getting Burned: Building Institutions While the Struggle Rages," *Sankofa: Journal of Nationbuilding and ReAfrikanization* 1, no. 2 (1999): 65.

13. See Ayi Kwei Armah, *Two Thousand Seasons* (Nairobi: East African Publishing House, 1973), 30–133.

14. Coleman, *Black Children Just Keep on Growing*, 141, 143.

15. Terrence E. Deal and Allan A. Kennedy, "Culture and School Performance," *Educational Leadership* 40, no. 5 (1983): 15.

16. The Imani Day School Computer Campus is a recent educational institution established by a former Uhuru Sasa teacher; the school provides a "cultural education from kindergarten to third grade." See *Caribbean Life*, June 12, 1999, 44.

17. J. K. Weusi, "The East Legacy," 16–17.

18. Shabaka, interview.

Epilogue: The East Family at Present

1. East Family Committee, "East Family Kwanzaa Reunion," *East Family Newsletter* 8, no. 1 (1998): 1, 5.

Appendix A

1. The Mashariki and Required Reading List (courtesy of the Salik Mwando Papers), 1–2.

Appendix B

1. I have intentionally sought not to edit this and other original documents to maintain their authenticity. For the most part, where grammatical changes would otherwise be needed, the text is intelligible and minor editing can be done while reading. The original document contains handwritten comments that suggest strong disagreements with the "singular ideology" of CAP and what appears to be some serious concerns about genuine collectivity, communication, and organizational management.

Appendix C

1. This document, like others, was transcribed without editing the content or format. The introduction reads like a "free form" poem. Otherwise, the document is intelligible and most necessary grammatical changes can be made by the reader without a problem.

Appendix E

1. Uhuru Sasa Shule, "Institutional Booklet," 17–20.
2. Algebricks and the approach using these manipulative tools are discussed in chapter 4.
3. Uhuru Sasa Shule, "Institutional Booklet," 21–23.
4. Ibid., 22.
5. "East Evening School," *Black News* 4, no. 5 (1979): 23.

Appendix F

1. *Annual Report* 1995, 1.
2. Ibid., 3; Smith, "Forward Ever," in *25th Anniversary Souvenir Journal*, 4. The African Marketplace has incredible array of wares, handcrafted items, international cuisine, cultural artifacts, and other related items.
3. Mari Toussaint, "Focus on the African Street Festival Talent Search," in *African Street Festival Souvenir Journal* (Brooklyn, N.Y.: African Street Festival, 1990), 11.
4. *Annual Report* 1995, 3.
5. Ibid., 3; Gayle DeWees, "24th African Street Festival Set," *New York Daily News*, June 30, 1995, 10.

Bibliography

Interviews

Bandele, Adeyemi. Aug. 17, 1998, Brooklyn, N.Y.
Bandele, Khadijah. Aug. 21, 1998, Brooklyn, N.Y.
Bandele, Lumumba. Aug. 7, 1998, Brooklyn, N.Y.
Barclift, Fela. June 30, 1998, Brooklyn, N.Y.
Black, Aminisha. Aug. 12, 1998, Brooklyn, N.Y.
Branch, John Watusi. Aug. 18, 1998, Queens, N.Y.
Bright, Martha. June 12, 1998, Brooklyn, N.Y.
Buyu, Okolo. Aug. 19, 1998, Brooklyn, N.Y.
Callender, Lauren (Latifah). July 13, 1998, Brooklyn, N.Y.
Clarke, Gladstone Modele. Mar. 10, 1999, New Paltz, N.Y.
Coard, Kuumba. Nov. 27, 1998, Brooklyn, N.Y.
Evans, Nekena and Nadira. July 4, 1998, Brooklyn, N.Y.
Holmes, Matthew. July 14, 1998, New York, N.Y.
Jones, Seitu. July 13, 1998, Brooklyn, N.Y.
Kierstedt, Cynthia (Fatima). July 13, 1998, Brooklyn, N.Y.
Leonard, Michael (Jumibia). July 26, 1998, Brooklyn, N.Y.
Lomotey, Kofi. June 16, 1998, Brooklyn, N.Y.
Mashariki, Job. Aug. 16, 1998, Brooklyn, N.Y.
Mchawi, Basir. Aug. 18, 1998, Bronx, N.Y.
Mitchell, Alfredo. July 31, 1998, Brooklyn, N.Y.
Mlimwengu, Mteteaji (Wakili) O. Aug. 2, 1998, Brooklyn, N.Y.
Moyo, Mzee. Aug. 17, 1998, Brooklyn, N.Y.
Mwando, Ngina (Beverly Blacksher). Sept. 21, 1998, Ithaca, N.Y.
Mwando, Salik. Nov. 5, 1998, Ithaca, N.Y.
Nyahuma, Jumibia. July 26, 1998.
Pou, Rosezina. Aug. 8, 1998, Queens, N.Y.
Rubie, Bernardo Osei. July 14, 1998, New York, N.Y.

Shabaka, Segun. Mar. 27, 1999, Brooklyn, N.Y.
Smith, Baraka. Aug. 1, 1998, Brooklyn, N.Y.
Wali, Kwesi Mensah. Aug. 8, 1998, Brooklyn, N.Y.
Waliyaya, Kubballa. Aug. 19, 1998, Queens, N.Y.
Waliyaya, Yusef. Aug. 3, 1998, Brooklyn, N.Y.
Weusi, Jitu. July 25, 1998, and Aug. 1, 1998, Brooklyn, N.Y.
Weusi, Msemaji. Aug. 20, 1998, Brooklyn, N.Y.
Wilcox, Preston. June 15, 1998, New York, N.Y.
Williams, James. June 26, 1998, Brooklyn, N.Y.

Primary Source Documents from The East

African Street Festival Annual Report (1995)
African Street Festival Souvenir Journal (1978 and 1990)
Black News (1969–86)
East Brotherhood Code Committee (n.d.)
East Family Newsletters (1996–98)
International African Arts Festival 25th Anniversary Souvenir Journal (1996)
"Kasisi Yusef Iman: The Pictorial Biography of a Great Renaissance Man" (n.d.)
Khadijah Bandele Papers
Mashariki Dress Code: Directive I
Minutes of Balozi Wazee meeting, Nov. 28, 1971–Sept. 26, 1972
Minutes of East Brotherhood Meeting, Nov. 22 (n.d.)
Salik Mwando Papers
The Aminisha Black Papers
The East Mental Ministry Report (1972)
The East Program and Curriculum of Uhuru Sasa Shule (1971)
The Principles and Institution of Baba Umoja
Uhuru Sasa Shule Curriculum (1978–79)
Uhuru Sasa Shule Institutional Booklet (1971)
Uhuru Sasa Shule Parent Handbook (1980)
Weusi Alfabeti (The Black Alphabets)

Books and Published Proceedings

Adamulekun, Ladipo. *Sékou Touré's Guinea: An Experiment in Nation Building.* London: Methuen, 1976.

Adeleke, Tunde. *UnAfrican Americans: Nineteenth Century Black Nationalism and the Civilizing Mission.* Lexington: Univ. Press of Kentucky, 1998.

Black Power Conference Reports. New York: Afram Associates, 1970.

Akoto, Kwame A. *Nationbuilding: Theory and Practice in Afrikan-Centered Education.* Washington, D.C.: Pan-Afrikan World Institute, 1992.

Anderson, James D. *The Education of Blacks in the South, 1860–1935.* Chapel Hill, N.C.: Univ. of North Carolina Press, 1988.

Ani, Marimba. *Yurugu: An African-Centered Critique of European Thought and Behavior.* Trenton, N.J.: Africa World Press, 1994.

Armah, Ayi Kwei. *Two Thousand Seasons.* Nairobi: East African Publishing House, 1973.

Baraka, Amiri. *The Autobiography of LeRoi Jones,* rev. ed. Chicago: Lawrence Hill, 1997.

———. *The Autobiography of LeRoi Jones.* New York: Freundlich Books, 1984.

———. "Individualism Brings Two Resignations from the Congress of African People." *Unity and Struggle* (1975).

———, ed. *African Congress: A Documentary of the First Modern Pan-African Congress.* New York: William Morrow and Company, 1972.

———. *The Meaning and Development of Revolutionary Kawaida,* 1974 (mimeograph).

———. "Revolutionary Culture and Future of Pan-Afrikan Culture." Paper presented at the 6th Pan-African Congress, Dar Es Salaam, Tanzania, June 19–27, 1974 (mimeograph).

———. "Toward Ideological Clarity." Paper presented at the African Liberation Support Committee Conference, May 24, 1974 (mimeograph).

———. "Kawaida: National Liberation and Socialism." n.d.

Bell, Derrick. "Learning from the Brown Experience." *Black Scholar* 11, no. 1 (1979): 9–16.

Berube, Maurice R., and Marilyn Gittill, eds. *Confrontation at Ocean Hill–Brownsville: The New York School Strike of 1968.* New York: Praeger, 1969.

Blackwell, James E. *The Black Community: Diversity and Unity.* New York: Harper and Row, 1975.

Blassingame, John W., and John R. McKiviyan, eds. *The Frederick Douglass Papers.* New Haven, Conn.: Yale Univ. Press, 1992.

Boahen, A. Adu. *African Perspectives on Colonialism.* Baltimore: Johns Hopkins Univ. Press, 1987.

Bosmajian, Haig A., and Hamida Bosmajian. *The Rhetoric of the Civil-Rights Movement.* New York: Random House, 1969.

Bouma, Gary D., and G. B. J. Atkinson. *A Handbook of Social Science Research*. New York: Oxford Univ. Press, 1995.

Bowers, Margaret A. "The Independent Black Educational Institution: An Exploration and Identification of Selected Factors that Relate to Their Survival." Ph.D. diss., Atlanta Univ., 1984.

Braun, Robert J. *Teachers and Power: The Story of the American Federation of Teachers*. New York: Simon and Schuster, 1972.

Briggs, John. *Fractals: The Patterns of Chaos*. New York: Simon and Schuster, 1992.

Brookins, C. C. "A Descriptive Analysis of Ten Independent Black Educational Models." M.A. thesis, Michigan State Univ., 1985.

Brown, Scot. *Fighting for US: Maulana Karenga, the US Organization, and Black Cultural Nationalism*. New York: New York Univ. Press, 2003.

———. "US and the Origins of Simba Wachanga: An Interview with Wesley Kabaila." *Umoja Sasa* 8, no. 2 (1996): 15–19.

Campbell, Leslie [Jitu K. Weusi]. "The Black Teacher and Black Power." In *What Black Educators Are Saying*, ed. Nathan Wright. New York: Hawthorn Books, 1970.

———. "The Difference." In *What Black Educators Are Saying*, ed. Nathan Wright. New York: Hawthorn Books, 1970.

Carson, Clayborne et al. *The Eyes on the Prize Civil Rights Reader*. New York: Penguin Books, 1991.

Cheek, William. *Black Resistance before the Civil War*. Beverly Hills, Calif.: Glencoe Press, 1970.

Clarke, John H. *African People in World History*. Baltimore: Black Classic Press, 1993.

Clarke, Gladstone Modele. "New York Family Schools: Head Start for Black Children?" Masters thesis, Columbia Univ. Graduate School of Journalism, 1979.

Coleman, Madeline, ed. *Black Children Just Keep on Growing: Alternative Curriculum Models for Young Black Children*. Washington, D.C.: Black Child Development Institute, 1977.

Connolly, Harold. "Blacks in Brooklyn from 1900 to 1960." Ph.D. diss., New York Univ., 1972.

Council of Independent Black Institutions. *Positive Afrikan Images for Children*. Trenton, N.J.: Red Sea Press, 1990.

———. *Fundisha!—Teach! The Newsletter of the Council of Independent Black Institutions*. Buffalo, N.Y.: CIBI, 1996.

———. *Members' Handbook*. Buffalo, N.Y.: CIBI, 1998.

Creswell, John W. *Qualitative Inquiry and Research Design: Choosing Among Five Traditions.* Thousand Oaks, Calif.: Sage Publications, 1998.

Cruse, Harold. *The Crisis of the Negro Intellectual.* New York: Quill, 1984.

Deal, Terrence E., and Allan A. Kennedy, "Culture and School Performance," *Educational Leadership* 40, no. 5 (1983): 14–15.

Delany, Martin R. *The Condition, Elevation, Emigration and Destiny of the Colored People of the United States.* Baltimore: Black Classic Press 1993 [1852].

Gayle DeWees. "24th African Street Festival Set." *New York Daily News,* June 30, 1995.

Doughty, James J. "A Historical Analysis of Black Education, Focusing on the Contemporary Independent Black School Movement." Ph.D. diss., Ohio State Univ., 1973.

DuBois, W. E. B. *Black Reconstruction.* New York: Kraus-Thomson Books, 1976.

Essien-Odom, E. U. *Black Nationalism: In Search of an Identity.* Chicago: Univ. of Chicago Press, 1962.

Ford, Donald H., and Richard M. Lerner. *Developmental Systems Theory: An Integrative Approach.* Newbury Park, Calif.: Sage Publications, 1992.

Foster, Gail. "New York City's Wealth of Historically Black Independent Schools." *Journal of Negro Education* 61, no. 2 (1992): 186–200.

Franklin, Vincent Paul. *Black Self-Determination: A Cultural History of African-American Resistance.* New York: Lawrence Hill Books, 1992.

Fu-Kiau, K. K. B. *Self-Healing Power and Therapy.* New York: Vantage Press, 1991.

Fu-Kiau, K. Kia B., and A. M. Lukondo-Wamba. *Kindezi: The Kôngo Art of Babysitting.* New York: Vantage Press, 1988.

Garmston, Robert and Bruce Wellman. "Adaptive Schools in a Quantum Universe." *Educational Leadership* 52, no. 7 (1995): 6–12.

Glasser, Ira. "The Burden of Blame: Report on Ocean Hill–Brownsville." *New York Civil Liberties Union* 16, no. 9 (1968): 1–8.

Gordon, Dexter B. *Black Identity: Rhetoric, Ideology, and Nineteenth-Century Black Nationalism.* Carbondale: Southern Illinois Univ. Press, 2003.

Haberstroh, Chadwick J. "Organization Design and Systems Analysis." In *Handbook of Organizations,* ed. James G. March. Chicago: Rand McNally, 1965.

Halisi, Clyde. *Kitabu: Beginning Concepts in Kawaida.* Los Angeles: US Organization, 1973.

Halisi, Clyde, and James Mtume, eds. *The Quotable Karenga.* Los Angeles: US Organization, 1967.

Hall, Raymond L., ed. *Black Separatism and Social Reality: Rhetoric and Reason.* New York: Pergamon Press, 1977.

Harris, Robert L. "Early Black Benevolent Societies, 1780–1830." *The Massachusetts Review* 20, no. 2 (1979): 603–25.

Higginbotham, Evelyn Brooks. *Righteous Discontent: The Women's Movement in the Black Baptist Church, 1880–1920.* Cambridge, Mass.: Harvard Univ. Press, 1993.

Hilliard, Asa G., III. *The Maroons Within Us.* Baltimore: Black Classic Press, 1995.

Hotep, Uhuru. "Dedicated to Excellence: An Afrocentric Oral History of the Council of Independent Black Institutions, 1970–2000." Ph.D. diss., Duquesne Univ., 2001.

Huggins, Nathan, Martin Kilson, and Daniel M. Fox, eds. *Key Issues in the Afro-American Experience.* New York: Harcourt Brace Jovanovich, 1971.

Hunter, Charlayne. "Black Intellectuals Divided Over Ideological Direction." *New York Times*, Apr. 29, 1975.

Imani Publications. "The East: A Model of Nationhood." *Imani* 5, no. 2 (1971): 28–39.

"Innovative, Challenging Program for Day School Students." *Caribbean Life* (Brooklyn edition), Jan. 12, 1999.

Institute of the Black World, ed. *Education and Black Struggle: Notes from the Colonized World.* Cambridge, Mass.: Harvard Educational Review, 1974.

Jones, Lesley. "Uhuru Sasa Shule Says Family Must Re-Educate." *New York Amsterdam News*, Jan. 15, 1972.

Joseph, Peniel E., ed. *The Black Power Movement: Rethinking the Civil Rights–Black Power Movement.* New York: Routledge, 2006.

Karenga, Maulana Ron. *The Roots of the US-Panther Conflict.* San Diego: Kawaida Publications, 1976.

———. *Kawaida Theory: An Introductory Outline.* Inglewood, Calif.: Kawaida Publications, 1980.

Keto, C. Tsehloane. *Vision, Identity and Time: The Afrocentric Paradigm and the Study of the Past.* Dubuque, Iowa: Kendall-Hunt Publishing Company, 1995.

Kushnick, Louis. "Race, Class and Power: The New York Decentralization Controversy." In *Black Communities and Urban Development in America 1720–1990*, Vol. 7, ed. Kenneth L. Kusmer. New York: Garland Publishing, 1991.

Landesman, Alter F. *Brownsville: The Birth, Development and Passing of a Jewish Community in New York.* New York: Bloch Publishing Company, 1969.

Lee, C. D. "Profile of an Independent Black Institution: African-Centered Education at Work." *Journal of Negro Education* 61, no. 2 (1992): 160–77.

Levine, Naomi. *Ocean Hill–Brownsville: Schools in Crisis, a Case History.* New York: Popular Library, 1969.

Lewis, Dan A., and Kathryn Nakagawa. *Race and Educational Reform in the American Metropolis: A Study of School Decentralization.* New York: SUNY Press, 1995.

Lomotey, K., and C. Brookins. "The Independent Black Institutions: A Cultural Perspective." In *Visible Now: Blacks in Private Schools,* eds. D. T. Slaughter and D. J. Johnson. Westport, Conn.: Greenwood Press, 1988.

Lomotey, K. "Independent Black Institutions: African-Centered Education Models." *Journal of Negro Education* 61, no. 4 (1992): 455–62.

Mabee, Carleton. *Black Education in New York State: From Colonial to Modern Times.* Syracuse, N.Y.: Syracuse Univ. Press, 1979.

———. "Brooklyn's Black Public Schools: Why Did Blacks Have Unusual Control over Them?" *The Journal of Long Island History* 11, no. 2 (1975): 23–38.

Malcolm X (with Alex Haley). *The Autobiography of Malcolm X.* New York: Ballantine Books, 1964.

Mayer, Martin. "The Full and Sometimes Very Surprising Story of Ocean Hill, the Teachers' Union and the Teacher Strikes of 1968." In *Black Protest in the Sixties,* eds. August Meier, John Bracey, Jr., and Elliott Rudwick. New York: Markus Wiener, 1991.

Mayo, Kierna. "Independents' Day." *City Limits* 22, no. 1 (1997): 20.

McAdoo, Bill. *Pre–Civil War Black Nationalism.* New York: David Walker Press, 1983.

McCartney, John T. *Black Power Ideologies: An Essay in African-American Political Thought.* Philadelphia: Temple Univ. Press, 1992.

McCoy, Rhody. "Why Have an Ocean Hill–Brownsville." In *What Black Educators Are Saying,* ed. Nathan Wright. New York: Hawthorn Books, 1970.

McCready, Lance. "Community Control of Schools." In *Encyclopedia of African-American Education,* eds. Faustine C. Jones-Wilson et al. Westport, Conn.: Greenwood Press, 1996.

Montgomery, M. Lee, ed. *The Perspectives Gained: Findings of a Five-Day Black Univ..* New York: National Association for African American Education, 1969.

———. "New Curricula for New Needs." *Foresight* 1, no. 1 (1969).

Moses, Wilson J. *Classical Black Nationalism: From the American Revolution to Marcus Garvey.* New York: New York Univ. Press, 1996.

———. *The Golden Age of Black Nationalism, 1850–1925.* New York: Oxford Univ. Press, 1978.

Munford, Clarence J. *Race and Reparation: A Black Perspective for the Twenty-First Century.* Trenton, N.J.: Africa World Press, 1996.

Newby, Robert G. "Desegregation Its Inequalities and Paradoxes." *Black Scholar* 11, no. 1 (1979): 17–28, 67–68.

Nkrumah, Kwame. *Class Struggle in Africa.* New York: International Publishers, 1970.

Nobles, Wade W., and Lawford L. Goddard. *Understanding the Black Family: A Guide for Scholarship and Research.* Oakland, Calif.: Black Family Institute Publication, 1984.

Nwasike, Dominic. "Weeksville: The Story of a Black Community." *Negro History Bulletin* 43, no. 3 (1980): 66–67.

Nyerere, Julius K. *Ujamaa: Essays on Socialism.* New York: Oxford Univ. Press, 1968.

Obadele, Imari A. *America the Nation-State: The Politics of the United States from a State-Building Perspective,* rev. ed. Baton Rouge, La.: The House of Songhay, 1991.

Paden, John N., and Edward W. Soja, eds. *The African Experience.* Vol. 1. Evanston, Ill.: Northwestern Univ. Press, 1970.

Pantell, Dora, and Edwin Greenidge. *If Not Now, When? The Many Meanings of Black Power.* New York: Dell Publishing, 1969.

Power, Edward J. *Philosophy of Education Studies in Philosophies, Schooling, and Educational Policies.* Englewood Cliffs, N.J.: Prentice-Hall, 1982.

Racism Research Project. *Critique of the Black Nation Thesis.* Berkeley: Racism Research Project, 1975.

Ratteray, Joan D. "Independent Neighborhood Schools: A Framework for the Education of African Americans." *Journal of Negro Education* 61, no. 2 (1992): 138–47.

Reed, Horace B., and Elizabeth L. Loughran, eds. *Beyond Schools: Education for Economic, Social and Personal Development.* Amherst: Univ. of Massachusetts, 1984.

Ridley, June Arden. "The Independent Black (Educational) Institution: An Exploratory Study with Implications for the Institutionalization of American Schools." Ph.D. diss., Univ. of Michigan, 1971.

Satterwhite, Frank J. *Planning an Independent Black Educational Institution.* New York: Moja Publishing House, 1971.

Semmes, Clovis E. *Cultural Hegemony and African American Development.* Westport, Conn.: Praeger, 1992.

Shujaa, Mwalimu J., and Nah Dove. "Catch a Fire Without Getting Burned: Building Institutions While the Struggle Rages." *Sankofa: Journal of Nationbuilding and ReAfrikanization* 1, no. 2 (1999): 65–70.

Shujaa, Mwalimu J., and Hannibal T. Afrik. "School Desegregation, the Politics of Culture, and the Council of Independent Black Institutions." In *Beyond Desegregation: The Politics of Quality in African American Schooling,* ed. Mwalimu J. Shujaa. Thousand Oaks, Calif.: Corwin Press, 1997.

Shujaa, Mwalimu J., ed. *Too Much Schooling, Too Little Education.* Trenton, N.J.: Africa World Press, 1994.

———. "Cultural Self Meets Cultural Other in the African American Experience: Teachers' Responses to a Curriculum Content Reform." *Theory into Practice* 34, no. 3 (1995): 194–201.

———. "Afrocentric Transformation and Parental Choice in African American Independent Schools." *Journal of Negro Education* 61, no. 2 (1992): 149–57.

Slack, Sara. "Franklin Kids Were Mad at Everybody." *The New York Amsterdam News,* Oct. 5, 1968.

Some, Sobonfu. *The Spirit of Intimacy.* New York: William Morrow and Company, 1999.

Strickland, William. "The Road since *Brown:* The Americanization of the Race." *Black Scholar* 11, no. 1 (1979): 2–8.

Stuckey, Sterling. *Slave Culture: Nationalist Theory and the Foundations of Black America.* New York: Oxford Univ. Press, 1987.

Sullivan, Joseph F. "Baraka Drops 'Racism' For Socialism of Marx." *New York Times,* Dec. 27, 1974.

Surfaro, Monica. "The East, A Black Culture and Education Center, Brings Bit of Africa to Brooklyn." *New York Times,* Aug. 17, 1977, 78.

Swan, Robert J. "Did Brooklyn (N.Y.) Blacks Have Unusual Control Over Their Schools? Period I: 1815–1845." *Afro-Americans in New York Life and History* 7, no. 2 (1983).

Tedla, Elleni. *Sankofa: African Thought and Education.* New York: Peter Lang, 1995.

Turner, James. "Black Nationalism: The Inevitable Response." *Black World* 20, no. 3 (1971): 4, 7–8.

———. "The Sociology of Black Nationalism." *The Black Scholar* 1, no. 2 (1969): 18–27.

Vann, Albert. "The Agency Shop." In *What Black Educators Are Saying,* ed. Nathan Wright. New York: Hawthorn Books, 1970.

Van Deburg, William L., ed. *Modern Black Nationalism: From Marcus Garvey to Louis Farrakhan.* New York: New York Univ. Press, 1997.

———. *New Day in Babylon: The Black Power Movement and American Culture, 1965–1975.* Chicago: Univ. of Chicago Press, 1992.

Wali, Abimbola, and Martha Bright. "The East Sisterhood: An Institution Beyond Walls." Paper presented at the annual Council of Independent Black Institutions conference, Fort Valley State Univ., Nov. 15–16, 2002.

Wesley, Charles H. *Prince Hall: Life and Legacy*. Washington, D.C.: The United Supreme Council Southern Jurisdiction, Prince Hall Affiliation, 1977.

Weusi, Aminisha. "Testimonial Dinner Held for Jitu Weusi." *Big Red* 19 (1978).

Weusi, Jitu. "The East Legacy," in *International African Arts Festival Souvenir Journal*, ed. International African Festival. Brooklyn, N.Y.: International African Arts Festival, 1996.

———. "From Relevance to Excellence: The Challenge of Independent Black Institutions." *Black Books Bulletin* 2, nos. 3–4 (1974): 20–22.

———. *A Message from a Black Teacher*. Brooklyn, N.Y.: East Publications, 1973.

Wilcox, Preston. "Education for Black Humanism: A Way of Approaching It." In *What Black Educators Are Saying*, ed. Nathan Wright. New York: Hawthorn Books, 1970.

Wilson, Amos N. *Blueprint for Black Power*. New York: Afrikan World InfoSystems, 1999.

———. *The Falsification of Afrikan Consciousness*. New York: Afrikan World InfoSystems, 1993.

Woodard, Komozi. *A Nation Within a Nation: Amiri Baraka (LeRoi Jones) & Black Power Politics*. Chapel Hill: Univ. of North Carolina Press, 1999.

Woodson, Carter G. *The Education of the Negro Prior to 1861*. Washington, D.C.: Associated Publishers, 1919.

Yeakey, Carol Camp. "The Public School Monopoly: Confronting Major National Policy Issues." In *Visible Now: Blacks in Private Schools*, eds. Diana T. Slaughter and Deborah J. Johnson. Westport, Conn.: Greenwood Press, 1988.

Index

African American Student Association (ASA), 26–31, 37, 89
African-American Teachers Association, 13, 17, 26, 37, 69, 88, 105
African-centered education, 21, 23–24, 65
African consciousness, 131, 134
African Cultural Association of Trinidad, 35
African District School, 6
African Free School, 5
Africanity, 31
African liberation, xxx, 35, 126
African Liberation Day, 76, 162
African liberation movements, 35, 126
African School No. 2, 4
African Society for Cultural Relations with Independent Africa, 34–35
African Society House, 21
African Street Festival, 114–18, 122
African Woolman Benevolent Society, 6
Afrik, Hannibal, 109
Afrikan Poetry Theatre, 37
Afrikan Street Carnival, 114–16. *See also* African Street Festival
Afro-American Investment and Building Company, 4
Ahmed, Lubaba, 66, 111
Akan, 62, 64
Akiba Mkuu bookstore, 60, 74–75
Alexander, E. Curtis, 58, 63–65, 109

Al-Karim Family School, 77, 107
angulia (attention), 97
anti-draft riots, 3–4
ASCRIA Speaks, 35
Ausar-Auset Society, 64

baba (father), 57
Baba Umoja (fatherly unity), 51
Balozi Wazee (council of elders), 48–50
Baraka, Amiri, 38–45, 143, 145, 147–49
Bazara Kazi (council work), 50
Bedford Stuyvesant, 3, 7, 89, 109
Bedford Stuyvesant Restoration Center, 69
Black, Aminisha, 55, 92
Black Arts movement, 136
Black Community Congress, 81, 109
Black Communiversity, 87
Black Consciousness movement, xx, 136
Black Experience in Sound, 28–29
Black nationalism, xxii–xxxii, 23, 29, 45, 70, 124–25
Black News, 65, 68–75, 82, 126–27
Black Panther Party for Self Defense, xxxi, 39
Black Power, xxx–xxxii, 2, 9, 24, 27
Black Power conferences, 27, 38, 43, 86–87
Black Solidarity Day, 32
Black students, 87–88

Black United Front, 81, 109
Boys and Girls High School, 116, 118, 122
Brooklyn Family Schools, 72, 107
Brown v. Board of Education of Topeka, Kansas, 22
Brownsville, 7, 37
buba (full top garment), 103
Burnham, Lynden Forbes Sampson, 34

California Association for Afro-American Education, 87
Carson, Sonny, 34, 45
Carver, George Washington, 94, 164
Churchville, John, 88, 98
Civil Rights movement, xxx, 1, 24–25, 86
Clarke, John Henrik, 95
Claver Place, 65, 67, 70–79, 108, 111, 113–15
colonialism, xxi, 5
Colored School No. 2, 4
Committee for United NewArk, 38–43, 46, 53
Commodore Barry Park, 122, 176
Communist Party, xxix, 54
community control, 1–2, 8–9, 14–16, 19, 24, 26, 88
Congress of African People, 38–39, 43–46, 53, 72, 147–49
Council of Independent Black Institutions, 65, 68, 89, 105, 108–12, 126
Cuisenaire-Gattegno system, 99–101
culture, 19–20, 22–24, 53, 64, 70, 93, 118–20, 124–25
curriculum, 4–5, 21, 92–103, 163–65

dashiki (loose-fitting shirt), 51–52, 83, 103, 153
December 12th Movement, 66
decentralization of schools, 10–18

decentralization of The East, 59–62, 72–73
Department of Record Keeping, 61–62
Dudley, George (Brother Z), 71

East Brotherhood, 48, 50–51, 139, 151–55,
East enterprises, 68–85, 91, 126, 133
East family, xx, 29–31, 47, 51, 54, 59, 63, 72, 79, 92, 138–39
East Family Kwanzaa Reunion, 138–39
East Kitchen and Caterers, 75–77, 169
East Sisterhood, 50–51, 54–56, 92, 139
Economic nationalism, 135
European (white) thought and culture, 31
Evening School of Knowledge, 64, 90–91, 104–5, 169–70

Family-based institutions, 56, 91, 130
Family Leadership Council, 60
Far-East, The, 37
Ferguson, Herman, 35, 143
Freedom Schools, 1, 86
Fundisha, 72, 148

Garvey, Marcus, xxix, 33, 41, 94, 98, 108, 116, 125, 130, 162–64
Ghana, xxii, 31, 126, 173
Global African community, 75, 117, 120, 131

Hannibal, 94, 164
harambee ("let us pull together"), 166–67
hekalu (temple), 40

ideology, 45, 50, 64, 96, 105, 115, 124, 128
Imamu (priest), 40, 42–43

Iman, Yusef, 37–38, 46, 96
Imani (faith), 41, 50, 92, 97
Imani Child Development Center, 91–96
Imani Day School Computer Campus, 112, 133
independent African-centered education, 21–22, 23–25, 65, 131, 133
Independent Black Institutions (IBIs), 87–88
institution building, xx, 22, 85, 124, 132–33
instructional methodologies, 97–100
International African Arts Festival, 113–23, 127, 173–76. *See also* African Street Festival
Ishilangu (security force), 40
Islam, xxxi, 64

Jumatatu, Nassoma, 92

Karenga, Maulana, 38–43, 86
Kawaida, 39–43, 45–46, 49–50, 118, 136
kazi (work), 47, 49, 127, 135, 153
Kenyatta, Jomo, 31
Kierstedt, Rashida, 66, 111
King, Anne, 34
King, Martin Luther, 1–2, 94, 162
Kiswahili, 31, 39–40, 43, 98–101, 104, 161, 165–70
Koch, Mayor Edward, 66
kufi (cap), 52, 103
Kujichagulia (self-determination), 41, 97, 164
Kununuana, 36, 78–82, 169
Kuumba (creativity), 41, 51, 96–97, 101–2, 165, 167
Kuzaliwa (birthday celebration), 41, 163
kwanza (first), 43

Kwanzaa celebration, 41–43, 46–47, 83, 118, 138–39, 163
Kwayana, Eusi (Sidney King), 34

lappa (skirt-like bottom), 103
Long Island Railroad, 107–8
Lynch, Acklyn, 34

Madhubuti, Haki, 45, 109
Malaikas (young women), 48
Malcolm X (Omowale), xxix, 33, 41, 86, 94, 125–26, 130, 143–44
mama (mother), 57, 162
Marxism, 45
Mashariki, 51, 65
Mashariki reading list, 47, 143–44
Maulana ("master teacher"), 40
Mavazi Clothing Cooperative, 36, 83
Mchawi, Basir, 71–75, 122
Message, The, 35
Mid-East, The, 38
mkuu, 90
Modern Academy, 77
Moore, Queen Mother Audley, 34
Musa, Mansa, 94

Naibu (counselors), 50
Nairobi College, 87
National Association of African American Education, 87
National Association of Kawaida Organizations, 118
National Black Assembly, 45
National Black Political Convention, 43, 76
nationalism. *See* nationalist
nationalist, xx–xxxii, 2, 9, 34–35, 38–39, 45, 64, 70–75, 84, 89, 125–28, 134

National Joint Action Committee, 35
nation building, xx, 20, 23–24, 36, 38, 125, 127, 152
nationhood, xxvi, 23–24, 26, 87, 89, 125–26, 132. *See also* Nation building
Nation of Islam, xxxi
New York City Board of Education, 5, 10, 27, 106–8
New York Eight, 66
New York Manumission Society, 5
New York Public School Society, 5
Nguzo Saba, 40–42, 46–47, 64, 68, 91–95, 118, 125, 136
Nia (purpose), 41, 97
Nkrumah, Kwame, xxii, 31, 52, 83, 143–44
Nkulunkulu, 40
Nyerere, Julius, xxii, 31, 83, 143–44

Ocean Hill-Brownsville, 7

pan-Africanism, 9, 31, 126, 144
Parks, Rosa, 94
pedagogy, 98. *See also* instructional methodologies
Penn Community Service Center, 89
Plummber, Viola, 66
polygamy, 57–58
polygyny. *See* polygamy
Purpose and Standards Committee, 65

Rebellion News, 68
relationships (family and personal), 48, 53–58, 62–64, 98, 131
Republic of Guyana, 31, 34, 36, 158
Republic of New Afrika, xxxii
Robert Conner Memorial, 77, 107

Satterwhite, Frank, 88
Saunders, Pharaoh, 28
self-determination, xx, xxvi, 23–24, 124, 131–33
Shabaka, Segun, 66, 77–73
shule (school). *See* Uhuru Sasa Shule
Shule ya Mapinduzi, 77, 107
sifa (praises, prayers), 139, 165, 167, 170
Simba (youth and paramilitary wing), 40
socialization, 19, 23–24, 133
Spirit House Movers and Players, 38
spirituality, xxx, 50, 62, 64, 136, 154–55
St. Peter Claver Catholic Church, 115
Super Simbas (young men), 48
Sweet-East restaurant, 77–78

talisimu, 41, 52, 153
Tanzania, xxii, 51, 83, 126
Teacher Training Institute, 98
Thabiti, Wambui, 92, 97
Thomas, Leon, 28
Tubman, Harriet, 94, 130, 164
Turner, James, 34

Uhuru Cultural Center, 59, 65, 75
Uhuru-East Bookstore and Cultural Center, 38
Uhuru Food Cooperative. *See* Kununuana
uhuru sasa (freedom now), 31
Uhuru Sasa Land Project, 36
Uhuru Sasa Shule, 31, 56, 64, 77, 86–113, 132–33, 161–71
Ujamaa (cooperative economics), 31, 41, 52, 78, 97, 155–57
Ujima (collective work and responsibility), 41, 70, 97, 155, 164, 167

Umoja (unity), 41, 68, 83, 97, 102, 159
Umoja Karamu (unity feast), 33, 50
United Brothers, 38
United Federation of Teachers, 11–18, 37
Unity and Struggle, 45
US Organization, xxxi, 39–43, 46

View from The East, A (radio program), 75

Walimu (teachers), 40, 90, 98, 162–63
Wanafunzi (students), 40, 162, 166–68
watoto (children), 93–95, 163–65
Waziri (ministers), 50, 59
Waziri Baraza (leadership council), 48, 50

Weeksville, 3–7
West, the, xxii, 31
Weusi, Jitu, 14, 24, 26, 29, 34, 45, 63–65, 68–69, 105, 108–9, 134–35
Weusi Kuumba Dance Troupe, 38
Weusi Shule (Johnson Preparatory), 77, 107, 133
Wilcox, Preston, 13, 87–88
Williams, Eric, 35

X, Malcolm. *See* Malcolm X (Omowale)

ya Salaam, Kalamu, 109
Yorùbá, 62, 64, 104–5